The Gospel in America

The Gospel in America

THEMES IN THE STORY OF AMERICA'S EVANGELICALS

JOHN D. WOODBRIDGE,
MARK A. NOLL, NATHAN O. HATCH

ZONDERVAN PUBLISHING HOUSE
OF THE ZONDERVAN CORPORATION
GRAND RAPIDS, MICHIGAN 49506

THE GOSPEL IN AMERICA: THEMES IN THE STORY OF AMERICA'S EVANGELICALS

Library of Congress Cataloging in Publication Data

Woodbridge, John D 1941-
The Gospel in America.

Bibliography: p.
Includes index.
1. Evangelicalism—United States. 2. Unites States—Church history. I. Noll, Mark A., 1946- joint author. II. Hatch, Nathan O., joint author. III. Title.
BR1642.U5W66 269'.2'0973 78-16129

ISBN 0-310-37240-2

Printed in the United States of America

To the millions of "ordinary" Christians
throughout American history
whose names, though absent
from these pages,
are not forgotten in the
Lamb's Book of Life.

Contents

Acknowledgments

The following individuals and groups read or heard parts of this book during its preparation and offered uniformly helpful suggestions for its improvement: Will Barker, James Hedstrom, Walter Kaiser, Kenneth Kantzer, William Lawhead, George Marsden, Egon Middelmann, Craig Noll, Timothy Philips, Lewis Rambo, Richard Reiter, David Schlafer, David Wells, the faculty of Trinity College (Deerfield, Illinois), and the congregation of Grace and Peace Fellowship (Saint Louis, Missouri). None of these, however, are in any way responsible for errors of fact or interpretation remaining in the volume.

We thank Joy Johnson and Dawn Phelan for their excellent typing at various stages of this project. Some of the funds for expenses relating to the preparation of the manuscript were generously provided by a summer study grant given to Mark Noll by Trinity College.

We thank our wives for their proofreading, typing, and other editorial assistance. Even more, Susan Woodbridge, Maggie Noll, and Julie Hatch are to be commended for their generous gifts of good sense, of which their academic husbands have more than occasional need.

This is an appropriate place, finally, to acknowledge the debt each of the individual authors of this volume owes to his two fellow-workers. John Woodbridge conceived the project and provided the first drafts of chapters 4 and 5; Mark Noll provided the first drafts of chapters 1-3 and 7; Nathan Hatch provided first drafts of chapters 6, 8, and 9. The process of rewriting the chapters to the reasonable satisfaction of all was long, occasionally difficult, but always harmonious. It is no small measure of the spirit behind this project that the authors remain friends after the process of refashioning each other's work, as well as laborers still joined by the commitment to offer historical study for the advancement of the Redeemer's kingdom.

Introduction

A White House "hatchet man," Charles Colson, finds forgiveness and renewal in Christ. His book *Born Again* sells into the hundreds of thousands of copies. One of the early leaders of the Black Panther Party, Eldridge Cleaver, proclaims a newfound love for whites, even those who most oppress the members of his race. The reason: life-changing faith in Jesus Christ. An unabashed Baptist, Jimmy Carter, is the thirty-ninth president of the United States. He urges his cabinet members to spend more time with their families. He reintroduces morality into United States foreign policy. He attends church regularly and occasionally teaches a men's Bible class.

Not without reason was 1976 called "The Year of the Evangelical." Pollster George Gallup's surveys showed that 34 percent of adult Americans claimed to have experienced the new birth. Campus Crusade for Christ's "Here's Life, America!" campaign focused evangelistic efforts in 165 metropolitan areas. Over 17,000 young people gathered at Inter-Varsity Fellowship's triennial missionary conference in Urbana, Illinois, to be challenged to more active service for God. The American Bible Society's *Good News Bible* sold a million copies in its first month of publication. Sales for *The Living Bible* climbed to over 2.2 million for the year. The three "finalists" in the presidential sweepstakes of that year all professed faith in Christ: the successful Carter, Episcopalian Gerald Ford, and Presbyterian Ronald Reagan. It's history now, but the evangelical strengths apparent in 1976 can still be seen: rapid growth in evangelical seminaries, increasing concern for a biblical witness in "mainline" denominations, telling evangelism on high school and college campuses, the explosion of the charismatic movement within and beyond traditional Pentecostalism, and a growing self-confidence for evangelical theology.

The current scene is by no means all sweetness and light for Evangelicals. Within there is continued disagreement over the way Evangelicals should relate to American culture. A complex debate on the nature of the Bible is fostering distrust and discontent. And differences in doctrine and practice that have existed since the Reformation give no sign of going away. Nor is nonevangelical America prepared to drape itself at the feet of Bible believers. Eighty million Americans are essentially unrelated to churches. Secularism shows no sign of giving up its hold in the public schools where a deterministic humanism prevails as often as not. The evangelical message seems to have made little impact on the American legal system, which, for example, often treats criminals and victims with equal callousness. Few Evangelicals have contributed distinctly Christian insights to the crises of energy and ecology or to the ongoing debate over the moral strengths and weaknesses of the American economic and political systems.

Evangelicals, in short, have recently been recognized as a force to be reckoned with in American life. Whether they will be able to live up to this new attention—providing answers to the pressing spiritual needs of individuals and to the impending crises in society—remains to be seen. One thing can be said for sure, however. Evangelicals in the present will have a better understanding of themselves and their place in American life if they know more about their past.

It is the purpose of this book to provide that knowledge. The searchlight of history cannot illumine the path to the future. But it can show us where we have been. And when we know that, we gain some balance for the road ahead.

At the outset several things need to be made clear about these chapters on the history of America's Evangelicals. The book is written for the pastor, layperson, college student, or seminarian who would like to know where Evangelicals have come from in the past and what that past has to say about the present. It is not a scholarly treatise designed exclusively for university professors and other inhabitants of the ivory tower. The book is a descriptive history of American Evangelicalism that tries to enlighten even where it seeks to instruct. It is not a partisan account making a special plea for any one denomination or narrow religious perspective.

Although the book takes theological questions seriously, it also is concerned about cultural, social, political, and intellectual manifestations of Evangelicalism. It is not intended primarily as an argument for what *evangelical* ought to mean in the abstract, but as an examination of the widest possible range of those who could be classed as Evangelicals.

Publishers in recent years have supplied a barrage of books talking about Evangelicals. We have been told about an *Evangelical Renaissance*, the *Evangelical Heritage*, the *Young Evangelicals*, and have been offered a series of essays under the simple title *The Evangelicals*. We have been informed *Why Conservative Churches Are Growing* and about the need for *Discovering an Evangelical Heritage*. Even *Time* magazine, which does about the same job of informing and entertaining the American people as the Bible itself did three hundred years ago, has reviewed the Evangelicals. In recent years it has covered the rapid growth of evangelical seminaries, described a *Battle for the Bible*, and taken note of other significant books by theological conservatives. Clearly, the time has come for a wide-ranging effort to trace the most important features of the history of Evangelicalism in America.

But who, after all, are we talking about when we speak of the Evangelicals? Harold Lindsell, retired editor of *Christianity Today*, might give one answer, and David Hubbard, president of Fuller Theological Seminary, another. William H. Bentley of the National Black Evangelical Association, David Preus of the American Lutheran Church, Mennonite scholar John Howard Yoder, feminist Lucille Sider Dayton, United States Senator Mark Hatfield, Harold Carswell of the Southern Baptist Convention, or charismatic Bob Mumford of Christian Growth Ministries would offer still others. Admittedly, if we concentrate on the issue of what evangelical *should* mean, it would be difficult to come up with a definition that would satisfy all of those in the country who call themselves Evangelicals or whom others commonly refer to by that name.

Better results can be obtained if we attempt to define the word in terms of its history. The first definition of *evangelical* in the authoritative *Oxford English Dictionary* is simply, "of or pertaining to the gospel." The gospel, as readers of the Bible's book of Mark recall, is that which Jesus proclaimed when he first began to preach: "The time is fulfilled, and the kingdom of God is at hand; repent, and believe in the gospel" (Mark 1:15). A clue to what Jesus meant by the gospel is found immediately thereafter in Mark's account: "And passing along by the Sea of Galilee, he saw Simon and Andrew. . . . And Jesus said to them, 'Follow me'" (vv.16-17). For Christians, the gospel has always meant first and foremost "following Christ."

Indeed, we speak of the four *evangelists*—Matthew, Mark, Luke, John—as the authors of the *gospels*, histories of the life of Christ. In the Greek language in which these records of Christ's life were written, "gospel" was simply "eu-angelion" or "good news." These "gospelers" proclaimed the joyful tidings that Jesus was God's promised Messiah, his unique Son who was "to save his people from their sins" (Matt. 1:21), "to preach good news to the poor . . . to proclaim release to the captives and recovery of sight to the blind, to set at liberty those who are oppressed, to proclaim the acceptable year of the Lord" (Luke 4:18-19).

If *Evangelicals* are people who are identified by the *gospel*, they are, thus, those who confess Christ as the one who delivers from the consequences of sin and who brings new life.

The word *evangelical*, however, is usually used more particularly than this. And with good historical reason. In Europe it is customary to designate the heirs of the Protestant Reformation as Evangelicals. These Evangelicals who took exception to the belief and practice of the Roman Catholic church preached a distinct message. They proclaimed that people were reconciled to God only by faith in the person and work of Christ and not by the things they did themselves. They also proclaimed that in religious matters the Bible was the ultimate authority, not the pope nor the traditions of the church. Later in eighteenth- and nineteenth-century England, the Evangelicals were those who emphasized the need for an experience of Christian conversion and who sought to carry out the Bible's commands rigorously in their personal and social lives.

The present use of the word *evangelical* in America partakes of all these usages. In its broadest possible use it is a synonym for Christian. Somewhat more frequently it is still used in its old European sense of "not a Roman Catholic." Much more frequently, however, it denotes a group or person who espouses distinctive Christian beliefs and who seeks to put those beliefs into practice.

The two beliefs that define Evangelicals most concisely are the following: (1) the conviction that people need to have a proper relationship with God, a relationship that can be brought about only when God forgives our offenses against himself and transforms us into people who can love him and do the things that please him, and (2) the conviction that the Bible has the last word on what man's responsibilities to God are and how God has provided a way for mankind to meet his demands and enjoy his friendship. In theological jargon, Evangelicals believe in justification by faith alone and in a uniquely infallible Bible. Within

Evangelicalism these two affirmations can admittedly be shaded with very different colorings.

In spite of evangelical differences on what exactly these two beliefs mean, most would see them as the important cornerstones of their religion. Most would also be unwilling to allow other aspects of their lives—whether ecclesiastical, cultural, or political—to define their essential religious commitments. Christ for Evangelicals is not only the Way of life but also the Truth of life. As a consequence, the kinds of definitions that Evangelicals are concerned about most are ones that involve their beliefs.

It would be wrong to think, however, that the forty-odd million Americans who are in general agreement about salvation by faith and the authority of Scripture see eye to eye on other matters. By no means. American Evangelicals pursue widely varied kinds of spirituality: from the liturgical-sacramental to the informal-fundamentalistic. They approach social and political matters from many points of view: some embracing American society wholeheartedly, others rejecting its values; some on the right politically, others on the left. Evangelicals also offer different kinds of definitions concerning the "worldliness" that they are to shun and that the power of Christ in them opposes. For some being "worldly" means drinking alcoholic beverages, for others it means watching television; for some it might mean going shopping or to the beach on Sunday, for others supporting the American military. In spite of these wide differences, however, professions of salvation by faith and biblical authority enable Evangelicals to understand each other and, when mistrust is set aside, to recognize their spiritual bonds. These shared affirmations stimulate a common desire to love God more purely, to understand him more completely, and to serve him more faithfully.

It is on the basis of these common affirmations that divisions can be made between those who are and who are not Evangelicals. In historical terms, Evangelicals include those who follow in the line of the orthodox theology of the Protestant Reformation and the piety of the eighteenth-century revivals. They are, in short, those who in spite of all the many changes since the sixteenth century still believe that salvation comes by God's grace through faith in Christ, who maintain that the Bible shows what man should believe about himself, God, and the way of salvation, and who affirm that such beliefs must determine the way they live. By this definition, then, widely contrasting groups can be regarded as evangelical. Bob Jones University (which shuns most other evangelical groups) and the Billy Graham Evangelistic Association (which cultivates relationships with a wide variety of Christians) would be included. As would Melodyland School of Theology, a charismatic institution with roots in recent American history, and the Christian Reformed Church, a Calvinistic body whose traditions reach back to early modern Europe. To make use of terminology proposed recently by Richard J. Mouw, the evangelical umbrella covers groups that could be called Fundamentalist, Neo-evangelicals (conservative, progressive, and militant), Confessional Evangelicals (with the same three subgroups), and Charismatics. (Many of these terms will be explained in the body of this book.)

On the other hand, anyone who affirms that man can find genuine liberation apart from Christ or ultimate truth apart from the Bible is not an Evangelical. Insofar as even a Protestant does not define salvation as an act accomplished for helpless sinners by the grace of God in Christ, he or she is not evangelical. Or to deny that the Bible and its revelation of Christ is the definitive authority for man in the search for forgiveness of sin, communion with God, and fulfillment in life, is to deny evangelical Christianity. In addition, groups such as the Church of Christ of Latter Day Saints or the Jehovah's Witnesses, no matter how "evangelistically" they live and propagate their beliefs, are not Evangelicals, for they do not find the finality of salvation in Christ nor the finality of revealed truth in the Bible.

Defining Evangelicalism in this way is like fishing with nets cast wide. The purpose is to haul in all the usable fish possible, even if some living creatures will be caught that are of no use. Similarly, our definition of *evangelical* here is wide in the effort not to exclude any of the fish that rightfully belong. In spite of inescapable limitations, the book does intend to talk about Evangelicals broadly and charitably defined.

And what a lively, interesting, controversial, exciting quantity of history there is to talk about! We begin with three connected chapters on evangelical theology. This may seem to be an imposing historical pill to swallow at the start of a book that is meant to be read. Fear should be set aside. Our discussion of theology stresses broad themes. It provides informal, nontechnical sketches of some of the names many modern Evangelicals recognize but have trouble placing—Jonathan Edwards, Charles Finney, Cotton Mather, Charles Hodge, C. F. W. Walther, Edgar Youngs Mullins, Edward Carnell, and others. It also provides a general historical framework for the more particular chapters that follow.

A full chapter on attitudes toward the Bible comes next. It outlines the ways in which the Bible has comforted and guided Evangelicals in America. In light of the recent controversy over the nature of the Bible, it also considers the history of crucial terms like "infallible" and "inerrant" at some length. Next are three chapters on the church. The first, on revivalism, discusses the periodic "awakenings" in America as events that have renewed the churches and increased their outreach. The second describes the general shape that the idea of the church has assumed in American history. The third looks at the process by which American evangelical churches have divided, subdivided, and occasionally reunited.

The final two chapters treat the history of evangelical interaction with American culture. The first looks at evangelical attitudes toward the nation, the second at evangelical responses to problems in society. A brief epilogue pulls together some of the themes running throughout the book. The volume concludes with a listing of further literature for those whose appetites have been whetted for more detailed knowledge than can be presented here.

In considering which subjects should be included in this volume, the authors had one primary goal in mind—to bring the light of the past to bear on distinctive features of American Evangelicalism that we experience today. We have thus been led to consider themes (like separatism) that are singularly prominent in evangelical history, as well as those (like theology) that are important one way or another in almost all religious histories.

The chapters themselves are meant to be read consecutively. Names, organization, events, and periods are defined most completely in the early chapters. Nevertheless, it is our intention that the individual chapters also stand as self-contained discussions of the topics under consideration. There is, thus, a limited amount of deliberate repetition. To provide variety and to avoid monotony, the chapters are designed to approach their subjects differently. Some are more chronological, some biographical, others thematic. Some are more concerned with how Evangelicals have expressed their beliefs, other with how they have acted. Some see more to criticize in the evangelical heritage than to praise, others just the reverse. In all, however, our aim has been to present readable and instructive accounts of the history behind the way Evangelicals have become what they are.

In no sense do we offer this book as the last word on the history of Evangelicals in America. We know well that we have neglected many important aspects of evangelical life: the missionary enterprise, the distinctive styles of life found in evangelical groups, the complex institutional worlds of publishing, summer camping, and philanthropy.

By giving our chapters the titles of gospel songs without anywhere treating worship or the arts, we point to another gap in our coverage. Much more could have been said about evangelical life in the black community. More too probably needed to be done for the contributions of women to evangelical history. And we are not equipped to offer the sophisticated kind of sociological analysis seen in Andrew Greeley's recent book *The American Catholic*. Other important topics—such as the influence of a Puritan work ethic, or the vacillation between optimistic and pessimistic attitudes to life in this world—had to be set aside in order to keep the book within manageable bounds. Conscious of all the worthy areas we have neglected, we nevertheless feel confident that the material here will profit a wide variety of Evangelicals, as well as outside observers with a general interest in American religious history.

The three authors write out of the Reformed-Presbyterian-Baptist strain of American Evangelicalism. As such we will miss nuances and sometimes more important features of other evangelical traditions. But we have tried to range widely in our reading and to be fair in our writing about these other traditions while not stinting our own. In addition, our efforts to keep things simple sometimes prevents us from doing justice to the bewildering complexity of modern Evangelicalism.

As committed believers in Jesus Christ and the authority of the Bible ourselves, we are convinced that the history of America's Evangelicals can provide valuable instruction to modern believers. In our history are countless examples of both good and bad evangelical practice. As evangelical *historians* we have tried to let the story tell itself, but as *evangelical* historians we have inevitably singled out the events and drawn the conclusions that seem most important from our perspective in late twentieth-century America. Our desire is that God would use this very fallible book as he has used his infallible written word: for teaching, for reproof, for correction, and for training in righteousness.

PART I:
EVANGELICAL THEOLOGY AND THE LIFE OF THE MIND

1

"Faith of Our Fathers"

From the Beginnings (1607-1870)

The word *theology* is not an exciting word for Americans, including most Christians. When we think of theology, we might picture medieval monks arguing long into the night about how many angels can sit on the head of a pin. Could anything be more irrelevant? Or, if we have lived for any time in Christian circles, we might think of learned scholars discoursing on the relative merits of supralapsarianism versus infralapsarianism. Could anything be less interesting? Perhaps we have also witnessed bitter battles in which the proponents of premillennialism dueled the proponents of amillennialism, or where defenders of free will and advocates of predestination went after each other in mortal conflict. Could anything be more disrupting in the church?

If these are the things that come to mind when *theology* is mentioned, it must seem strange to begin a book with three whole chapters on theological developments. Yet there is another way of looking at theology which makes it an appropriate place to begin the story of America's Evangelicals. If we look upon theology as merely Christian thinking about God and his work, rather than the obscure mumbo jumbo of academicians, it makes more sense as the first consideration in this book. For thinking about God is really what theology means. Defined in this simple way, every Christian, at his or her own level, is a theologian.

In these first three chapters we look at American evangelical theology as two, closely related activities. We want, first, to explain as simply and clearly as possible what American Evangelicals have thought about God, his actions, and the ways he makes himself known to mankind. To do this, we must naturally discuss the men, and occasionally women, who as ministers and teachers have devoted their lives to systematic study of the Bible. Our aim throughout, however, has been to translate the sometimes complicated and confusing statements of these persons into language that all can understand.

We want, secondly, to see theology as the process of "bridge building" between biblical truth and American culture. It is there that "the life of the mind" becomes important. The theologian who talks about God is always influenced, one way or another, by the world in which he stands. The Puritans in the 1600s lived in a different world than the revivalists of the 1740s, or the missionary-reformers of the 1830s, or the Fundamentalists of the 1910s. To explain how Evangelicals brought their thinking about God to bear within their various historical situations is, then, our second task in describing theology, broadly conceived.

The first three chapters, in short, tell a story that Evangelicals in the present day should find interesting. How do our views on salvation or the end times, for example, differ from those who have gone before? How have they remained the same? It is of course impossible to tell the entire story of evangelical theology even in three lengthy chapters. The individual denominations are filled with men and women who have made important theological contributions. Although we will not be able to treat, or even mention, all of these, we can give a general sense of the path that evangelical thought has taken to the present. And we can indicate as well some of the significant differences that mark off groups within Evangelicalism from each other. We hope that the simple survey which follows will entice readers to delve further into the theological treasures of their denominations and to catch a sense of how rich the various evangelical theological traditions remain to this very day.

THE BEGINNINGS: 1607-1730

In one very important respect, the shape of "American" theology was set before the first English settlers arrived in Virginia and Massachusetts. As Protestants, American Evangelicals have always believed that salvation is by faith and not by works, and that the Bible and not the pope or tradition is the supreme authority for the church. As such, they continue in the principles announced first in modern times by the German reformer Martin Luther. In addition, American

Evangelicals, however much they have disagreed among themselves, usually talk about salvation in terms of God's sovereignty and man's will, of Christ as prophet, priest, and king, and of the need for faith. And these are themes which the reformer John Calvin spelled out particularly in his *Institutes of the Christian Religion* at least seventy years before the settlement of America. We could even argue that the work of John Wesley, who lived in the 1700s well after the founding of America, contributed to American evangelical theology as much as Luther or Calvin through his emphasis on holy living.

The point in mentioning Luther, Calvin, and Wesley here is that American theology rests on a sturdy European base. One of the ways, in fact, that the story of theology in America can be viewed is as a series of modifications adapting the European heritage to the New World. That is not to say that Americans have merely copied what Europeans have done. Nor is it to say that Americans ever abandoned the Bible as the final source for all Christian thought. On the contrary, from the time of the Puritans, the thinking of Christians in America has borne a distinct and self-consciously biblical character. To the distinctives of the first American Protestants we now turn.

The Christians among America's earliest settlers were firmly committed to the faith of the Reformation. The Puritans of New England, most of the Anglicans of early Virginia, the early Dutch settlers of New York and New Jersey, and later the Scotch-Irish of Pennsylvania were all Calvinists. (Or to state it more accurately, they were "Reformed," the general term for the theological position of which Calvin was one part.) It was not as if these early settlers slept with Calvin's *Institutes* under their pillows, for the English Reformation had produced many theologians whose works had a wider readership in America than Calvin's. (The theology text at Harvard in the early days was, for example, William Ames's *The Marrow of Theology*.)

It is true, nevertheless, that these early colonists held convictions that we associate with Calvin's name. They believed that God's law was clearly set forth as the absolute standard for all human behavior, that all men fell short of God's standard because of the sinful human nature inherited from Adam and because of personal sinning, that sinful human nature could do nothing spiritually good by itself, that only God's grace in Christ—received by faith—could bring salvation to the sinner, and that without God's supernatural work in the individual life, no sinner would desire God nor turn from evil to faith in Christ.

Undergirding these specific theological ideas were more general attitudes toward God's character and the way in which he communicated with man. The Puritans were strenuous moral athletes because they had a high view of God as "a Spirit, infinite, eternal, unchangeable in His being, wisdom, power, holiness, justice, goodness, and truth" (Westminster Shorter Catechism of 1646). Such a being deserved all the love, dedication, energy, and devotion that the creature, by God's grace, could give back to him. The Puritan also believed that God had spoken truly and clearly through the pages of the Bible and that these pages contained all that he needed to know in order to organize his personal life, his life in society, and his church life.

The New England Puritans, and to a lesser extent Reformed Christians in the other colonies, used a "covenantal" vocabulary to describe the relationship between God and man. They spoke of a mutual contract in which God and man fulfilled certain obligations to each other. From the Old Testament the Puritans saw that a covenant was sometimes a conditional agreement between God and man, sometimes an unconditional gift of God demanding a response of obedience to God's law. The New Testament, the Puritans noted, spoke of a new covenant from God in Christ. Puritan theology adopted both the Old and New Testament concepts of the covenant as a means to proclaim God's grace while maintaining the authority of his law.

In the covenants God's perfect law set the standard by which people were measured, and God's grace offered an opportunity to fulfill the conditions demanded by the law. Mankind, spiritually incapacitated by sin, was unable to live up to the original standards of God's righteousness as these had been set forth in a "covenant of works." But God in mercy sent his Son to pay the debt of mankind for breaking the law. Jesus was the substitute for covenant-breaking man as he felt the brunt of God's righteous anger on the cross. Because of Christ's work on man's behalf, God established the covenant of grace with the elect. The condition of salvation was now not the fulfilling of the law (which had proven impossible in the Garden of Eden), but faith in Jesus. It was a covenant of grace because God provided the faith for belief in Christ. The believer's part of the bargain was to love God and obey his law, a task which by faith in Christ could now be taken up with hope.

The virtue of a covenantal system in explaining the plan of salvation was twofold: it preserved the Reformed view of God's grace while retaining an important place for the law. Only supernatural grace could overcome total depravity, but the ability to love and keep God's law indicated that a person was a child of God. Following the law did not save a person, but a saved person did follow the law.

The two early Americans who put these ideas best were Thomas Hooker (1586-1647) of Connecticut and John Cotton (1584-1652) of Boston. Both had arrived on board the same ship to the New World in 1633. Both were powerful preachers. Both dominated the religious lives of their respective colonies as long as they lived. Both were very influential in establishing the "Puritan Way" in their colonies. Theologically, works such as Hooker's *A True Sight of Sin* or Cotton's *Purchasing Christ* proclaimed the supreme place of grace in redemption and drove home the covenantal system as the best explanation for God's work among men. Along with these basic similarities, the theology of the two leaders also contained shades of difference that would be magnified by later evangelical theologians into distinct commitments.

When Cotton talked of the covenant of grace, he emphasized the Holy Spirit's immediate work in the heart of the elect. Hooker tended to emphasize the holy living which that same covenant both demanded and made possible. Where Cotton labored to preserve God's glory in conversion, Hooker glorified God in the labors of the converted. Substantially united, yet differing in significant details, their work set a high standard for later American theologians.

DISSENT AND DECLINE

A few dissenters from the point of view expounded by Cotton and Hooker did exist in seventeenth-century America. Anne Hutchinson (1591-1643), for example, was exiled from Massachusetts in 1638 because of her dangerous theology. The authorities there thought she was overlooking the connection between God's grace and good works. Anne Hutchinson seemed to say that grace could exist as a result of the Holy Spirit's special action without good works necessarily following. The Puritans replied that although there are no spiritually profitable good works before conversion, good works show that God's grace has actually come into a life. To them, Anne Hutchinson seemed to attack the holy character of God's law and its important place in the Christian's life.

The other best-known dissenter in early New England, Roger Williams (1603?-1683), would later be acclaimed for his defense of religious freedom (for details see chapter 7). It is important to note in our discussion of theology, however, that his dissent in practical matters had a doctrinal base. Williams was probably the most consistent Calvinist, theologically, in early New England. So thoroughly did he believe in the sovereignty of God's grace—so thoroughly did he deny the possibility of salvation through human works—that he attacked all efforts of whatever kind to "help" God's work. State support of the church, for instance, was illegitimate for a theological reason: the church, as God's work, must be supported only by God's people, and that only as they are moved by the Holy Spirit to contribute. Unlike many Evangelicals before and since, Williams would make no concessions for getting along in the world if it forced him to transgress a theological principle.

In general, however, frontal attacks on Puritan theology in the seventeenth century were rare. What did happen as years went by was that the fine distinctions the early Puritans had made began to blur. The talk continued to be of God's power in salvation and of the divine origin of good works, but gradually the emphasis was shifted. More and more stress was placed upon the need to "prepare" for salvation by doing good works. More and more attention was paid to human responsibility for good works before and after conversion. More and more concern was shown for formal religious responsibilities, less and less for inner spiritual realities.

This gradual dilution of Puritan thought was matched by a progressive cooling of the religious fervor that had characterized many of the country's first settlers. The second and third generations, in New England particularly, did not have the same enthusiasm for God that their fathers and grandfathers had had when confronted by spiritual deterioration in England. The very fruitfulness of the New World posed a problem as well. With increased opportunities for wealth came also increased temptations to snobbery, social alienation, and self-sufficiency. And these traits corroded the common Christian foundations upon which Puritan theology had rested.

Toward the end of the seventeenth century, a heavy series of blows brought added discouragement to believers in the English colonies. War with the Indians saw the destruction of many lives and much property (1675-1678). In 1684 the English Parliament revoked Massachusetts's charter under which it had established its Puritan way of life. The hysteria over witchcraft in Salem, Massachusetts, in the early 1690s testified to the severe strains present in colonial society. It is hard to say exactly which caused which, but without doubt the Puritan society and the Puritan theology were both falling on hard times at the end of the seventeenth century.

This is not to say, however, that the era lacked substantial religious thought. A long series of sermons preached by the Boston minister Samuel Willard (1640-1707) was published after his death in 1726 as *The Compleat Body of Divinity*. This work was the closest thing to a systematic theology that Puritanism's covenantal thought ever received. It was also the largest book published in America to that time. Through detailed exegesis of Scripture, weighty argumentation, and sturdy reliance on the Westminster Confession of Faith, Willard again proclaimed the sum of Puritanism: God's sovereignty, man's covenant dependence upon the Trinity, the joys and labors of sanctification. Unfortunately for such a substantial work, the times had passed it by, and very few heeded its message.

The works of Cotton Mather (1663-1728) received a better hearing. This brilliant, if overbearing, heir of the Puritan tradition saw himself as a mediator between the values of the past and the needs of the present, between thought in Europe and life in America. Mather struggled to recall Americans to their Puritan heritage even as he absorbed Europe's newest learning (Isaac Newton on the laws of the physical world, John Locke on the "laws" of the mind). He battled for Puritan orthodoxy at the same time as he championed the new pietism from awakened Germany with its stresses on Christian activism and godly feelings.

The theology Mather expressed in his spiritual history of America, *Magnalia Christi Americana*, and his proposals for doing good, *Bonifacius*, was a subtle blend of the old and the new. From the past it drew on Puritanism's love of God's law and its preoccupation with his grace. From the present it drew a concern for cause and effect relationships from the new science and a concern for godliness active in love from the new pietism. Although Mather died with no immediate disciples to carry on his work, his effort to fuse doctrinal orthodoxy and active piety would be repeated, with much greater success, in the colonial Great Awakening.

In spite of the solid works of Willard and Mather, American theology in the early years of the eighteenth century was less potent than at the end of the seventeenth. Even in New England it was obvious that times had changed greatly from the days of Hooker and Cotton. Some colonists were uneasy about the temptations of prosperity. A few were concerned about the emergence of deism in Europe and its questioning of traditional Christian doctrines. Some noted a growing surge of Arminianism, a perspective which gave man more responsibility for his own salvation. Some, like the young Ben Franklin, poked fun at the efforts of old-guard Puritans to patch up old ways. Others turned away from theology altogether, perhaps to the disputes between "court" and "country" that were entering American politics. Theology in the early eighteenth century was uncertain because American life itself was uncertain as it faced the adjustments demanded by an increasingly modern world. The settled world of Puritan religion from which Puritan theology had sprung was no more.

THE GREAT AWAKENING AS A THEOLOGICAL EVENT: 1730-1770

Religious stirrings in the 1730s and the Great Awakening of the 1740s did not bring innovation in theology so much as renovation. It did not change the theological principles of the Puritans, but it did proclaim them with a new and urgent voice. When the Dutch Reformed church in Raritan, New Jersey, received its new minister in 1720, it received a man who had been trained in the centers of European pietism. For Theodore Frelinghuysen (1691-1747) attitudes of the heart were more important than formal religious orthodoxy. As he warned his parishioners with increasingly pointed language that formal religiosity by itself would not save them from the wrath to come, his preaching created a stir. He called upon his people to seek a warmhearted relationship with God rather than a cold alliance.

Frelinghuysen's Presbyterian neighbor in New Brunswick, Gilbert Tennent (1703-1764), picked up the cry and gave it even stronger language: repent and believe the gospel or suffer the fires of God's wrath directed at those who do not believe. About this same time in Northampton, Massachusetts, Jonathan Edwards (1703-1758) was preaching an effective series of sermons on justification by faith, a doctrine that had been obscured for the preceding generation. And then in the late 1730s came the Grand Itinerant, George Whitefield (1714-1770). Whitefield's theology was neither profound nor novel: he proclaimed the awful plight of the damned and the glorious prospects of those whose sins had been forgiven.

The importance of the Great Awakening for American revivalism is considered at length in chapter 5. Its importance for evangelical theology lay more in its aftermath than in its unfolding. It was as ministers began to reflect on the theological implications of what had taken place that important developments occurred. It was particularly as Jonathan Edwards bent his great mind to study the revival in the light of the Bible and of the best modern learning that American theology moved into a new era.

Edwards's theological accomplishment was twofold: first, he restated the Calvinistic doctrine of salvation in terms that would dominate American theology for at least a century and influence it to the present. Second, he examined the nature of proper Christian behavior with the sophisticated categories of modern thought.

Edwards's *Freedom of the Will* (1754) set out, in new and forceful language, traditional Calvinistic ideas on the nature of man and the source of salvation. Edwards argued that there was no such entity as a "will" inside people. Rather, people "willed" to do something in accordance with the strongest motive within themselves, a motive that may have come from the environment or from the essential nature of the person. In other words, Edwards said that people always act in a way that is consistent with their internal character: good trees do not produce bad fruit, nor bad trees good. This discussion of "willing" was important theologically. It meant that a sinful person would never *want* to act in a way pleasing to God unless God himself changed that person's character. Because a sinful nature would never "will" to love God and follow his commands, God himself must change the sinner before the sinner could love God and obey his word. (In theological terms, Edwards was arguing that regeneration—God's act—was the basis for repentance and conversion—our acts.)

Edwards's opponents reacted to this treatise by inquiring how Edwards knew so much about the nature of sinful man. Edwards replied in his book *Original Sin* (1758). This volume argued that humanity as a whole was present in Adam when he sinned and that all people as a consequence shared the bent toward sinning that Adam had brought on himself. In later years many American Christians would take exception to Edwards's formulation of the doctrine of salvation. But for at least a century after his death in 1758, when Evangelicals talked about salvation, they did so in terms made famous by Jonathan Edwards.

Edwards's examination of religious experience had a less obvious impact on the history of evangelical theology, but it was still important. His book in 1746 on the *Religious Affections* (or emotions) stated a profound truth that Evangelicals have sometimes forgotten to their sorrow. It is not the quantity of religious emotions or their intensity that proves their reality. It is rather that they originate in a heart that has been changed to love God and seek His pleasure. Truly Christian emotions may be intense and prolific. The final test of their validity, however, is that they flow from a heart that has been made new by God and that they result in a lifetime of loving service to God.

A posthumous work published in 1765, *The Nature of True Virtue*, defined virtue as "love to Being in general." Edwards argued that to be truly good was to treat everything (from God as purest being to man and the creation as beings made by God) according to its true worth.

Thus, for example, to treat God like a man or a man like God violated virtue and led to sin.

These two works were not as argumentative as the strictly theological tomes, and their careful philosophical style makes them difficult reading. Nevertheless, they have helped to shape the way that Evangelicals evaluate religious emotion and Christian behavior.

The numerous followers of Jonathan Edwards came to be known as the proponents of a New Divinity. They constituted the dominant theological strand in America until the start of the nineteenth century. With an ardor that many would find strange today, these New Divinity men went round and round on the subject of salvation: what exactly was the effect of Adam's sin today? Could people take free actions to bring about their own salvation? Was "self-interest" a valid Christian motive for repenting of sin and believing in Christ? Did Christ's death on the cross have the same meaning for those who would be saved and for those who would reject the gospel? A small but growing number of Baptists argued that the theology explained so well by Jonathan Edwards fit their practice of believer's baptism for adults better than it did the traditional baptism of infants. Such issues were debated endlessly by ministerial graduates of Harvard, Yale, and Princeton. Laymen also took the questions seriously. At least as far as the general level of theological interest and knowledge was concerned, the fifty years after Edwards's death was probably the high point of evangelical theology in American history.

The followers of Edwards could not match their master's philosophical brilliance or theological depth. They did make a contribution to later developments, however, by providing a Calvinistic system that nineteenth-century theologians would modify for the American environment of their day.

Samuel Hopkins (1721-1803) developed Edwards's ethical insights into a consistent system. "Disinterested benevolence" was the catchword he used to describe how love to God and fellow creatures, apart from love for ourselves, should be the guideline for our actions. Hopkins also maintained a heightened sense of God's sovereignty by suggesting that people should be willing even "to be damned for the glory of God."

Joseph Bellamy (1719-1790) argued for God's absolute control in redemption and against man's efforts to save himself. But he also modified slightly the traditional idea of how that redemption was accomplished. This modification went a step further with Bellamy's pupil, the son of the great Edwards, Jonathan Edwards, Jr. (1745-

1801). Apparently swayed by the preoccupation with law in Revolutionary America, the younger Edwards proposed a "governmental theory" of the atonement. That is, Christ died to satisfy God's standards of justice rather than to appease his wrath at sin.

Opponents of the New Divinity included "Old Calvinists" like Ezra Stiles (1727-1795), president of Yale College. Stiles much preferred a pietistic emphasis on God's love and Christ's mercy to the elaborate rational efforts of Edwards's followers. Other opponents, like the increasingly self-confident Unitarians, were beginning to write off most discussions of man's depravity and God's absolute sovereignty as antiquated remnants of the past. In a way, the New Divinity men proved to be their own worst enemies. Jonathan Edwards, Jr., for example, saw his New Haven, Connecticut church lose more than four-fifths of its membership. The people simply were not being nourished spiritually by the dry, rationalistic scholarship that they heard from this theologian of the New Divinity. Sad to say, the style of the younger Edwards was all too typical for this theological persuasion.

THE AMERICAN REVOLUTION AS A THEOLOGICAL EVENT: 1770-1800

In another sense, however, theology of every stripe was something on the fringe of American society, for the great age of theological discourse following Edwards was also the great period of nation building. While New England Congregationalists, Pennsylvania Presbyterians, and Carolina Baptists argued about how men were freed from sin, colonists all across America spoke even more eagerly about being freed from Parliament. The great public concern for independence and for the construction of a new nation also exerted an influence on the course of theology in the country. The ideals that patriots fought for during the Revolution and that underlay the founding documents of the new country had an impact on theology as well. When the Declaration of Independence proclaimed "that all men are created equal, that they are endowed by their Creator with certain unalienable Rights," theologians also listened. The convictions that men had rights by nature, that the pursuit of personal happiness was an inalienable right, that all men were essentially equal, and that personal freedom was necessary for societal well-being influenced the thinking of church fathers as well as founding fathers.

The trend in American Evangelicalism away from Reformed, Calvinistic theology did not arise with the Revolution nor cease with its success, but the period of nation building did ease the way for movements opposed to the Reformed theology of earlier American history. Take the so-called Five Points of Calvinism. The idea of total depravity did not stand up well to the belief that individuals had the inherent capacity to shape their own destinies. The concept of unconditional election also seemed to deny that people were fully capable of determining the course of their own lives. The Calvinistic idea of a limited atonement in which the benefits of God's action in Christ were restricted to the "elect" was an affront to the equality of which the Declaration of Independence spoke. Irresistible grace seemed offensive to the American idea that uncontrollable power was evil. True, American Evangelicals might continue to believe in the perseverance of the saints, but they did so as much for their confidence in themselves as in God. Those who opposed the Calvinistic ideas most strenuously became Unitarians or abandoned Protestant Christianity entirely, and thus were cut off from Evangelicalism properly so-called. But the ideas of the new nation had their effect on proper Evangelicals as well. Without the Revolutionary backdrop, the history of evangelical theology in the first two-thirds of the nineteenth century would be difficult to comprehend.

THE BIG PICTURE AT 1800

It would be well to pause at this point to take a long view of American theology at the start of a crucial century. As the nation itself was entering a new era, so too was the church. The United States was experiencing the enthusiasm ("Westward Ho!") and doubts (Could we really remain independent?) that often characterize a new country. The settlers who streamed across the Appalachians sacrificed stability and a settled life for novelty and the prospect of better things. Many of those left behind were also caught up in the heady excitement of the day. A spirit of change gripped American society, not least the Christians in its midst.

Where theology was concerned, at least five major developments were underway by 1800, developments that would permanently alter the ways in which Evangelicals thought about God and communicated that thinking in the world. First, the relative theological unity of Evangelicalism was beginning to break up. Where most American Christians before 1800 were Reformed (or, broadly speaking, Calvinistic), many after this date would be Arminian (see the sections on the Methodists and Charles Finney in this chapter and on the Holiness movement in the next). By the end of the nineteenth century, three other points of view—liberalism, dispensationalism, and pentecostalism—would dilute evangelical theological unity even further.

Second, the evangelical perspective was dominating American life less and less and cooperating with it more and more. This caused no problems so long as American society remained at least vaguely Christian—as in the first two-thirds of the nineteenth century. Indeed, this partnership could even appear as a great advantage. But when significant segments of American society turned from traditional Christianity, as they did in the last third of the century, it was a great shock for evangelical theology. No longer could it take for granted a sympathetic audience, nor assume that everyone was predisposed to think along the same lines about God, man, and the world.

A third, related change concerned the evangelical attitude toward the country itself. Developments here are covered at considerable length in chapter 8. For now, it is enough to say that much of the enthusiasm for the church and God's activity in America was being transferred to America itself, which was seen increasingly as the agent for doing God's work in the world. This assumption has major theological consequences. Some Americans developed a supreme confidence in the unquestionable truth of their doctrinal points of view. They often held them to be as uniquely blessed of God as their country was.

Fourth, evangelical theology by 1800 was exporting fewer ideas into American culture and importing more from it. Jonathan Edwards and other ministers had set the tone for American intellectual life in the mid-eighteenth century. By 1800 the statesmen and governmental leaders were performing this function. By 1870 the scientists had begun to assume this role. Theology, in other words, no longer reigned as "queen of the sciences" in the American kingdom of thought.

A fifth change was taking place in the relationship between the mind of the church and the life of the church. These two aspects of Christian existence always influence each other, with life sometimes following thought, sometimes vice versa. Where before 1800 the mind of the church (its theology) had tended to control the life of the church (its practice day by day), after 1800 the life exerted more control over the mind. To cite just one example of this, which is explained fully in chapter 5, revivalistic practice in the eighteenth century developed under the constraints of the dominant Calvinistic theology. In the nineteenth century it altered the shape of the Calvinism.

None of these changes took place overnight. Some of them were well underway by 1800; some had only just begun. Together, they contributed to the creation of a new theological landscape for American Evangelicals in the nineteenth century.

PROTESTANTISM AT ITS PEAK (1800-1870): REFORMED

The Second Great Awakening that began in the 1790s had even more impact on the shape of evangelical theology than the great revival fifty years earlier. Both the New England and frontier phases of this second Awakening served to modify the Reformed heritage in America. The spectacular camp meetings in Kentucky and Tennessee and the calmer, yet no less powerful, stirrings in New England differed in many outward respects. Traveling evangelists such as the Presbyterian James McGready (1758?-1817) led the more emotional revival in the mid-South while in New England the president of Yale College, Timothy Dwight (1752-1817), led a movement that drew great strength from the colleges and settled pastors of that region. The labors of Dwight's most well-known theological student, Nathaniel William Taylor (1786-1858), were particularly important in giving a theoretical foundation to the northeastern revival (for a full account of this revival, see chapter 5).

The frontier revivals and the more organized resurgence of Evangelicalism in the east shared much in common theologically, however. In both, the prevailing Calvinism of the eighteenth century was giving way to a more Arminian construction of the gospel. Where Jonathan Edwards in 1740 proclaimed that mankind's original sin prevented any movement toward salvation apart from the Holy Spirit's specific work, Nathaniel Taylor and the frontier revivalists called on people to exercise native powers to make the choice for Christ. Seen from another angle, the earlier theology had stressed the various inabilities of people in order to preserve God's sovereignty unto himself. Now the increasingly dominant theology of the nineteenth century stressed the abilities that God had lovingly bestowed on all people and not merely on a limited number of the elect.

Since the time of Edwards and Whitefield, the revival had been accepted as the best way of "harvesting" souls, but in the early nineteenth century it began to reflect new theological emphases. Revivalists now preached that the reality of conversion could be grasped immediately by the person taking hold of Christ. Edwards and Whitefield would have urged those responding to their messages—the "hopefully converted"—to examine their lives to see if God had truly done a work of grace in their hearts. But nineteenth-century revivalists were prone to assure individuals of their place in the family of God as soon as the believer had exercised his or her God-given natural capacities.

Evangelical theology did not follow this path unanimously. At the same time that these newer theological accents gained currency, other influential theologians restated the traditional Reformed theology of the eighteenth century. Chief among these was Charles Hodge (1797-1878) of Princeton Seminary. Although his massive, three-volume *Systematic Theology* was not published until the early 1870s, his theological point of view had been taught to some 3,000 seminarians in a crucial generation and a half of American church history. Hodge's frequently quoted assertion that "there had never been a new idea at Princeton" has been the butt of unfair laughter. What he intended to say was that Princeton desired to transmit the tried and true Reformed theology to new generations of Americans. To do this he relied more on the Westminster Confession of Faith (1643-1646) and the works of an earlier Swiss theologian, François Turretini (1623-1687), than on the modern ideas of man's innate capabilities.

To cite just one of the theological controversies in which Hodge was engaged, he took decided exception to the views of Nathaniel Taylor on salvation. To Taylor's idea that human guilt arose only from one's own sins, Hodge held out the traditionally Reformed idea that Adam's guilt was imputed to all the human race. To Taylor's idea that people possessed a "freedom to the contrary" in their natural ability to choose God, Hodge replied with the old Reformed view that man, because of sin, was not capable of doing anything for his own salvation. To Hodge salvation was an absolute gift of the absolutely sovereign God. Although Hodge and the Princeton school of theologians were somewhat wary of Jonathan Edwards (he appeared too speculative and philosophical for comfort), they came as close as any group during the nineteenth century of carrying on his Calvinistic tradition.

PROTESTANTISM AT ITS PEAK (1800-1870): THE METHODISTS AND CHARLES FINNEY

In this period as in other ages of American history, evangelical theology was being shaped by more than just the transmission and modification of older ideas. In the early nineteenth century evangelical theology received another powerful stimulus from overseas in the form of John Wesley's Methodism. Methodists had been active in the colonies before the Revolution. But because they were *English* missionaries, their work suffered during the War. The Christmas Conference at Baltimore in 1784 created a distinctly American Methodism that soon assumed a distinctive cast of its own and made a significant impact on Evangelicalism. American Methodism is known best for the genius of its organization under such energetic leaders as Francis Asbury and Peter Cartwright. By 1844 it had emerged as the largest Christian body in America. But Methodism also left a deep imprint on American theology.

John Wesley (1703-1791) had been a "Puritan" in his attitude toward Christian life in the world. Believers were to take their actions, duties, and responsibilities in this life seriously, and they were to spare no pains in the energetic pursuit of truly Christian behavior. To these Puritan perspectives Wesley added a basically Reformed view of man, a creature lost in sin without any hope of salvation apart from the grace of God. What separated Wesley from the Reformed tradition was his view of that divine grace without which man was lost. As Wesley read the Bible and the fathers of the church, he concluded that all people had been given a "prevenient" grace (a grace which "goes before") that now bestowed upon each individual the power to accept or reject Christ. With this view, and in opposition to strict Reformed theology, Wesley held that Christ's death had in fact atoned for all men. He felt that God's grace was in fact resisted by those who were lost. And he believed that the saints could consciously and deliberately lose their salvation.

Wesley's most influential teaching, however, dealt not with these alterations to Reformed theology but with his view of the believer's task after conversion. The particular genius of Wesley's Methodism—the great Christian principle that shook English society in the eighteenth century and American society in the nineteenth—was his insistence that the experience of the believer's daily life required the same zeal as the experience of conversion itself. In this, Wesley was transmitting influences from the pietistic movement in Germany that had exerted such an important influence on himself. Many years before, Cotton Mather had longed to see a more active, energetic pietism in America. Not until Methodism exerted its full impact on this side of the Atlantic, however, was his desire fully realized. In theological terms, Wesley infused the idea of sanctification with the same enthusiasm that he and other revivalists gave to justification. For Wesley, the proper goal of every believer was Christian perfection, gained through the special work of the Holy Spirit.

The American exponents of Wesley's thought promulgated his ideas with love, with zeal, and with great effect. Even as they played down the more objective parts of the Protestant tradition such as formal creeds, formal liturgy, and formal sacraments, they stressed the subjectivity of the new birth and of Christian perfection. Thus, while Charles

Hodge and Nathaniel Taylor debated in learned theological journals about the Atonement, the nature of human freedom, and the imputation of Adam's guilt, Methodist itinerants like the convincing Mrs. Phoebe Palmer proclaimed in the highways and the byways the enthralling prospect of perfection in the Holy Ghost. Methodists in the nineteenth century never lost a feeling for the necessity of initial conversion to Christ, but their great contribution to American theology lay in pointing newborn babes in Christ to the prospect of a perfect adulthood in the Holy Spirit. From this point on in American Evangelicalism, the theology of Christian life became almost as important as the theology of Christian conversion.

The significance of this concern for sanctification can be seen in the theology of Charles Grandison Finney (1792-1875), the greatest revivalist of the nineteenth century before Moody. While not himself a Methodist, Finney succeeded in combining elements of the American Reformed heritage and the newer strivings for a Christian perfection. After his conversion in 1821, Finney joined the Presbyterians. While yet a member of this denomination, he imbibed freely of the ideas of Nathaniel Taylor that had influenced many of Presbyterianism's New School wing. In particular Finney was attracted to the idea that people had the ability within themselves to choose Christ and to choose to live the Christian life. Finney expounded this view during the "age of the common man" when Andrew Jackson publicized a new concern for the plain folks of the country. Much of what President Jackson was doing for politics, Finney was doing for theology. He brought the message of salvation into the highways and byways of "the common man." He proclaimed that energetic personal effort, with God's ready help, could overcome any obstacle to the life, liberty, and happiness of a Christian.

Later, in the mid-1830s, after Finney had left Presbyterianism, he pastored the independent Broadway Tabernacle in New York City. While in New York, and apparently apart from Methodist influence, Finney came to the conclusion "that an altogether higher and more stable form of Christian life was attainable, and was the privilege of all Christians." Shortly thereafter Finney read Wesley's *Plain Account of Christian Perfection* and was confirmed in his belief about "entire sanctification." This teaching became the trademark of Oberlin College in Ohio, where Finney had gone after leaving New York City. At Oberlin a vocabulary of the Christian life that prevails widely in evangelical circles to the present day came into existence when professors began to teach and write about "holiness," "Christian perfection," and "the baptism of the Holy Ghost." The first president of Oberlin, Presbyterian Asa Mahan, has been a neglected figure who did much to spread concern for this theology of the Christian life.

Finney, Mahan, and like-minded teachers worked out their concern for "holiness" in very practical terms. Much of the evangelical protest against slavery, drunkenness, discrimination, and other evils in nineteenth-century American life was led by those dedicated to "Christian perfection." Theologically considered, Finney's concern for both justification, understood as an Arminian interpretation of the Reformed theological heritage, and sanctification, understood as an American variant of the Wesleyan theological heritage, made him perhaps the most visible symbol of mainstream evangelical theology in the period from 1820-1870.

PROTESTANTISM AT ITS PEAK (1800-1870): THE MAINSTREAM

That theological mainstream, as we have seen, was by no means united in every respect, but it did share the broad heritage of Reformation Protestantism and an overriding interest in the doctrines of personal salvation. This mainstream, from Hodge to Finney, shared orthodox Protestant beliefs about the Trinity, the deity of Christ, and the authority of the Bible. Although significant differences existed in interpretations of particular biblical passages, most approached Scripture in much the same way. They tried to make sense of the whole Bible while focusing on the great acts of God in Christ, as narrated in the Gospels and interpreted by the New Testament Epistles. All in the mainstream looked forward to Christ's return to earth. None of them, however, made eschatology as important as the Adventists of that period or the dispensationalists later on. To be sure, the traditionally Reformed idea of God's sovereignty had been altered in an Arminian direction: Wesleyans spoke triumphantly of "grace for all." N. W. Taylor, when describing salvation theologically, put more emphasis on natural human ability than had his Reformed predecessors. And Finney's revivalistic "new measures" moved the practice of conversion away from the Reformed models of the eighteenth-century Great Awakening. Yet all still spoke of the grace of God revealed in perfect love through his son, the Lord Jesus Christ, as the bedrock of their theologies.

All, too, were relatively comfortable with the distinctively American cast of their theologies. America in the pre-Civil War days was an optimistic and practical land. Visions of a great country stretching from the Atlantic to the Pacific, and even beyond, danced in the minds of political leaders. The practical task of winning the West and subduing the wilderness took precedence over critical discussion of the American character. Visions of a great surge in Christian influence danced no less enthusiastically in the minds of this period's leading theologians. Charles Hodge and Charles Finney differed in their regard of man's inherent abilities, but they were equally optimistic concerning the spread of the gospel. They differed in their beliefs concerning how the gospel would work best, but they agreed on the fact that it was enjoying a notable success in this "golden day of democratic evangelicalism," as historian Sydney Ahlstrom has named the period.

The banks of this theological mainstream spread wide enough to include representatives of all major Protestant denominations. Congregationalist turned Presbyterian Lyman Beecher (1775-1863) preached revival and moral reform with equal fervor. In his New England pastorates and as president of Lane Presbyterian Seminary in Cincinnati, he was a lively exponent of N. W. Taylor's views on human responsibility in salvation and Christian action.

Balancing the "Old School" Presbyterianism of Charles Hodge was "New School" theologian Henry B. Smith. (The "Old School-New School" split in nineteenth-century Presbyterianism receives separate attention in chapter 7.) Smith felt that Hodge laid too much stress on God's formal decrees concerning mankind. He preferred a focus on the mediating work of Christ, and thought that this emphasis could provide a rallying point for Protestant theology in general.

Dissident Presbyterians, Barton W. Stone and Alexander Campbell, who founded the "Christian" or "Disciples" movement, are also discussed at greater length in chapter 7 as well as in chapter 6. But they too shared the basic theology of the period although with a greater emphasis on the simplicity of Christian truth.

Even the churches of European origin participated in the mainstream. Lutheran Samuel Schmucker (1799-1873) eventually came to be called an "American" Lutheran because of his desire to share the doctrinal emphases of his countrymen. After study at Presbyterian Princeton, he still relied on his Lutheranism as a bulwark against impiety, but he also added more American convictions. Included among these were his approval of revivalism. He was also unwilling to hold the traditional Lutheran belief, expressed in the Augsburg Confession, that the Lord's Supper was an objective means by which God's grace came to people. A similar "Americanization" can be seen in other denominations. The evangelical wing of the Episcopal church, for example, showed its affinity with the theological mainstream by putting more weight on preaching than on the Lord's Supper, by soft-pedaling the traditional Anglican sense of baptismal regeneration, and by removing most pictures and images from their churches. The mainstream of evangelical theology in the nineteenth century was indeed divided into discernibly different currents. It nevertheless retained a substantial unity due to its general acceptance of Reformed doctrine, or modifications thereof, and its common expression of that doctrine in terms congenial to the American environment.

PHILOSOPHY AND THEOLOGY IN THE NINETEENTH CENTURY

One other factor seemed to unify Protestant theology of this period, a commonly accepted philosophical point of view that was relatively new in nineteenth-century America. To one degree or another, many theologians of this period held to a philosophy called Scottish Common Sense Realism. As its name implies, this system arose in Scotland. It was carried to the New World by influential books and by John Witherspoon, a Scotsman who became president of Princeton College in 1768. As its name also implies, it stressed the reliability of common sense approaches to truth. The theologians adapted this perspective in different ways. For Nathaniel Taylor, it was merely "common sense" that human guilt arose from the individual who had sinned. For Charles Hodge, it was "common sense" that true theology came into existence by taking individual pieces of scriptural revelation and building them into a common whole. For Alexander Campbell, it was "common sense" to root Christian life in the New Testament era rather than in later church history.

This perspective offered strong support against the philosophical scepticism that had gained ground in Europe since the early 1700s. It encouraged a more systematic analysis of human capacities and Christian responsibilities. In so doing, it provided revivalism and reform movements a method of simplifying problems and applying specific Christian solutions to them. Common Sense Realism was, in short, a helpful way to find a place for everything theological and to put everything in its place.

For all its strength, this philosophical position also had some drawbacks. It was unwilling to rest with traditional tensions in Christian thought: for example, how divine sovereignty and human responsibility could exist together, or how the sacraments could be valuable for salvation without denying justification by faith. Most theologians in the nineteenth century were not content until they had "settled" these difficulties. In addition, people who looked at reality from the perspective of human common sense found it difficult to duplicate the kind of awe in which Jonathan Edwards stood before the untold glories of God's holiness. Finally, the position failed to deal with some issues, such as the value of "proofs" for God's creation of the world, which would one day pose considerable difficulties for evanglical thought. Taken as a whole, however, Scottish Common Sense Realism offered a helpful way for evanglical thinkers of different persuasions to relate the Bible to daily concerns. It provided a valuable framework for mainstream theology in the nineteenth century and has retained considerable influence in evangelical circles to this day.

BEYOND THE MAINSTREAM: 1800-1870

It would be wrong, however, to think that this mainstream exhausted evangelical theology in the mid-nineteenth century. True, by 1850 the distant roots of the sixteenth-century Reformation of Luther and Calvin and the more recent graftings from Wesleyan stock had all assumed distinctively American foliage. But there were other theological stirrings in America during this period that deserve at least a brief consideration, among which were important theological labors in the German Reformed Church, among Lutherans in America, and among the downtrodden untouchables of American life, the blacks.

When Philip Schaff (1819-1893) left Germany and his post at the University of Berlin in 1841 to come to the obscure little seminary of the American German Reformed Church in Mercersburg, Pennsylvania, his colleagues must have wondered about his mental health. Yet from this tiny seminary during the 1840s and 1850s came a significant, independent evangelical theology that flowed in a different channel from the more visible mainstream.

For his part, Schaff's monumental historical scholarship (a three-volume *Creeds of Christendom* and a seven-volume *History of the Christian Church*, both still standard works) presented the tacit case for a more comprehensive, a more catholic Evangelicalism. His book *The Principle of Protestantism* made the case explicitly. It called upon Americans to view the history of the church, even medieval Roman Catholicism, as a rich reservoir for present spirituality. American Evangelicals who saw themselves as the last, best hope for mankind sometimes took offense when Schaff urged believers to heed the Christian traditions passed on from earlier days. (He was in fact tried for heresy, but acquitted, in the German Reformed Church.) After leaving Mercersburg for Union Theological Seminary in New York, Schaff himself drew closer to the theological mainstream. His work on the American Revised Version of the Bible and for the cooperative Evangelical Alliance made him more acceptable, although he never abandoned commending the riches of the entire Christian tradition to Americans.

Schaff's colleague at Mercersburg, John Williamson Nevin (1803-1886), presented an even more explicit counter-evangelicalism to American theology. His sharp tract of 1843, *The Anxious Bench*, weighed the theology of Finney-style revivals in the balance and found it sadly wanting: such revivalism was "unfavorable to deep, thorough and intelligent piety . . . absolutely fatal to the idea of devotion and . . . injurious to the worship of God."[1] Nevin was particularly concerned about the American tendency to make theology exclusively subjective and internal. He feared that the emotionalism of the revivals and the intense scrutiny paid to the inner life were driving out the essence of Christianity—God's objective work in the incarnate Christ.

As his positive antidote to subjectivism, Nevin proposed a renewed appreciation of the Calvinistic concept of the Lord's Supper. His book entitled *The Mystical Presence* stated that "Christianity is grounded in the living union of the believer with the power of Christ; and this great fact is emphatically concentrated in the mystery of the Lord's Supper."[2] The Lord's Supper did have a subjective aspect in which the believer drew near to Christ, but its chief aspect was objective, the drawing near of Christ to the believer.

Nevin and Schaff thought American Evangelicalism was too emotional, too individualistic, and too subjective. Their proposals for a better-balanced evangelical theology in which God's love for us was the fountain from which our love for Him was drawn did not influence the mainstream greatly, but it did offer a significant evangelical dissent to the dominant theology of the nineteenth century.

A similar dissent came from America's Lutheran churches during this same period. In the East a third-generation American, Charles Porterfield Krauth (1823-1883) of the Lutheran seminary in Philadelphia, led a movement to call Lutheranism back to its original character. In St. Louis an immigrant from Germany, Carl Ferdinand Wilhelm Walther (1811-1878), labored to keep traditional Lutheran convictions alive among the vast numbers of Germans and Scandinavians coming to the Midwest in the nineteenth century. Krauth's most influential work, *The Conservative Reformation and Its Theology* (1871), called on Lutherans, and all American Evangelicals, to place a higher value on the historic confessions of the church and to give "the sacrament of the altar" its proper due in worship, doctrine, and practice. It was not as if

Krauth desired to abandon the Bible as the source of Protestant standards. Rather, he felt that the labors of the church universal throughout the centuries, and particularly during the Reformation, should not be discarded because of the supposedly novel situation in America.

Walther argued in his *Proper Distinction Between Law and Gospel* that God's grace must never be ignored as the source of salvation and as the source of a proper church life. He challenged Lutherans to renounce the reliance on self that had crept into their practice in America. He challenged American Evangelicals at large to recapture the historic confessons of Protestantism and their teaching of justification by faith. And he worked to infuse a less individualistic, more communal concept of the church into the practice of the Lutheran Church, Missouri Synod. Together Krauth and Walther urged American Evangelicals to avail themselves of the fruits of Protestant history as a means to live God-pleasing lives in rambunctious America.

The theological influence of the Mercersburg theologians and of the Lutherans came from outside the evangelical mainstream. Theologizing by America's blacks came from underneath that mainstream. Because blacks were not encouraged to express their Christian beliefs in the writing of systematic theologies, we know more about the Christian beliefs of blacks from their songs than from their treatises, from the comments of slaveholders than from the slaves themselves. Given the kind of life that faced Negroes in early America, it is amazing that any would have accepted the Christian beliefs of their oppressors. Yet millions of blacks, slave and free, gave evidence of a profounder grasp of Christian truth than did many white Evangelicals. Modern historians have had to dig deeply to find out about black Christianity, but they have succeeded in reconstructing the following picture.

The cornerstones of the inarticulate black theology were the forgiveness of sins, awe of God, religious ecstacy, self-respect in Christ, ethical earnestness, and hope. As very few whites in the nineteenth century, blacks experienced the profound paradox of the love of God and the harsh facts of a sinful world. In the face of systematic efforts to degrade black people and to destroy black family life, Christianity provided blacks with the ability to affirm the worth of mankind in general and themselves in particular. The many recorded instances of blacks who had forgiving attitudes toward their slavemasters gave evidence that this central truth had burrowed deep into the soul of black Christians—only the person who is conscious of how much he has been forgiven by God can forgive the one, such as the slaveholder, who inflicts so much pain on him.

Finally, the theology of the black Christians was a true theology of hope. Listen to the words of an old slave woman who comforted her master's daughter after that master had died: "Missus, don't cry; it vex de Lord. I had t'irteen children, and I ain't got one left to put even a coal in my pipe, and if I did not trust de Lord Jesus what would become of me?"[3] Black theology never became a dominant force in American Evangelicalism, but it had a profound grasp of Christian truths that white Evangelicals could well have used as a powerful source for their more systematic theological efforts.

SUMMING UP: THE NINETEENTH CENTURY TO 1870

Perhaps the best way to provide a summary to this point is to look at a contrasting pair of principles that influenced theology in the nineteenth century. The desire to "get back" to Christian roots combined with the desire to "get with" the prevailing spirit of nineteenth-century American culture helped to shape a distinctive evangelical theology. The desire to get back to Christian basics can be seen almost everywhere in this period, although its expression took strikingly different forms. American representatives of the traditional European fellowships harked back to their founders and attempted to recapture the pure spiritual visions that had moved these great men. Confessional Lutherans like Krauth and Walther returned to a renewed study of Luther and the Augsburg Confession. Old School Presbyterians like Hodge reasserted the importance of Calvin and the Reformed systematic theologies of the seventeenth century. Some Methodists worked to revise Wesley's stress on personal holiness. Barton W. Stone and Alexander Campbell desired an unfettered New Testament practice for the groups of "Christians" and "Disciples" arising under their leadership.

In almost every instance, however, these movements toward restoration were matched by movements more in accord with the spirit of the times. Campbellites were at the forefront in affirming the ideals of independence and self-reliance so prominent in the era of Andrew Jackson. But other groups were not far behind. "American" Lutherans like Schmucker felt that nothing was amiss in accepting the American revivalistic tradition or in revising the Augsburg Confession to make it fit the American theological scene. New School Presbyterians like Henry B. Smith made the most of American revivalism and hesitated to pour this new wine back into old wineskins of traditional Reformed thought. The evangelical party in the Episcopal church was reluctant to abandon the accommodation that it had made with prevailing forms of American Protestantism. And many Methodists were very happy indeed that Wesley's teachings had been brought into the mainstream by de-emphasizing the power of God's grace and reemphasizing the power of mankind.

Sometimes these efforts to "get back" and to "get with it" existed right beside each other in the same person. The Charles Hodge who revived the Reformed theologies of the seventeenth century was the same Charles Hodge who succumbed to American sentimentalism. Hodge, in a break with traditional Reformed thought, held that all infants who died were saved. The same tension can be seen in Charles Finney. He looked back to New Testament standards of holiness, but he also partook generously of the optimistic, Jacksonian view of mankind. What we see, in short, during the first two-thirds of the nineteenth century is an evangelical theology joined by strong ties to both the past and the present. It definitely was a child of the basically Reformed theological heritage in America. It was also just as definitely a young adult coming to maturity very much on its own.

The American nation in the nineteenth century was full of great optimism. Evangelical theology felt the tug of that optimism and let itself be pulled along quite happily. Even the many Protestants dissatisfied with the American present looked eagerly to the future and a Christian righting of the country's wrongs. Only the wisest at midcentury could have foreseen the shocks that would descend on evangelical theology in the half-century after the Civil War. For the first two-thirds of the nineteenth century, America was the rising galaxy of the universe, and Protestant theology was its highest star.

2

"My Anchor Holds"

A Great Divide (1870-1930)

A ten-year old American in 1870 could probably have cared less about the future. If he or she lived in rural America, as over half the population still did in that year, a full round of agricultural tasks would very likely have filled up the day. If the child was a city-dweller, there might have been less physical labor—in which case free time could have been spent in building models, enjoying excursions to the beach, or playing a new game that would soon be called baseball. It might, however, have meant much more work if he or she was among the thousands of children employed by American industry to sweep its floors or man its light machinery. Whatever the child's circumstances, however, it would have taken a very lively imagination to foresee the changes that lay in store over the next sixty years.

If our imaginary child had lived to be the biblical three score and ten, he or she would have seen a significantly altered America. Messages that once were carried by foot, or horse, and then by the miracle of telegraph, would be sped on their way by the telephone. And by 1930 the radio would cast its life-changing magic throughout the country. In 1870 visions of material success might have danced in the head of a ten-year old boy. Perhaps he could envision becoming a great tycoon and do in some business endeavor what John D. Rockefeller was doing with oil or Cornelius Vanderbilt with the railroads. By 1930 the boy-become-man would have experienced the wildly fluctuating cycles of the American economy. He might have made (and lost) large amounts of money. And in the early years of the Great Depression he might have experienced severe disillusionment with the American god of material success.

The ten-year-old whose father may have served in the Civil War would have lived to see war with Spain in the 1890s and, as a senior citizen, "The War to end all Wars"—World War I. His life would have spanned the time when America came of age in world politics. In 1870 most Americans had little concern for the world beyond their own shores, or for that matter beyond their individual communities. Hardly anyone would have thought that an American president, Woodrow Wilson, would one day lead the fight for a world-wide League of Nations.

The same youngster would have lived to see American journalism transformed. Now the whole nation could be caught up with the "news." The presidents, like Teddy Roosevelt, Wilson, and Warren G. Harding, became truly household names for the first time in America. Red Grange, Babe Ruth, Jack Dempsey, and Gene Tunney became, if anything, even more famous than the presidents. And before the 1920s were out, American journalism would tranform a youthful stunt pilot, Charles Lindbergh, into the greatest public hero America has ever known.

Life would have changed for our ten-year-old, and it would have changed fast. If the youngster was a girl, she might have eventually participated in the struggle for women's suffrage, the right for women to vote. If our child was black, he or she might one day have experienced a solid glow of satisfaction as the educational work of Booker T. Washington achieved national recognition—or thrill to the challenges for black dignity set forth by W. E. B. DuBois and Marcus Garvey. If the child was fashion conscious, the changes to be observed would have seemed absolutely revolutionary—mass production of clothing, the invention of nylon, and—by 1920—skirts above the ankle and rising rapidly.

The years between 1870 and 1930 were years of rapid change in the internal life of the country as well. Not only telephones, the five-dollar-a-day wage, and the radio were new. So were the ideas, the values, and much of the morality that shaped American life. By 1930 the great moral experiment of Prohibition was in its last years. A government that had been unable to ban the bottle effectively was nevertheless the object of great public attention. By 1930 more and more people had begun to look toward Washington for solutions to the country's pressing problems. New philosophies of life—with names like "pragmatism"—had made their influence felt. More people were going to high school, and even college. And in these schools the role of science grew larger and larger. "Do we have a problem? Let science provide us with the answer."

Evangelical theology, as well as American society, also underwent a tumultuous sixty years from 1870-1930. If this period marked the Great Divide in American life, it marked no less a divide for the theology of American Protestants. What was to be done with America itself, the supporting partner of evangelical thought throughout much of the nineteenth century? What did evangelical theology have to say about the increasingly urban character of the country? Its growing industrialism? The hordes of new citizens from overseas? How should evangelical theology respond to the the new ideas from Europe that challenged traditional Protestant values? How were the growing divisions within Protestantism, including a new "liberalism," to be handled? And what kind of theology would Evangelicals themselves come up with during this period? Any of these questions would provide problems enough for its own chapter, or even its own book. Our story here will be content to sketch the broad outlines of this vital period. What was happening to the theological world of our ten-year-old? There is no better place to begin than with a closer look at the new forces confronting traditional evangelical theology.

THE CHALLENGES OF MODERN LIFE

Although the challenges to evangelical theology from modern life were extremely complex, they can be stated simply enough: evolution, the "scientific" study of religion, and the changing patterns of American life. The first challenge, evolution, received its strongest impetus when Charles Darwin's famous book, *The Origin of Species*, was published in 1859. Briefly stated, Darwin concluded from extensive observations of plants and animals that the kinds of living things presently on the earth had developed from simpler forms of life through a process of "natural selection." This process, which came to be known as "the survival of the fittest," suggested that natural forces determine which species (kinds) of living things best adapt to conditions in the world and are able to reproduce.

The challenge of evolution was twofold. In its earlier, more scientific phase it called into question the usual way of understanding the Bible. Did not Genesis 1:25 say that *God* had made "the beast of the earth after his kind"? This first aspect of evolution also called into question a treasured proof for God's existence, the 'argument from design'. Protestant and Roman Catholic theologians alike had long argued that the world itself—with all its splendor and complexity—could not be explained except by the kind of creating and sustaining God of which the Bible spoke. Did not the manifold variety of the creation demand an all-wise Creator? Evangelical theologians in America, particularly with the frame of thought provided by the Scottish Common Sense philosophy, had used this 'argument from design' to show that belief in God was intellectually, as well as spiritually, respectable.

Evolution also posed a more direct challenge. A later book of Darwin's, *The Descent of Man* (1871), suggested that mankind was not exempt from the evolutionary processes described in *The Origin of Species*. By implication, Darwin was saying that neither God nor the Bible's story of Creation were necessary to explain man's presence on the earth. Natural selection could do it all. Even more offensive was the work of Darwin's "popularizers" like English sociologist Herbert Spencer. (His major work was the multivolume *Systematic Philosophy*, 1862-1893.) Much more than even Darwin, Spencer argued that evolution provided a whole philosophy of life. Mankind, indeed all of life, was progressing from simpler to more complex forms, from worse to better ways of life, from primitive to sophisticated states. Christianity might have been helpful in aiding primitive man to cope with life. But now we knew better. Because life in all its variety is always at its highest and best stage of evolution, primitive beliefs like Christianity could be abandoned without harm. American Evangelicals who read Darwin were usually troubled. Those who read Spencer were aghast.

The second general challenge to evangelical theology came principally from Germany where by 1870 the "scientific" study of religion had been going on for nearly a century. Germany had been the first western society to develop higher education of a modern sort. The stress there on scientific inquiry and on freedom for research took academic life out from under the control of the churches. This freedom was added to the foundation laid by the general European Enlightenment of the eighteenth century. That movement had greatly advanced the cause of humanism and secularism at the expense of Christianity. Detached German scholars often had much the same attitude toward traditional Christianity as did Herbert Spencer. When people were ignorant, of course they needed the myths of Christianity. Now that mankind had matured, however, these myths could be set aside. German scholarship did not always lead in these directions, but it did so often enough to breed deep suspicion in the minds of many American Evangelicals.

Evangelical theologians were particularly offended by some of the extreme conclusions which German scholars drew from their research. (1) A rapid increase in knowledge about the ancient world led some academics to consider Christianity as just one of the many "magical" religions of the ancient Near East. If other cultures had their stories about great floods or the appearance of gods on earth, how could Christianity be so special? Scholars who were not this radical often distinguished between Christianity's "spiritual values" (to be retained) and its "historical dress" (no longer valuable). (2) When scholars rejected the possibility of God's direct intervention in human history, another attack on traditional Christianity followed. Because the miraculous was just a figment of the primitive imagination, then the prophecies, healings, and other wonders described in the Bible must have been fabrications. (3) A great interest in ancient texts combined with these perspectives to call the Bible itself into serious question. Obviously, what we read in the Bible was only the attempts by religious people to make some sense out of their existence. Figures like Abraham and Moses might not have even existed. David and Solomon certainly did not do all that the Bible says they did. And for Jesus—while a Jewish figure of that name probably existed, our accounts of his life are fuzzy to say the least.

Because of its academic prestige, Germany had long been a mecca for American scholars. Over three hundred of the seven hundred scholars listed in the American *Who's Who* in 1900, for example, had studied in Germany. The theologians who took academic pilgrimages to Germany, or elsewhere in Europe, often returned to America with new perspectives on the evangelical heritage. Some would use these perspectives to broaden and deepen orthodoxy; some would run it into the ground. Theologians who stayed in America, and who took time to become familiar with European scholarship, were like unsuspecting sleepwalkers shocked with a bucket of ice water in the face. Some reacted with anger. Others were curious. Without exception they knew that traditional evangelical theology faced a stern challenge.

The last major difficulty for evangelical theologians in this period was American life itself. Society no longer presented the settled values that had prevailed before the Civil War. Cities grew rapidly. Immigrants—Roman Catholic, Jewish, or even unchurched—inundated the city parishes where American Evangelicals had once held forth. Even the many Lutherans from overseas, not even to speak of the non-Protestants, simply did things differently than America's traditional Evangelicals.

American government and American business had struck a momentous bargain. Government gave business wide leeway to expand and develop. Business gave America in general, and many Americans in particular, unprecedented prosperity. It also produced the depersonalization of gigantic industrialism, appalling working conditions for many laborers, cutthroat competition, and a mad dash for the dollar. Many Evangelicals took note of the rise of big business. Only a few felt confident enough to ask where industrialization was taking the country. What were the costs in human terms? What did the avid pursuit of material gain do to Christian faith and practice?

Evolution. The "scientific" study of religion. An industrial and urban America. These challenges provided the context for evangelical theology and the life of the Protestant mind in the last three decades of the nineteenth century and the first three of the twentieth. Before we look at the properly evangelical theology of this time, we must first take note of the great split among Protestants that divided the evangelical mainstream into two markedly different channels.

THE LIBERAL ACCOMMODATION TO MODERNITY

The rise of modern America coincided with the rise of a "modern" theology within Protestantism. For the first time in American history a broad and influential theology developed which was not evangelical. Protestant Liberalism represented an accommodation to the new ideas from abroad and the new stirrings at home. It came to regard the older evangelical theology of the nineteenth century as out of date. New ways of looking at the history of mankind (evolution), at the religious faiths of primitive peoples (comparative religion), and at the development of religious writings (higher criticism) seemed to question the uniqueness of the Bible and the supernatural history of the life of Christ. As early as 1889, for example, the Presbyterian scholar Charles A. Briggs could say of the Bible: "The sacred Scriptures do not describe for us all questions of orthodoxy.They do not answer the problems of science, of philosophy or of history. They do not cover the whole ground of theology."[1]

Evangelicals could have agreed that the Bible did not directly treat many of the specific developments of modern life. But they did not concede with Briggs that the "truths" of modern science modified, changed, or advanced beyond the truth of the Scriptures.

Nor could they quietly accept the redefinition of traditional Christian doctrines which became so much a stock in trade of Liberalism. When, for example, the Baptist theologian William Newton Clarke spoke about the resurrection of the dead from his evolutionary standpoint, he did not speak for American Evangelicalism: "If the coming of Christ is conceived as spiritual, not visible, and as a process, not an event, . . . no simultaneous resurrection of humanity on earth will be expected . . . . According to this view resurrection is not simultaneous for all, but continuous, or successive."[2]

Some Protestants were led to question older styles of evangelical thought because of the new conditions of American life. The America that faced the theologian in 1900 seemed a vastly different one from that which had confronted his predecessor in 1850. A basically agricultural economy had given way to industry. The rural, small-town character of American life was being replaced rapidly by an urban, big-city influence. The rising tides of immigration were coloring the traditional Anglo-Saxon fabric of American society. Some Protestant theologians looked for new religious categories to cope with the changing situation. In particular some asked what the gospel could offer to society at large. Among these were basically evangelical theologians such as the German Baptist Walter Rauschenbusch who linked social reform with the spiritual message of the gospel. As Rauschenbusch put it: "In personal religion the first requirement is to repent and believe the Gospel . . . . Social religion, too, demands repentance and faith: repentance for our social sins; faith in the possibility of a new social order."[3] Unfortunately, many of the Protestant theologians who followed Rauschenbusch forgot about personal repentance and faith and translated Christian theology into simply another plan for social betterment. The full flowering of the "social gospel" often reversed the injunction of Christ: it sought first justice and equity in American society with the hope that the kingdom of God would be added to that.

By the 1920s these Protestant responses to the new ideas and conditions of American life had developed into a distinctly new religious perspective, known then as "Modernism" and later as "Liberalism." One of its chief spokesmen, Shailer Mathews of the University of Chicago, outlined its affirmations in a book entitled *The Faith of Modernism* (1924). Evangelicals who read the book knew that their theology and the theology of Liberalism had parted company. Said Mathews:

> If we think of God as creating man through the process of divinely guided evolution, we shall set forth salvation as a continuation of the processes by which humanity from its first days more and more has appropriated God's personal influence . . . . The Modernist will not insist upon miracles, but he believes that God is active and

> mysteriously present in the ordered course of nature and social evolution.[4]

Modernistic theologians fought hard to establish their right to the evangelical Protestant tradition. Although Evangelicals reacted from different perspectives, they were quick to contend that a wide gap now separated this new religion from the traditional faith.

THE EVANGELICAL TASK

The theological task for Evangelicals was, however, much greater than just arguing against Protestants who had abandoned evangelical convictions. For Evangelicals were also called to make a response to the trends that had produced Protestant Liberalism. The three-fold task in this period included this agenda: (1) to defend the name of true Christianity against the Modernists who wanted the sanction of Protestant tradition without the substance of Protestant faith, (2) to maintain the vitality and integrity of evangelical theology in the face of the great changes in American life, and (3) to make a convincing response to new forms of thought, particularly evolutionary science.

From the perspective of half a century or more, it is fair to conclude that Evangelicals succeeded better with the first task than with the last two. Evangelical theology did mount a telling and effective defense of its right to the Protestant heritage. And it did so through contributions from almost all points of the evangelical compass.

DEFENDERS OF THE FAITH

Later on we will look more closely at the systematic theologies produced by Evangelicals in this period. But it is appropriate to note here that the meaty volumes from Shedd, Strong, Hodge, Berkhof, Pieper and others testified that many strains of evangelical thought retained their vitality in the face of Liberalism.

At this point, however, it would be appropriate to cite one systematic theologian's exposition of the old faith in the New World. In the 1880s and 1890s American Methodists were a good deal more concerned about the debate over holiness and the second blessing in their own ranks than about liberal trends as such. In addition, the heirs of Wesley, with their strong emphasis on Christian experience, had never been as concerned for orthodoxy as such as had the Presbyterians and the Baptists. Nevertheless, the *Systematic Theology* of John Miley (1813-1895) provided an evangelical answer to liberalism that drew on the Methodist heritage. Miley, professor of theology at Drew University, published his two-volume systematics in 1892 and 1894. It argued that

Christian faith rests on four sturdy pillars: proofs for God from nature, the truth of the Bible, man's own religious character, and the experiential facts of a religious life. Miley did place more stress on man's essentially free nature than earlier Methodists had done. (Wesley had seen free will as a gift of God's prevenient grace; Miley took it to be something of a human "right.") But Miley's theology nonetheless posed this important reminder to Methodists: to be swept away by new ideas was to forsake a heritage of evangelical thought that had been tried and found true.

The currents of liberalism flowed strongly in American Methodism, and Miley's theology did not by any means stem the tide. Some later Methodists, however, also spoke out for historic Evangelicalism. Prominent among these was a church historian, also at Drew, John Alfred Faulker (1851-1931). Early in his career this scholar had studied in Germany and had accepted much of the new approach to theology. But his own personal experience and his own study brought him back to a traditional Wesleyan perspective. His books, such as *Modernism and the Christian Faith* (1921) and *Burning Questions in Historic Christianity* (1930), called on modern man to look honestly at history and their own experience. If they would only do so, they would cease to belittle the faith of the fathers. Faulker wrote clearly and persuasively to defend the deity of Christ, his Virgin Birth, the destructiveness of human sinfulness. He based his defense of historic Christianity on "the language of facts" which, as he put it, was "the best apology of Christianity."

Southern Baptists resembled the Methodists in not being as caught up in the debate with Modernism as other groups. Yet one of the most persuasive defenders of evangelical Christianity at the turn of the twentieth century was the president of the Southern Baptist Theological Seminary in Louisville, Edgar Youngs Mullins (1860-1928). In 1905 Mullins published a book whose title asked, *Why is Christianity True?* Mullins replied that physical nature, the New Testament, Christian experience, and Christian history raised their combined voices to proclaim the truthfulness of the historic faith. Mullins was moderate in tone but resolute in his convictions. He was not afraid to adopt a moderate kind of theistic evolution. But he was also not afraid to challenge the supposed results of modern science when they presumed to call Christianity into question.

Mullins felt that the experience of believers was a vastly neglected support for Christianity's validity. His treatment of Christian experience in *The Christian Religion in Its Doctrinal Expression* (1917) stated his conviction gently but also forthrightly: the countless personal experiences of God's grace must stand as firm witnesses for the faith. His book published in 1924, *Christianity at the Crossroads*, argued that Christian experience was such a valuable proof of the faith because it brought individuals face to face with "the irreducible Christ . . . irreducible as the eternal Son of God and Saviour of men, sinless, crucified for our sins, risen from the dead, reigning in glory, and destined to come again in his own time."[5]

Effective as theologians such as Faulker and Mullins were in their own circles, the staunchest defense of evangelical orthodoxy came from the Presbyterians. Late in his life, Charles Hodge had taken note of modernizing trends in American theology and had spoken to them directly (see below on Hodge's book *What is Darwinism?* and on his systematic theology). Later Presbyterians would continue to argue the case for orthodoxy with consummate skill throughout this period. Although they would fail to win over large segments of their own denomination, they provided orthodox theological grist for the mills of many who were not of the Presbyterian communion.

In the 1890s the learned B. B. Warfield (1851-1921), professor of theology at Princeton Seminary, argued cogently against the detractors from Scripture. The only acceptable view of the Bible that accorded with its own statements and the testimony of the church through the centuries was scriptural infallibility. Warfield expanded his views on Scripture in several scholarly articles in the *International Standard Bible Encyclopedia* (1915), which were later gathered together into a single volume published by the Oxford University Press. Warfield's argument that the Bible is absolutely without error in all of its statements, when approached with the accepted practices of interpretation, has not been passively accepted by all later Evangelicals. Yet it is a position which sharply and effectively rebutted the attitudes of Protestant Modernists to the Bible (see chapter 4 for more on Warfield and the Bible).

The secretary of the Board of Foreign Missions of the Northern Presbyterians for forty-six years, Robert E. Speer (1867-1947), carried the fight into another arena. Some conservatives thought Speer should have exerted more care in assuring that mission funds not go to liberals, but they could not fault his dedication to Christianity itself. Modernism had placed in doubt the necessity of the missionary task. If Christianity is just one of the world's many expressions of God, why waste so much effort and money in sending Christian missionaries to foreign lands? To this Speer replied with an emphatic defense of the missionary task. On his wide travels and in his many books, he argued that Christian missions are necessary because Christ is necessary. His *Christianity and the Nations* (1910), for example, admitted that the Protestant missionaries had sometimes added inessential matters to the preaching of the gospel. Speer did not concede, however, that occasional mispractice did away with the necessity of preaching Christ to the whole world. His masterful work, *The Finality of Jesus Christ* (1933), summed up the burden of a lifetime. Missions is necessary because Christ is the divine, sinless, and unique Savior of mankind.

J. Gresham Machen (1881-1937), a student of Warfield's who also became a professor at Princeton, encapsulated the Presbyterian response to Modernism in a book with the simple title *Christianity and Liberalism* (1923). The famed journalist Walter Lippman called this volume a "cool and stringent defense of orthodox Protestantism."[6] Recently a nonevangelical historian has commented that "even after a half-century it remains the chief theological ornament of American Fundamentalism."[7] The book stated the case against Liberalism clearly, vigorously, and decisively. Machen contended that Protestant Modernism simply did not deserve the name Christian. As he put it: "The chief modern rival of Christianity is 'liberalism.' An examination of the teachings of liberalism in comparison with those of Christianity will show that at every point the two movements are in direct opposition."[8] In carefully written chapters, Machen drove home this argument by considering the different attitudes held by Christianity, properly so called, and Liberalism about God and man, the Bible, Christ, salvation and the church. In Machen's volume Evangelicals of the 1920s, and also to the present, possessed a classic counterpoise to the drift of Protestant Liberalism away from Christian truth.

Modern historians sometimes leave the impression that reactions to Liberalism were frantic, frenzied, and foolish. No one who reads the works of Miley, Faulker, Mullins, Warfield, Speer, or Machen could make such a mistake. True, these evangelical thinkers differed among themselves on significant issues. Warfield did not like Miley's Arminianism; nor Miley, Warfield's Calvinism. Machen eventually separated from the Northern Presbyterian church, while Speer remained with that communion. Other internal differences abounded. Yet together these Evangelicals stood firm against the destructive aspects of modern thought. Man was a sinner in need of grace. Christ was both God and man. He did die for the salvation of mankind. The Bible was God's authoritative message to us. In these—and other points of dispute—the intramural dissonance gave way to a harmonious affirmation of the faith once delivered to the saints.

THE FUNDAMENTALS

The most noteworthy response to Liberalism, however, was not individually produced by such men as Mullins or Machen, but by a large team of Evangelicals working in concert. Between 1910 and 1915 the Testimony Publishing Company, located on the grounds of Moody Bible Institute in Chicago, produced twelve booklets that bore the collective title *The Fundamentals: A Testimony of the Truth.* Financed by Lyman and Milton Stewart, owners of the Union Oil Company of Los Angeles, *The Fundamentals* were sent without charge to pastors, evangelists, missionaries, theological professors, seminary students, and YMCA/YWCA secretaries throughout the English-speaking world. As many as three million booklets were distributed. The reported 200,000 letters of commendation received by the series editors testify to the impact of these publications upon the evangelical world.

These articles constituted a solid defense of the basics, or fundamentals, of the faith that Liberalism was calling into question. Authors for the series were drawn from throughout the English-speaking world and from a wide spectrum of Protestant affiliations. As in all projects of this nature, there were some lightweight articles of no lasting signficance. But *The Fundamentals* also included many well-conceived and carefully written defenses of Christian truth for which no Evangelical in the early years of this century, or later, had cause to be ashamed.

The bulk of the nearly one hundred articles met the liberal challenge head on. The Bible *was* the inspired word of God. It was historically accurate and, even more important, was totally and authoritatively reliable in presenting the way of salvation. Jesus Christ was not mere man or merely a godlike teacher, but the actual Son of God in human flesh. Christ was born of a virgin; he did live a sinless life; he did die on the cross to reconcile God and man; he did rise triumphant over death in an actual bodily resurrection; he did ascend into heaven; and he would return at the end of the age to judge the living and the dead. The booklets also stressed other essential Christian doctrines: sin was not just a figment of uneasy imaginations but real offense against God; reconciliation with God came about through faith in Christ and not by mankind's own efforts; the church was God's creation to nurture believers and provide a staging ground for evangelization. The articles discussing these cardinal doctrines provided meaty and scholarly presentations of the gospel. It is one of the great disappointments in modern American history that the word *fundamentalist* later became a party label of fierce pride or unreasoning scorn. When this happened, it kept many from reading the solid and competent evangelical theology gathered in *The Fundamentals*. Unlike the negative tone of some later fundamentalistic activities, *The Fundamentals* offered calm, well-reasoned, and well-balanced testimony to Christian truth.

Another striking feature of these volumes was their evangelical ecumenicity. Presbyterians joined Methodists; Baptists wrote alongside Episcopalians; ministers of independent churches aided seminary professors in presenting a first-class evangelical theology. Those who would later separate from the traditional denominations worked side by side with those who stayed in. In the face of the liberal threat, the evangelical mainstream subdued its differences to defend principles of the common faith. To cite just one example of this cooperative spirit, *The Fundamentals* included an article by B. B. Warfield, the Reformed spokesman, and also one by C. I. Scofield, the promoter of a theological position, dispensationalism, that differed in many significant respects from Warfield's.

In sum, the response of evangelical theologians to Protestant Modernism was sure-handed and effective. In individual works as well as *The Fundamentals*, Evangelicals lodged a very strong claim for their right to speak as the voice of historic Christianity. The response to Liberalism revealed as well that in spite of intramural differences, Evangelicals were capable of working with each other in the face of a grave external threat.

A THEOLOGY FOR MODERN AMERICAN LIFE?

From our perspective today, it is possible to wish that evangelical theologians had expended a little less energy in combating Liberalism and a little more in coming to terms with conditions in American life. Early in the century, of course, no one could foresee the self-defeating disillusionment that Liberalism led to in the 1930s and 1940s. Nor was it possible to predict the great influence that newer, non-Christian patterns of life would obtain in American society. Or the new situations that would confront America as a world power. The much greater involvement of government in personal life, the increasingly pluralistic character of American culture, the "de-Christianization" of public education, American leadership of the noncommunist world—all of these situations demanded evangelical response. Unfortunately, the great efforts at combating Modernism often seemed to leave little energy for providing theological guidelines in the crises of the twentieth century.

Evangelical thought did not exactly head for cover at the great changes taking place in America at the end of the nineteenth century. In fact, recent scholarship has shown that even many premillennialists, who often have been accused of abandoning social concerns, maintained a positive attitude toward the Christian's social responsibilities. And individual Evangelicals often spoke directly in public forums to express their Christian concerns. Presbyterian layman and presidential candidate, William Jennings Bryan (1860-1925), considered many of his public positions to be the outgrowth of Christian convictions. When Bryan argued for peaceful arbitration in international disputes, for women's suffrage, for better conditions for labor, against the liquor trade, and against evolution in the schools, he did so from a grasp of Christian truth. Bryan did tend to confuse the sovereignty of God and the innate goodness of the American "people" in his thinking. He nevertheless sought valiantly, and laudably, to activate Christian doctrine in public practice.

Fundamentalist leader John Roach Straton (1876-1929) provides an even better example of someone who tried to put his theology to work in society. His little book, *The Salvation of Society* (1909?), argued that the Atonement, "individual salvation," was the key to theology. Right next to the Atonement, however, was the Incarnation. Because Christ came to earth as a real human being, Straton argued, we can perform our responsibilities on this earth with the expectation of Christ's blessing. Because Christ came, "The dignity and value of earthly life is immeasurably advanced and a new emphasis is given to the importance of service in the present world . . . . Thus we are led to believe that Christianity is a means of *social* salvation, as well as a means of individual salvation . . . . That Christ's purpose was to establish an ideal social order upon the earth, as well as to save the individual soul, is plain upon every page of the Gospels."[9]

After the disillusioning days of World War I, Straton became the minister of Calvary Baptist Church in New York City, where he served until his death in 1929. He gained fame as a penetrating preacher and for attacking immorality in the theater. But he was also busy implementing his "incarnational theology." The selfishness of capital and labor, the exploitative character of some industries, maldistribution of industrial profit, failure to legislate against the liquor traffic, official tolerance of prostitution, the "paganism" of the great prize fights, the Ku Klux Klan—these were only some of the aspects of American life that felt his lash. With equal forthrightness he spoke out for women's rights, equality for Jews, and justice for blacks, whom he welcomed in his church and received as members. Without a great deal of elaboration, Straton's theology for society nevertheless bore significant fruit.

Yet while there were these positive contributions, Evangelicals as a whole did not advance against the secularization of society with half the fervor that they showed against the liberalization of doctrine. One of the reasons for this may have been the trauma induced by bitter controversies within the denominations over fundamentals of the faith. An even more important reason may have been the great fear of the "social gospel."

Traditionally, American Evangelicals had always shown significant concern for society and for the role Christians should assume in it. Puritan ideas of government and social cohesion had come out of Puritan theology. Early attacks against slavery had grown out of the theology of the Quakers and the New Light Calvinists. The moral reform movements in the first half of the nineteenth century arose as a direct product of the activistic theology of Lyman Beecher, Charles Finney, and the Methodists. But in the late 1800s the situation changed. Evangelicals saw that Protestant Liberalism was tying itself ever more closely to the social "gospel" that ignored the truths of individual responsibility for sin and of God's forgiveness through grace. In the effort to combat theological liberalism, Evangelicals forgot their heritage and began to combat social applications of the gospel in general. It was thought that such efforts were only thinly veiled attempts by Modernism to evade the preaching of repentance and faith. The final result was that evangelical theology no longer spoke positively to society. It no longer applied biblical principles in a systematic way to the needs of its culture. In this Evangelicals rolled back their history and left themselves without a rudder in the violent seas of twentieth-century American life (see also chapter 9 on the evangelical response to social problems).

A THEOLOGY OF SCIENCE?

The response of evangelical theology to the intellectual trends that lay behind Protestant Liberalism must also be given mixed reviews. In one sense, evangelical theology began in the late nineteenth century to pay the price for having been the dominant force in American religious life for so long. In the early 1700s Jonathan Edwards had made a dedicated effort to thoroughly digest and, where necessary, refute modern currents of thought. But this kind of effort had simply not been taking place in the nineteenth-century evangelical mainstream. A "common sense" philosophy was enough to satisfy most Americans. The great success of revival provided Christians with better things to do than worry about European philosophy.

There would have been no difficulty with this kind of evangelical thought if the intellectual world had not been changing so dramatically. But when higher critics called the Bible's unique revelation into question, Evangelicals were better equipped to respond with assertions than with arguments. When comparative religionists reduced the Judaeo-Christian tradition to just another oriental mysticism, evangelical theologians were sometimes left speechless. Or what was even worse, they were reduced to a snide ridicule—as when Evangelicals called evolution the "bestial hypothesis" of man's orgins (to which evolutionists, however, replied in kind by labeling the biblical concept of special creation as the "mudman theory").

Throughout the nineteenth century American evangelical theology had been more interested in debate among its various strands than in sensitive dialogue with modern intellectual trends. Evangelical theology was by no means destroyed when modern ways of thinking came to prominence, for strong works building on evangelical tradition continued to be written in this era. The difficulty was, rather, that fewer and fewer people outside orthodoxy understood traditional theological vocabularies. Evangelical theologians seemed unable to show why people in the modern world should spend time thinking about such apparently outdated ideas as human depravity, the Virgin Birth, or the substitutionary atonement.

It would be wrong to think that the picture was entirely bleak. Taking evolution as an example, there were positive, distinctly Christian responses to this newly publicized idea. Evangelical thinkers spoke with one voice in rejecting the atheism of evolution taken as a total philosophic scheme. All rejected, that is, the kind of popularized Darwinism that Herbert Spencer offered as a comprehensive picture of reality. Then as now, however, considerable difference of evangelical opinion existed on how much evolution could be accepted within Christian orthodoxy.

One of the most clear-headed early rebuttals to Darwinism came from the pen of Charles Hodge. His volume *What is Darwinism?* (1874) argued that Darwinistic evolution was nothing short of atheism. Hodge contended that Darwin's principle of natural selection denied God's role in the design of the universe. Eliminate God's creation of the individual species, Hodge said, and you are well on the way to eliminating Him altogether. Hodge's work was carefully conceived and logically executed. It set a high standard for future responses to Darwin.

The New School Presbyterian Henry B. Smith (1815-1877) went

part way in agreement with Hodge. He too condemned Darwinism when it was used to account for man's existence apart from God. Unlike Hodge, however, Smith saw a place for development in nature when this was placed under God's control. One historian of New School Presbyterianism has put Smith's position like this: "Progress was an integral part of Smith's theological system, and he consistently affirmed that there was a proper place for the theistic 'law of growth.'"[10]

Other, more extensive forms of Christian evolution were worked out by the eminent Harvard botanist, Asa Gray (1810-1888), and the Calvinistic theologian, George Frederick Wright (1838-1921). Gray's book *Darwiniana* (1876) provided an indirect counter to Hodge. Gray argued that a Christian, particularly one who has done his scientific homework, could very well accept Darwinism as a scientific theory. But, Gray went on, Darwinism-as-science was very different from Spencer's Darwinism-as-total-philosophy. Gray's review of Hodge's *What is Darwinism?* had asserted that "evolution may be as profoundly and particularly theistic as it is increasingly probable. The taint of atheism which, in Dr. Hodge's view, leavens the whole lump, is not inherent in the original grain of Darwinism . . . but has somehow been introduced in the subsequent treatment."[11] And in his introduction to *Darwiniana*, Gray summed up his postion by calling himself "one who is scientifically, and in his own fashion, a Darwinian, philosophically a convinced theist, and religiously an acceptor of the 'creed commonly called the Nicene,' as the exponent of the Christian faith."[12]

George Frederick Wright, a friend of Gray's and an amateur geologist as well as a thoroughly evangelical theologian, presented an even more interesting attempt to integrate orthodoxy and the scientific aspects of evolution. His article in 1880, "Some Analogies Between Calvinism and Darwinism," tried to show that evolutionary science and traditional Reformed theology pointed to the same kind of universe. Both, Wright suggested, helped explain human degeneration and the sovereignty of general Law over sentimental individualism. Wright eventually became professor of theology at Oberlin. And then late in life he wrote three articles for *The Fundamentals*. His first two defended the historical reliability of the Old Testament books of Moses. His third, entitled "The Passing of Evolution," represented a more restrained approach to scientific evolution than he had taken earlier. Wright contended, first, that the evidence for systematic evolution was not as good as it had once seemed. But then he suggested that even if the evidence were there, Darwinism (as science) would not detract from the God of the Bible or from the Bible itself. Wright thought that large-scale evolution, demanded, if anything, even more of God's control of each individual part of every single creature than a one-time creation of the various species.

The real difficulty for evangelical theology and science came not with these earlier responses to Darwin. Hodge's outright denial of evolution, as well as Wright's construction of a Christian evolution, both represented serious work. They did indeed offer different approaches to the problem of integrating science and theology. But they agreed in rejecting the atheistic implications that Darwinists like Spencer drew from evolution. In that agreement lay a prospect for fruitful discussion.

The problem lay, rather, in the general nature of the reaction to Darwin. Evangelicals tended to be strongest in affirming the accuracy of the Bible and validity of science in its proper place. But they were weakest in actually doing the nitty-gritty science required to come to terms with evolution. The earlier responses also would have benefited from a more sensitive approach to the Bible. Important questions that did not receive satisfactory treatment in this respect were ones such as these: How much of modern science could be accepted while still retaining the authority of biblical passages such as Genesis 1-3 and Romans 5 (both of which speak much of Adam)? Is it possible to find new interpretations of the Bible, perhaps even at the urging of modern science, that preserve the intent of the scriptural texts as penned by their human authors under the inspiration of the Holy Spirit?

Unfortunately, these types of questions did not receive sustained attention. Nor did the potential dialogue between Hodge's position and that of Wright ever get off the ground. The fight against Liberalism was too intense. Battles within the denominations consumed too much time. Finally, the shock of World War I made Evangelicals, and many other Americans, very suspicious of anything smacking of Germany—whether its language or the prestige of its scientific scholarship, which had seemed such a part of its culture. The cumulative weight of all these factors kept Evangelicals from the kind of fruitful dialogue with modern science that both Charles Hodge and George Frederick Wright had begun in the nineteenth century.

This is not to imply that a more intense evangelical wrestling with Darwinism would have carried the day in American society. So firmly entrenched had philosophical evolution become by the 1920s that any Christian who questioned evolution became an object of ridicule for America's "enlightened" opinion makers. This inability to see any sort of evangelical case against Darwinistic evolution manifested itself most clearly in the famous Scopes trial of 1925.

An unbiased person who reads the transcript of that trial (and not the slanted play based on it, *Inherit the Wind)* would note that William Jennings Bryan's evangelical theology was not as clumsy as later commentators have taken it to be. When, for example, Clarence Darrow tried to get Bryan to concede that the Bible taught the world was created in 4004 B.C. or that the days of Genesis 1 were 24-hour days, Bryan replied that these were matters about which Christians differed among themselves. As Bryan stated in his testimony, the defense in the trial was not so much concerned with the biology teacher, John Scopes, who had taught evolution to his high school class, or even with a calm examination of the truth of evolution. As Bryan saw clearly, Clarence Darrow "came here to try revealed religion" and "to slur at the Bible."

Only because a hopelessly prejudiced press had given itself over to modern ideas long before the Scopes trial did the nation see Bryan as a laughable buffoon and Darrow as an urbane champion of modern science. In fact, Bryan's evangelical commitment to the activity of God in the world provided him with a sure basis to counter this most explosive manifestation of the modern American spirit.

Bryan, however, was not a systematic thinker. As an active politician, he was not the man to propound a definitive answer to a perplexing intellectual question. Yet his response to Darwinism was seen as the best Evangelicals could muster. And perhaps it was. Too little effort had gone into the task of clarifying relationships between evolution and Scripture, between science and the Christian faith. Given the nature of the time, it is perhaps understandable that more serious evangelical thought was not devoted to this effort. But with Evangelicals having put off the task of integrating their theology with modern science in the first third of this century, the job—with all its complexity, its potential for controversy and misunderstanding—has remained an unfinished task for the generations since.

SHIFTING FOCUS: FROM RESPONSE OUTWARDS TO DEVELOPMENTS WITHIN

On balance, then, evangelical theology sailed through rough seas as it faced outward in this period. It waged its defensive task manfully and with considerable success against its erstwhile Protestant friends. But it did not do so well in its efforts to proclaim Christian theology forthrightly to an America that was racing to shuck off its nineteenth-century evangelical heritage. We must not overlook the significant accomplishments of the period. But we must also confess that much work remained to be done, particularly in developing a biblical theology that could speak to modern America and to the relationship of science and the faith.

But surely, someone will say, Evangelicals were doing more than just *reacting* during this period. Surely there must have been positive theological contributions as well. True enough. Even as evangelical theology reacted, it also acted along several positive lines. For one thing, the underlying substratum of theology—the ongoing life of the church—retained considerable vitality. The day to day life of Christian people went on, and this provided the support for the more rarified theology that is the concern of this chapter. In the next chapter we look at greater length at the kinds of support that undergirded the theological effort. Many of the factors mentioned there could apply as well to the years before 1930: dynamic preaching, faithful instruction in the Christian faith, serious work in the interpretation of Scripture, publication for popular audiences, and so on. Evangelical theology did not exist apart from this life of the church. The health of one reflected the health of the other. As Christian life in general was shaken by the assaults of modernity, so was its theology. Where by God's grace Evangelicals triumphed in their daily lives, so by the same grace did theologians make positive contributions. To these we now turn.

A FLOWERING OF SYSTEMATIC THEOLOGY

It may seem strange at first that during a period of crisis Evangelicals produced many significant works of theological synthesis. The five authors we will consider briefly here—Presbyterians Charles Hodge and William G. T. Shedd, Baptist Augustus H. Strong, Lutheran Franz Pieper, and Reformed Louis Berkhof—published their systematics from 1872 to 1932, at the very time of great shock for American Evangelicalism. On closer inspection, however, the apparent irony evaporates. The systematic theologies of Hodge, Shedd, and Strong were in effect the flower of the evangelical heyday earlier in the nineteenth century. Their works were not blind to the modern world, but they drew most of their strength from the nineteenth century and before. Pieper, of German stock, and Berkhof, a Dutch immigrant, restated highly developed European heritages for American immigrant constituencies. In every case, the systematizers were the beneficiaries of long and relatively stable traditions, even though they wrote in the turmoil of a changing America.

The five works selected for brief discussion here have a double importance. All extended the personal influence of their authors, which had been great in every case already. All have also been reprinted in recent years as a further testimony to continuing influence.

A recent centennial commemoration of the publication of Charles Hodge's *Systematic Theology* spoke of that work as "stout and persistent." The phrase is apt. Hodge's three-volume systematics (published 1872-1873) was in fact a summation of conservative Reformed orthodoxy in America. Hodge (1797-1878), professor at Princeton Seminary for over fifty years, gave definitive expression to American Calvinism first as a teacher. In writing his theology he continued to draw from the same resources and emphasize the same themes as he did when teaching. He made use of Calvin, the Westminster Confession of Faith, and particularly the *Theological Institutes* of François Turretini, a Genevan of the seventeenth century. The glory of God, the regenerating power of God's grace in Christ, the all-sufficiency of Scripture, the helplessness of man apart from God's effective call to salvation—these are the themes that frame the work. Hodge did not pay a good deal of attention to the threats of liberalism and modern thought. His major opponents were still Roman Catholicism and liberal Calvinists such as Nathaniel W. Taylor from earlier in the century. Nevertheless, the work is a nearly comprehensive summation of Reformed thought (although Hodge, surprisingly, does not discuss the church). Hodge's personal influence was great during his own lifetime. In the years since his death the *Systematic Theology* has continued to exert a powerful influence on American Evangelicalism, particularly its Reformed wing.

The *Dogmatic Theology* (3 vols., 1888-1894) of William G. T. Shedd (1820-1894) has not been as widely-used as Hodge's work, but it too is a powerful statement of Reformed doctrine. Shedd had a varied career before beginning a tenure of twenty-eight years as professor of theology at Union Seminary in New York City: a minister of Congregationalist and Presbyterian churches, a professor of English at the University of Vermont, and professor of church history at Andover Seminary in Boston. Shedd, like Hodge, was a proponent of "Old School" Calvinism. Unlike Hodge, however, Shedd took more notice of modern intellectual trends. Against these Shedd set his vast reading in church history. For him the works of Athanasius (on the Trinity), Augustine (on the nature of sinfulness), Anselm (on the existence of God), and the Reformers of the sixteenth century (on the Atonement) were still standards of the faith. More like Philip Schaff than most American Evangelicals of his time, Shedd looked to the entire history of the church as a resource for theology. He took modern philosophy seriously, but contended that "the Augustino-Calvinistic" tradition had more than enough resources—biblical, theological, and philosophical—to sustain the church in its confrontation with new ideas.

Another strain of American Reformed thought was summarized by the multivolume *Systematic Theology* (1886, rev. ed. 1907) of Augustus Hopkins Strong (1836-1921). Strong, a Baptist, was president of Rochester Theological Seminary (New York) and its professor of biblical theology for forty years. His work showed great affinities with Hodge and Shedd, except in its commitment to adult, believer baptism by immersion. Like Shedd, Strong took an active interest in new strains of modern thought. He was, on balance, more receptive to these than any other evangelical theologian of the period. "Neither evolution nor the higher criticism," Strong wrote in the introduction to the 1907 revision of his work, "has any terrors to one who regards them as parts of Christ's creating and educating process." Strong tempered this openness to the newer ideas with a strict adherence to orthodox doctrines. The same introduction of 1907 noted regretfully that the new critical mentality had led some to deny Christ's divinity or the Atonement. Strong saw his Calvinistic-Baptistic work as an antidote to these trends. He felt that a faithful presentation of Christ—as "the one and only Revealer of God, in nature, in humanity, in history, in science, in Scripture"—was the single best means of combating infidelity and encouraging godliness. For Baptists and for a wide constituency beyond Baptist circles, Strong's theology has remained a powerful exposition of the sum of Christian faith.

The *Christian Dogmatics* (1917-1924) of Lutheran Franz August Otto Pieper (1852-1931) differed in significant respects from the previous theologies. For one thing, although published in St. Louis, the theology was written in German. For another, it carried on more dialogue with contemporary European theologians than even Strong had. It was also written for a group, the Missouri Synod Lutherans, who were not part of the general Reformed heritage shared by so many American Evangelicals. Yet Pieper's work reflects many of the same commitments as the Reformed theologians—an absolute fidelity to infallible Scripture, a determined defense of justification by faith, and a stout resistance to the exaltation of modern science over the Bible and the creeds of the church. Beyond these common affirmations with his Reformed brethren, however, Pieper did devote considerable attention to the distinctives of "confessional Lutheranism." Against "modern rationalizing Lutherans," he argued for the identification of the Word of God and the Bible. Against American Evangelicals (whether Reformed or Arminian), he contended for the 'real presence' of Christ in the Lord's Supper and the regenerating powers of baptism. Both, Pieper held, were true channels of God's grace. He also took time to combat the "errors" of "millennialism and the general conversion of the Jews," which he saw as distinct problems of the time. In sum, Pieper's work offered American Lutherans sure guidelines as they grew less familiar with theology past and more familiar with the American experience.

Louis Berkhof (1873-1957), professor of theology (and eventually president) of Calvin Seminary (Michigan), performed this same function for immigrants from Holland. Berkhof's *Reformed Dogmatics* (3 vols., 1932) drew heavily on the work of European Calvinists even as it provided theological pointers for life in modern America. In many respects Berkhof's treatments of the standard Reformed doctrines resembled those of Hodge, Shedd, and even Strong. He differed most from these other Reformed Americans by employing insights from Abraham Kuyper and Herman Bavinck, Dutch thinkers of the previous generation. In particular, Berkhof drew on these theologians to outline a distinctly evangelical theology of culture. In no small measure as a consequence of Berkhof's instruction, ministers and teachers in his Christian Reformed Church have been leaders among American Evangelicals in bringing Christian principles to bear on education, politics, and the fine arts. Perhaps most importantly Berkhof offered to the Dutch immigrants, and to their children, a sturdy summary of the traditional faith for their altered circumstances in the New World.

Many common affirmations bind these theologians together—faithfulness to a high view of Scripture, the belief that salvation is first and last God's work, the conviction that God was in Christ reconciling the world to himself. Their intramural differences should not be overlooked. Hodge's reliance on seventeenth-century Reformed thought, Shedd's commitment to the formulations of church fathers, Strong's Baptistic principles and his relative openness to new ideas, Pieper's sharp attacks on American practices of baptism and the Lord's Supper, Berkhof's ties to his Dutch antecedents—these and other distinctives set the theologians apart. Yet together they speak with one voice in giving glory to God, in praising the gift of his Son, in honoring the life-sustaining revelation of Holy Scripture. With perhaps only one or two exceptions, American Evangelicalism has not seen better systematic theology since these writers. For that reason their work remains a faithful resource for better understanding of the faith. For that reason they commend themselves, even after the passage of years, to those who wish to know more of the whole counsel of God.

DISPENSATIONALISM

It would be a grave error to pass over the period 1870-1930 without pausing to account for other significant developments. In particular two movements still of great importance for modern evangelical theology had their origin at the turn of the twentieth century. One of these movements, dispensationalism, arose from the predominately Reformed part of the evangelical mainstream, the other, Pentecostalism, came from the Methodist component.

Theologians throughout the Christian centuries have spoken of "dispensations," or special periods marked off from each other by God's different ways of dealing with mankind. Before the rise of modern dispensationalism, Calvinists, Lutherans, and Anglicans were accustomed to speak of a dispensation before Christ (the Old Testament period) and one after His coming (the New Testament and beyond). Modern dispensationalists mean something more than this simple division, however, In order to see what they do mean, we will sketch a history of this theological persuasion and then describe it in greater detail.

In modern times this special way of treating God's dispensations came to the fore in the work of John Nelson Darby (1800-1882). Darby, an Englishman prominent in the growth of the Plymouth Brethren, later was instrumental in forming the Exclusive branch of the Brethren movement. Darby's massive theological writings (collected in 32 volumes) described several distinct periods in history during which God had set differing standards for salvation. Darby himself carried his theological views to America in the mid-nineteenth century, and his writings influenced other theologians than merely those within the Brethren movement.

Partially as a result of Darby's stress on biblical prophecy, but also from a native desire to understand that subject better, major conferences studying the Bible's teachings on the end times took place in the late 1880s. Those who attended these conferences generally held a premillennial view of the Lord's return. They interpreted Rev. 20:2-7 literally and taught that Christ would return to the earth for a reign of one thousand years before the final judgment. (Premillennialism is, thus, the belief that Christ would come before [pre] a literal one thousand year [millennium] reign.) Not all the premillennialists at these conferences or among later Evangelicals were dispensationalists, even though all dispensationalists at that time and since have been premillennialists.

The most influential formulation of dispensational teaching appeared in 1909 when the Oxford University Press published the Scofield Reference Bible. The editor of this text, C. I. Scofield (1843-1921), had been a lawyer before becoming a Congregationalist minister. After a long period of private study, he published an annotated Bible as an aid to properly understand its message for the present and its significance for the future. The impact of the Scofield Reference Bible (rev. ed. 1967) has extended well beyond the original centers of dispensationalism to influence a wide spectrum of American Evangelicals in a dispensational direction.

A student and colleague of Scofield's, Lewis Sperry Chafer (1871-1952), eventually provided the best summation of dispensational theology in his eight-volume *Systematic Theology* (1947). The work has been aptly summarized as "unabridged, Calvinistic, premillennial, and dispensational." As the first president of Dallas Theological Seminary and the editor of its journal, *Bibliotheca Sacra*, Chafer has been the most influential dispensationalist theologian in the United States.

The principles upon which dispensationalism rests place it within the American evangelical heritage, but they also bring to the fore new emphases. Dispensationalism stresses, first, that the Bible must be interpreted literally. In this connection dispensationalists differ with other Evangelicals in being very reluctant to interpret any Bible passage figuratively unless there is overwhelming evidence within that passage itself to demand such a figurative interpretation. Thus, the fact that "one thousand" is used elsewhere in the Bible as a figure of speech meaning "a very great or complete number" (as Deut. 7:9; Pss. 50:10, 90:4) does not make the one thousand year reign of Rev. 20:2 figurative, since it is not clearly labeled as a figure of speech in the Revelation passage. Dispensationalists in general also place great stress on prophecy that is not as yet fulfilled. Indeed, the most well-known works by dispensationalists in the twentieth century deal with biblical prophecy (as Hal Lindsey's *Late Great Planet Earth*).

Given the stress on literal interpretation of the Bible and on future events, dispensationalists also make a sharp distinction between national Israel and the church. In God's dispensational plan, promises to the Jews made in the Old Testament will someday be fulfilled, even if the Jewish rejection of Christ did postpone the final fulfillment of these prophecies and allowed God to gather a church of Gentiles in the intervening period. Finally, dispensationalists order their theology around God's plan for the world in general—culminating in the triumphant millennial kingdom—rather than in God's plan of salvation for individuals. It is not as if personal salvation is slighted but rather, as one contemporary dispensationalist, Charles C. Ryrie, puts it: the "saving program of God is not the only program but one of the means God is using in the total program of glorifying Himself. Scripture is not man-centered as though salvation were the main theme, but it is God-centered because His glory is the center."[13]

Various divisions of God's dealings with mankind have been proposed by dispensationalists, although the seven-fold plan offered by C. I. Scofield is the best known. According to Scofield, God established periods of Innocence (before Adam's sin), Conscience (to the time of Noah), Human Government (from Noah to Abraham), Promise (from Abraham to the Ten Commandments), Law (under the Ten Commandments), Grace (from the time of Christ's first to his second coming), and finally Kingdom (the millennium). In each dispensation God set up certain standards for men that they were not able to meet. God in his mercy, after each human failure, gave mankind further opportunities to be reconciled to himself.

Critics of dispensationalism have often accused it of teaching two or more distinct ways of salvation. Although incautious dispensationalists do sometimes leave this impression, it is not strictly true. The careful dispensationalism for which Dallas Theological Seminary provides a forum, for example, argues for a single plan of salvation. In every dispensation salvation is based on the work of Christ, received by faith, and directed to the glory of God. Dispensationalists do teach, however, that the content of faith differs from period to period. God displays his grace in different ways in different periods (as through the rainbow to Noah after the Flood or through the Mosaic law or through Christ) and, thus, to be saved meant responding to different aspects of God's progressive revelation in the different dispensations.

Dispensationalism has had a widespread influence in recent evangelical theology. It is very strong in Baptist and independent churches. It has pockets of strength among others in the Reformed tradition. And it has even penetrated some of the various groups of European origin, as branches of the Mennonites or the Evangelical Free Church, an offshoot of Scandinavian Lutheranism. Dispensationalism's appeal comes from its no-nonsense approach to the Bible and its easily grasped plan of biblical interpretation. Critics of dispensationalism contend that it has oversimplified the task of scriptural interpretation. They remind dispensationalists that while the Bible's message of salvation is certainly understandable by all, its teaching in such areas as prophecy may be more complex and involved than it seems on first reading.

Dispensationalism's particular concentration on the end times has also had an important effect on evangelical theology. The unity shown in *The Fundamentals* among dispensationalists, Reformed theologians, and members of other evangelical persuasions has not been sustained since that time. One of the sources for this internal strife has been the distinctive teachings of dispensationalism, a fact that defenders of this orientation concede. It is certainly a cause for regret when premillennialists—whether dispensationalists or not—are regarded as virtual heretics by some Reformed, Lutheran, or Episcopalian Evangelicals. It is an equal cause for regret when churches or schools under dispensational influence criticize too harshly Evangelicals who think Christ's second coming will occur without a literal millennium.

Dispensationalism also marks a significant break in the Reformed tradition for many Evangelicals. Although this theological position arose within Reformed thought, it has severed many of its connections with it. C. I. Scofield was a Congregational minister. Lewis Sperry Chafer was a Presbyterian. Yet the theological emphases of dispensationalism have set it apart from the Reformed heritage of Congregationalists and Presbyterians. It is no longer the doctrine of personal salvation that holds center stage for many dispensationalists, but a particular theory concerning the kingdom of God. Dispensationalism with its detailed attention to the end times also tends to be "otherworldly," where the Reformed tradition was more concerned about bringing life in this world into subjection to Christ. Dispensationalism, in sum, has opened new vistas in the study of the Bible to many men and women from all walks of life, but in so doing it has also cut its adherents off from some valuable aspects of the American evangelical heritage.

THE HOLINESS MOVEMENT AND PENTECOSTALISM

The second major development of the period 1870-1930 within Evangelicalism came from the Wesleyan heritage. Throughout the nineteenth century, Methodists had been torn by schism when it was felt that Wesley's emphasis on sanctification was being compromised. Even before the Civil War, "Wesleyan Methodists" and "Free Methodists" split off from the main Methodist churches, at least in part because the parent bodies were not teaching or practicing the second blessing with sufficient zeal. In 1867 the National Holiness Association was formed within Methodism to promote these concerns. Later in the century new groups arose that emphasized a crisis of sanctification. This experience removed remaining sinfulness and prepared the believer to live without sin if he set himself diligently to the task. When the bishops of the Southern Methodist church denounced the Holiness movement in 1894, separate bodies were formed to preserve the Holiness emphasis. This, in brief, is the history behind the Church of the Nazarene and the Church of God of Anderson, Indiana.

Perfectionist and holiness ideas were widespread in the late nineteenth century. They had a large place in the thought of A. B. Simpson (founder of the Christian and Missionary Alliance) and William and Catherine Booth (whose Salvation Army had invaded the United States by the 1880s). The British Keswick movement (named for an evangelical summer fellowship meeting from 1875 onward in the north English town of Keswick) exerted a transatlantic influence also. Although its Reformed sponsors spoke more of a gradual process of spiritual maturity than of an immediate crisis experience, their talk of "practical holiness" encouraged Americans to persevere in the search for personal holiness. An influential book by Hannah Whitehall Smith, *The Christian's Secret of a Happy Life* (1875), added fuel to the Holiness flame. Smith set out in considerable detail how total personal commitment to Christ could lead to a deeper and more victorious Christian life. President Asa Mahan of Oberlin also encouraged a more systematic and scholarly exploration of the Holy Spirit's work in the believer.

Drawing from these various influences, Holiness groups began to reach wider and wider circles with the message of a higher spirituality to which a Christian could ascend by firmer, more absolute trust in Christ. In this process renewed stress was placed on the role of the Holy Spirit. Well before the end of the nineteenth century, Holiness theologians had begun to speak of the "baptism of the Holy Spirit" as a way of describing what took place at the time of the 'second blessing'. The Holiness thrust to Wesleyan theology—in reality an intensification of John Wesley's original teaching rather than an alteration of it—was well established by the turn of the century. It has continued to be a powerful influence in American Evangelicalism. Like dispensationalism, it has affected many Evangelicals who are not connected with the Methodist movement.

From the Holiness movement and in particular from its discussion of the Holy Spirit emerged a distinctly new emphasis in evangelical theology—Pentecostalism. A recent historian of the Holiness-Pentecostal movement has summarized the movement with the adjectives: "Arminian, perfectionistic, premillennial, and charismatic."

About the turn of the twentieth century, a Bible school teacher in Kansas, Charles F. Parham (1873-1929) who had ties to the Holiness revival, began to teach that "the baptism of the Holy Spirit" was something more tangible than just the experience of the 'second blessing'. Relying very heavily on his reading of the book of Acts, Parham urged his students to search out the special, or supernatural, gifts of the Holy Spirit that had appeared in Acts, particularly speaking in tongues and miraculous healings. Parham reasoned that if these phenomena characterized the early church in the book of Acts, they should also mark the modern church.

Early in 1906 one of Parham's black students, W. J. Seymour (d.1923), received an invitation to speak at a Negro Holiness church in Los Angeles. When he arrived, he chose Acts 2:4 as his text and as his theme the proposition: "Anyone who does not speak in tongues is not baptized with the Holy Spirit." To his Holiness listeners who had long thought of the baptism of the Holy Spirit as the 'second blessing', Seymour's teaching did not make sense. They asked him to stop spreading such ideas in the Holiness churches. But Seymour was undaunted. He continued to hold meetings in private homes, and finally on April 9, 1906, "the fire came down," as later Pentecostals would describe it. People spoke in tongues and testified to an ecstatic baptism of the Holy Spirit. Seymour rented an old Methodist church on Azusa Street in Los Angeles, and from this Azusa Street Mission went out teaching on the gifts and baptism of the Holy Spirit that has shaken the Christian world in the twentieth century. It deserves more than a passing notice that this movement, more than any other twentieth-century development in evangelical theology, owes its origin and continued life to the spiritual vitality of Bible believers from the black community.

Theologically, Parham and Seymour only extended the doctrines of the Holiness movement. They taught that the baptism of the Holy Spirit, marked always by tongues speaking and frequently by miraculous healings, was a third stage in the believer's life after conversion and after the sanctification of the 'second blessing'. Later Pentecostal leaders such as W. H. Durham (who received the baptism of the Spirit at Azusa in 1907) taught a two-stage doctrine of the Christian life. He believed that the baptism of the Holy Spirit with its attendant "signs" was the only post-conversion experience that a believer should expect. Sanctification, rather than being an immediate experience, was a lifelong process of "self-abandonment to God's power." Not surprisingly this view that differs so markedly from the Wesleyan-Holiness idea of sanctification, has come to be known as "the Baptist understanding of sanctification."

Other disputes within Pentecostalism focused a great deal of attention inward at the same time as other American Evangelicals were waging battles against external foes. In 1914 the Assemblies of God, holding to a "finished work" view that saw sanctification complete at justification, split off from the main body of Pentecostals. The more dominant "second work of grace" position continued to regard the charismatic signs as the distinguishing marks of the sanctifying experience. About this same time a "Jesus only" movement led to further controversy. The adherents of this view, who later formed the black Pentecostal Assemblies of the World and the white United Pentecostal Church, insisted that God the Father and God the Holy Spirit were only different names for Jesus. This "Pentecostal Unitarianism" was a major source of contention until its defenders separated into their own bodies. Attention paid these internal matters tended to keep Pentecostal interests separate from those of the Evangelicals involved in controversy with Modernism. The fact that Pentecostals had little use for the Calvinism of the American Reformed tradition and that other Evangelicals often distrusted Pentecostalism's "enthusiasm" kept the movement pretty much on its own. As a result Pentecostals largely escaped the traumas of Fundamentalists' battles. They were thus in a better position to expand during the 1930s than other Evangelicals who had been through the "religious wars."

The spread of Pentecostalism in the twentieth century has been nothing short of phenomenal. It quickly claimed many adherents from the Holiness movement who frequently organized groups with the name "Assembly of God." Belief in a special baptism of the Holy Spirit spread rapidly to Scandinavia, England, Germany, and India. Pentecostalism's most spectacular growth has been in South America where something over three-fourths of the Protestants are thought to follow this theological persuasion. And since World War II, an emphasis on Spirit baptism and the "sign" gifts of healing and tongues speaking have appeared in many of the more traditional denominations—Methodist, Lutheran, Episcopalian, Baptist, and even Roman Catholic. This latter development has usually been called the charismatic movement (*charismata* = gifts) to distinguish it from the exclusively Pentecostal churches.

Pentecostalism has not been without its critics. Reformed theologians have been quick to contend that it is an illegitimate movement, since the supernatural gifts of the Holy Spirit were designed for that period after the ascension of Christ before God's final revelation could be gathered in the pages of the New Testament. This position has been maintained in Reformed circles from the time of B. B. Warfield (see his *Counterfeit Miracles*, 1918) to the present (the 1976 General Assembly of the Orthodox Presbyterian Church denied the validity of tongues speaking in this postapostolic age).

Other critics in the Reformed-Baptist tradition who would not go quite this far argue that Pentecostalism's stress on a second work of the Holy Spirit hamstrings the biblical doctrine of the New Birth. These critics argue that the baptism of the Holy Spirit takes place at the time of conversion. If tongues speaking is valid at all (and there is disagreement here), it is only as an aid to worship and devotion. In the eyes of these critics, Pentecostalism has created the false and dangerous impression that a person who has not spoken in tongues is a second-class Christian citizen. Finally, strong criticism of Pentecostalism has come even from the Holiness movement. Holiness theologians argue that Pentecostalism's emphasis on the supernatural gifts of the Holy Spirit distorts the proper biblical teaching on sanctification.

The broad sweep of the Pentecostal movement has had a great impact on recent evangelical theology. Not all charismatic Evangelicals reflect the distinctive two-stage or three-stage description of God's saving acts as these were formulated early in the century. But all do affirm that the Holy Spirit's ministry has been neglected and that it needs to be revived. This emphasis on the work of the Holy Spirit has had a wide effect. Noncharismatic churches make much more now of the gifts of the Holy Spirit (see the popular books by Ray Stedman, *Body Life*, and by David Mains, *Full Circle*).

Evangelicals have in Pentecostalism an example of ardent dedication to God and his work. The prominence of laymen in the charismatic movement has been one of the factors behind the vigorous growth of lay renewal that is active all the way from home Bible studies to week-long inspirational retreats. Pentecostalism is a child of the Holiness thrust of American Methodist theology, but it has grown to be an adult that has influenced almost every phase of American Evangelicalism in the twentieth century.

SUMMING UP

Odds are that the ten-year-old with whom we began this chapter would not have taken a deep interest in the theology of the times in which he lived. But if he had, he would have seen a great divide in

American theology. In 1870 evangelical theology was still the dominant religious orientation in the country, and one of the strongest general forces in America. By 1930 Evangelicalism was one among several competing theological points of view. It may or may not have lost ground in the population at large, but it certainly had considerably less importance for the opinion makers of the country. By 1930 Evangelicalism as a whole had retreated into something of a domestic exile. Our next chapter begins with a description of that exile and continues by telling the story of a return by evangelical theology from exile.

The period from 1870 to 1930, however, was by no means filled with wasted years for the evangelical life of the mind. On "defense," Evangelicals mounted a very respectable campaign against Protestant Modernism. On "offense," systematic theologians produced some of the best work in American evangelical history. The rise of dispensationalism and Pentecostalism marked the presence of vital, if controversial, theological systems. True, the challenges of modern life—particularly science and industrialized American society—had given the theologians pause. Yet even in these areas seeds were planted which would later yield good fruit. If a modern observer focused exclusively on the Fundamentalist-Modernist debates of the 1920s, he might see only defeat and despair for the evangelical cause. Our ten-year-old of 1870 who lived through the entire period would have known differently. Significant successes mingled with the defeats. Considerable progress in communicating the gospel—systematically, coherently, and comprehensively—coincided with garbled transmissions of the faith.

3

"Great is Thy Faithfulness"

Regrouping and Renewal (1930-1978)

EXILE

Exile is a strong word, but not too strong to describe the situation of theological conservatives in the 1930s. Particularly in the North, Evangelicals often became what one writer has called "a despised minority sub-culture." Evangelicals within the mainline denominations suffered from the general reaction against Fundamentalism and, as a consequence, had little influence in setting the direction of their churches. Some self-avowed Fundamentalists, on the other hand, gloried in the breach with mainline Protestants and made separation from Liberalism and the corruptions of American life a badge of honor. Southern Baptists, Lutherans, and Pentecostals were insulated from wider trends in Protestantism by the inward looking character of their groups. And black Christians remained isolated from whites in general because of longstanding racial antagonisms. In brief, Evangelicals had little access to the levers of power that guided American Protestantism or that shaped the mores of the nation.

The burdens of this exile were great. Most everyone had heard stories of young people who had gone to state universities, only to lose their faith in the study of secular philosophy or science. Students who did try to speak up for the Bible's teachings at prestigious private colleges or at state universities were often mocked as culturally backward. An entire generation of evangelical scholars withdrew from the marketplace of ideas, leaving serious books and journals to the non-Evangelicals. Some believers even felt reluctant to speak out on matters of public concern—repeal of Prohibition, the Depression, or the coming of World War II—under the impression that they were too insignificant to affect life in America.

The exile was not entirely burdensome, however. An interconnected community of "safe" churches, camps, mission societies, Bible schools, colleges, seminaries, presses, and denominations arose as compensation for lost influence in the wider society. In these organizations Bible believers lost their sense of loneliness and felt safe from the dangers and temptations of the "world." So effective were these substitute organizations that many Evangelicals were able to live out their lives without sensing the estrangement of their exile from the dominant culture of the age. Only in the Bible-believing black churches, cut off from the larger society by the racism of both conservatives and liberals, did the sense of alienation remain sharp.

In the sections that follow we will spend more time looking at the resources for evangelical theology within the evangelical community than we have in early chapters. Although American evangelical theology reflects European influence, it has always been strongly affected by American evangelical life, and this relationship can be observed most clearly in the recent past. Accordingly, after we examine the impact of the Depression on evangelical thought, we will look at broadly based developments in recent Evangelicalism that provided the indispensable reservoir for a return from exile. Only by understanding the popular movements will we be in a place to understand the more significant developments in evangelical thought after World War II. We will once again observe the continuing impact on American Evangelicalism of Christian thought from the rest of the world.

THE IMPACT OF THE DEPRESSION

The Depression era brought more than an economic burden to the American churches. As other traumatic national events had preoccupied the public mind, so too the Great Depression stole attention from spiritual concerns. Liberal and evangelical churches alike suffered losses in both membership and self-confidence. Beside the grievous burden of distressingly hard times, Evangelicals also were suffering the aftershocks of the Fundamentalist-Modernist controversy. Although, as we have seen, evangelical theology did not in fact fare too badly in the struggles of the 1920s, a hostile national mood, directed by self-appointed champions of the new secular humanism, had declared the forces of Modernism the victor and draped scorn and ridicule on the name Fundamentalist.

Some Evangelicals in the 1930s accepted the analysis of conservative Protestants supplied by the secular press. Of this group, a good number would continue to call themselves Fundamentalists into the 1960s and 1970s and would continue to exhibit what many Evangelicals considered intellectual narrowness and petty legalism. In so doing, they left behind many of their fellow Fundamentalists of the 1940s and 1950s who had meant to defend the essentials of the Christian faith but who had no desire to be needlessly strait-jacketed in the forms created by the traumatic controversies of the 1920s. Most Evangelicals, however, were more in shock than in reaction. With Protestant Liberals they waited for less convulsive times when churches and individuals could resume more normal pursuits.

Having said all this, it would yet be wrong to see the Depression era as theologically insignificant. In fact, it could be claimed that later evangelical advances in theology could not have taken place without the trauma of the great collapse. For it was in the 1930s that the newly won trophies of American Liberalism began to tarnish before they had hardly been set on the shelf. In the 1920s Modernists had scoffed at the evangelical view of man as a sinner; they had pointed to the theory of evolution as proof positive of an inexorably advancing world; they had found in themselves no weaknesses, no deficiencies, that required the healing touch of the Fundamentalists' God-man, Jesus Christ. If the Depression did not see a resurgence of evangelical theology, it did see a widespread crisis of confidence in the religion of Liberalism. Mankind did not seem to be getting better and better. Selfish competition waxed instead of waned. From Europe came disturbing sounds of the breaking of glass and the wail of homeless Jews. Even the last fond hope of some Modernists, the benevolent "dictatorship of the Proletariat" in Soviet Russia, became a source of disillusionment as the kindly mask of Joseph Stalin fell off to reveal a ruthless butcher of all who did not live in fear of his power. Fundamentalist talk about human evil and the need for a Savior seemed less and less a vestige of mankind's vanished childhood.

Evangelicals found allies in the attack on secular Liberalism from unexpected quarters. Out of the ashes of European Liberalism, for example, came the powerful voices of Karl Barth and Emil Brunner. Although Evangelicals had trouble understanding the philosophical existentialism underlying the neoorthodoxy of Barth and Brunner, and although they could not agree with much that these theologians said about the Bible or the exact nature of salvation, they found themselves agreeing with their critique of Liberalism. Evangelicals, too, thought that Modernism had seen too much of man in God and too much of God in man. Evangelicals also felt it necessary to talk about Christ as the Mediator and of God as man's absolute Lord.

Even more surprising to American Evangelicals were the strange words from American Modernism. Evangelicals did not mistake Reinhold Niebuhr's *Moral Man and Immoral Society* (1932) for a definitive exposition of evangelical theology. But they did agree with Niebuhr's attack on the optimistic view of man's nature and the visionary delusions of the social gospel. When it came time to analyze the positive contributions of theologians such as Barth, Brunner, and Niebuhr, Evangelicals lost no time in pointing out serious deficiencies. Yet the service of these neoorthodox thinkers in clearing away the weeds of modernistic humanism was a valuable one in preparing the American theological soil for more expressly evangelical plantings.

KEEPING THE FAITH

When these theological seedlings were put down in the 1940s and 1950s, they found soil that had been well prepared. Throughout the Depression, World War II, and into the post-War era, popular Evangelicalism had succeeded in maintaining considerable vigor. No startling theological breakthroughs marked this period of preparation, but the main themes of evangelical theology were aired by competent and dedicated figures of national influence. Over the airwaves, Walter A. Maier proclaimed from 1930 on the strictness of God's law and the tenderness of his grace on "The Lutheran Hour." Charles A. Fuller's "Old Fashioned Revival Hour" (which enjoyed many years on the Mutual and CBS radio networks) spread a more Americanized, yet no less evangelical message into millions of homes. During the 1930s and 1940s periodicals such as *Sunday School Times*, *Christian Life*, and *Eternity* proclaimed the gospel message of traditional Evangelicalism simply but effectively. Dynamic personal leaders such as John R. Rice and Carl McIntire may be faulted for overly separatistic and negative attitudes in more recent decades, but in the 1930s these feisty individualists spread the gospel message to thousands upon thousands of common people who learned the doctrines of God's grace in Christ along with the more idiosyncratic concerns of these leaders. Periodic revivals of mostly a local and limited character kept this mode of evangelical activity alive until the day in 1949 when Billy Graham's extended crusade in Los Angeles pushed American mass evangelism into a new era. Evangelical colleges and seminaries continued to educate a considerable number of young believers in the basics of evangelical thought. And the growing number of Bible schools—from tiny institutions attached to local churches to large schools like Moody Bible Institute—provided basic training in the faith for many more.

Although it breaks the chronological sequence somewhat, it would not be inappropriate to note that such popular evangelical forces have continued into the present as a backdrop to more systematic theological efforts. The radio voices of J. Oswald Hoffman on the modern "Lutheran Hour" and Joel Nederhood on the "Back to God Hour" (Christian Reformed Church) have continued to proclaim evangelical truths with great integrity in a public forum. In recent years many have become acquainted with Christian teaching through evangelical television programs, particularly those sponsored by charismatic groups. *Christianity Today*, founded in 1956, and *The Reformed Journal*, founded in 1951, have provided an outlet for high quality, popular evangelical theology. The Billy Graham ministries continue to attract widespread attention to evangelical ideas and to direct large numbers of awakened believers toward deeper theological effort. Evangelical Bible schools, colleges, and seminaries are growing in enrollment and educational quality, and these environments prove to be the training grounds for many evangelical theologians.

Without the efforts of such organizations and individuals of mass appeal, the theological enterprise would never get off the ground. Or what is worse, it would degenerate into an exclusive club of academicians whose work is out of touch with the concerns of the church at large. The advance of evangelical theology in recent years, however, has required more than just a large supporting public alive to evangelical programs and quickened by basic Christian truths. Evangelical theology required also a new self-confidence in dealing with the source of its labors, the Bible.

Although Evangelicals never stopped studying seriously the Bible, the inroads of higher criticism retarded evangelical biblical scholarship in the early years of this century. The assurance with which learned scholars spoke of three or more "Isaiahs" or of the committees that put together the Gospels late in the second century drove Evangelicals for cover. At the same time Fundamentalists stoutly defended the authority of the Bible, they tended to let diligent and detailed study of Holy Scriptures take second place to polemical, evangelistic, or eschatological concerns. All this began to change in the early 1940s as Evangelicals once again began to deal deeply and systematically with the biblical text. Along with those who labored to keep evangelical ideas alive among the general population, evangelical biblical scholars share the credit for the rise of evangelical theology in recent decades.

To mention only a few of the thorough works of recent Biblical scholarship does an injustice to those not cited. Nevertheless, certain works stand out historically. The Old Testament labors of Oswald T. Allis (*The Five Books of Moses*, 1949) and E. J. Young (*An Introduction to the Old Testament*, 1949) in the 1940s gave forceful examples to Evangelicals of men who were not afraid to call the bluff of higher criticism and who presented solid, scholarly work of their own on the Old Testament. The New International Commentary on the New Testament, a joint product of American and English Evangelicals, provided weighty and learned commentaries on the New Testament.

The field of biblical theology mediates between biblical commentary and systematic theology by analyzing the comprehensive thought of just one biblical author or book. This discipline also began to see excellent work by Evangelicals. Geerhardus Vos's *Biblical Theology* (1948), marked by a fresh reapplication of Reformed insights to Scripture and a particularly sensitive treatment of Old Testament themes, broke fresh ground for those who would follow. The works of George Ladd (from *Crucial Questions About the Kingdom of God*, 1952, to *A Theology of the New Testament*, 1974) have provided Evangelicals, and particularly evangelical theologians, with diligent, first-class expositions in the New Testament field.

A number of evangelical journals have also provided outlets for more serious treatment of theological matters. The *Concordia Theological Monthly* (founded by Concordia Seminary of the Lutheran Church—Missouri Synod of St. Louis in 1920) and the *Westminster Theological Journal* (founded at Philadelphia's Westminster Seminary in 1938) were only two of the excellent "house journals" that have provided forums for weighty theological, biblical, and homiletical studies. More recently the pages of the *Gordon Review* (founded 1955) and its successor *The Christian Scholar's Review* (1970) have offered Christian perspectives on academic and cultural matters. The journals of the Evangelical Theological Society (founded 1949) and the Wesleyan Theological Society (1965) are also recent significant evangelical publications; these two periodicals have provided evangelical theologians with means to bring their studies to a wider public.

Many of the contributors to these journals teach at the growing network of rejuvenated evangelical seminaries. It is much harder to calculate influence for institutions than for individuals. Nevertheless, it is altogether likely that seminaries such as Asbury, Bethel, Calvin, Concordia, the Conservative Baptist seminaries, Dallas, Fuller, Gordon-Conwell, Reformed, Trinity, and Westminster among others have been an even greater factor in reinvigorating evangelical biblical scholarship than the individuals mentioned here.

Along with radio pastors, evangelists, and educators, the efforts of biblical scholars gave evangelical theologians a constituency and a fund of biblical knowledge for the construction of more distinctly theological work.

STABILITY REGAINED

The task of evangelical theology since the Fundamentalist-Modernist controversy has been threefold. It has been necessary to regain sure footing, to overcome the shocks of harsh religious warfare in the 1920s and desperate social conditions in the 1930s. The second task was carried over from earlier in the century—the need to present an attractive and well-reasoned case for orthodoxy against its enemies, both within and outside of the Protestant camp. And the third task has been the effort to make positive statements about Christian doctrine that clarify the mind and actions of the Lord to the theological community and to the church at large.

The effort to recover stability, to restart the theological engines, so to speak, has been a long one. Neither the country at large nor Evangelicals in particular were much concerned about theological self-confidence in the 1930s. In the 1940s, however, a group of well-trained Evangelicals began to right the ship of evangelical theology.

Edward J. Carnell (1919-1967) of Gordon and Fuller seminaries was a pioneer in this effort. His many books and articles presented a clear, articulate, and evangelical faith. Unlike many of his immediate predecessors, moreover, Carnell did not restrict his efforts to evangelical circles. He earned doctorates at Harvard Divinity School and Boston University. He wrote critically, but with appreciation, of theologians such as Søren Kierkegaard and Reinhold Niebuhr whom Evangelicals had usually shunned as too complex or too suspect. He published in evangelical magazines like *Christianity Today* and Inter-Varsity's *His* but also in "mainline" journals like the *Christian Century*. His range of interests extended from the Christian's use of television to academic defenses of the faith. He criticized what he called the "cultic" aspects of American Fundamentalism while seeking to proclaim "orthodoxy" in the marketplace of American thought. His books such as *Christian Commitment: An Apologetic* (1957) and *The Case for Orthodox Theology* (1959) put Evangelicals and non-Evangelicals alike on notice that sane, reverent, evangelical theology could still be written in twentieth-century America.

Another leader in the reassertion of evangelical stability was Baptist theologian Bernard Ramm (b. 1916). His book on *The Christian View of Science and Scripture* (1954) punctured the myth that had pictured Evangelicals as unanimously hostile to the practice of modern science. Ramm gave hearty endorsement to the scientific enterprise, and only cautioned it not to make unfounded philosophical or religious statements beyond the competence of its rightful domain. This work marked an important public redirection for America's Evangelicals. No longer need science be an object of general suspicion. Ramm's many other publications—on subjects as far-ranging as the interpretation of the Bible, the work of the Holy Spirit, the defense of the faith, and Christian conduct—have also given Evangelicals invigorating theological insight. Like Carnell, Ramm seemed to want to regain a middle ground for evangelical thought. He thus criticized Fundamentalists (for divorcing the Bible from God's work in the world) while at the same time attacking the proponents of non-Evangelical Protestantism (for divorcing knowlege of God in the Bible from the believer's experience of God).

Most important in reasserting the self-respect of evangelical theology was Carl F. H. Henry (b. 1913), professor at Fuller and Northern Baptist seminaries and in 1956 the founding editor of *Christianity Today.* Henry's own works in the 1940s *(Remaking of the Modern Mind,* 1946; *The Protestant Dilemma,* 1948) pointed out the staying power of evangelical theology by comparing it to the distress of Protestant Modernism. But his most important services to evangelical theology were his editorial labors. In the pages of *Christianity Today* he gave evangelical theologians of all kinds a visible and effective platform from which to testify to the vitality of orthodox and pietistic Protestant thought. He also edited a very valuable series of composite works which drew authors from the many theological componenets of American (and European) Evangelicalism *(Contemporary Evangelical Thought,* 1957; *Revelation and the Bible,* 1958; *Basic Christian Doctrines,* 1962; *Christian Faith and Modern Theology,* 1964; *Jesus of Nazareth, Savior and Lord,* 1966). In much the same way as *The Fundamentals* had done, these volumes competently restated the basics upon which evangelical theology was constructed. Although none of these works became a best seller, they all gave uncertain ministers and laymen the assurance that evangelical theology was far from dead. The work of Carl Henry in recent years has encouraged American Evangelicals by providing highly visible coordination for serious evangelical thought. In sum, the books of Carnell, Ramm, Henry, and like-minded scholars signaled to the world that whatever difficulties evangelical theology had undergone in the 1920s and 1930s, it was now determined to make its presence felt in the American religious scene.

APOLOGETICS

Although evangelical theology could now be considered to have regained its feet, there was still much to be done. The challenge of modern thought and of deviant Protestantism remained to test the mettle of evangelical theologians. As far back as the 1920s J. Gresham Machen had produced solid theological works challenging liberal departures from the faith. His book on *The Origin of Paul's Religion* (1921) incisively attacked the modernist contention that Paul had taught a different faith than Jesus. His study of *The Virgin Birth of Christ* (1930) is unsurpassed to this day as a statement of the importance of this doctrine for Christian life and as an argument against liberal detractors from the Virgin Birth. Later in the century, theologians such as Carnell and Henry would also mount telling defenses of evangelical truths against Protestant liberals and secular humanists.

Evangelical theologians have also shown themselves to be competent "defense artists" in the technical field of apologetics. As those who have heard evangelical scholars such as John Warwick Montgomery or Cornelius Van Til in person know, there is nothing "apologetic" about "apologetics." Rather, apologetics is simply the technical name for what one dictionary defines as "the use of theology in order to justify Christianity before men, in the claims it makes to be the ultimate truth, in the demands it makes on its followers, and in its universal mission." Although many Evangelicals have done sturdy work in this area, the two men already mentioned are good representatives of dominant strands of evangelical apologetics.

John Warwick Montgomery, a scholar of the Lutheran Church—Missouri Synod, is a historian. In works such as his *History and Christianity* and *The Suicide of Christian Theology*, he argues for the truth of the Christian faith because of its historical accuracy. As a Lutheran, Montgomery stresses the historical Christ as the key to convincing nonbelievers of the truth of the gospel. He argues that when the records of history are examined fairly and without prejudice, they lead to the inescapable conclusion that Jesus in fact rose from the dead. Such an unusual event demands an explanation. Of all the possible ways of interpreting the resurrection of Jesus, Montgomery contends that Jesus' own account is best—he is the Son of God come in the flesh. Once granting this, it follows that all that this Son of God says is true.

Because Christ told the truth about human sinfulness, about the need for reconciliation with God, and about his own substitution for sinful mankind, we can accept these doctrines as true Christian theology. And because Christ also sanctioned the Bible as the written word of God, we can have utmost confidence in its truthfulness as well. The arguments which Montgomery uses to drive home his contentions are logical, forceful, and persuasive, even though they are not the kind of apologetics that all Evangelicals think best.

Cornelius Van Til, professor emeritus at Westminster Theological Seminary and an Orthodox Presbyterian, views the Christian's apologetic task differently. Van Til argues that no person can fairly and without prejudice examine the historical facts of Christ's life. Van Til makes much of the fact that people are either lost in their sins or born again by God's grace. If they have not been changed by God's grace, they will consciously distort the facts of Christ's life and his claims upon themselves. Van Til's system of apologetics is called "presuppositionalism" because it asks people to consider their underlying attitudes and beliefs (their "presuppositions") with which they approach the Christian message. Van Til argues that only a person with presuppositions that accept the Bible as absolutely authoritative and Christ as the authoritative Absolute will be able to avoid contradiction in his own thinking and despair in his own life. Van Til has used this method to attack European neoorthodoxy *(The New Modernism,* 1946) and other varieties of antievangelical beliefs (as in *The Defense of the Faith,* 1955). Much more philosophical than Montgomery's historical approach, Van Til's apologetic has provided a strong theological stance for many Evangelicals going out to face a hostile world.

What may be an even more encouraging sign for evangelical thought in general is that evangelical philosophers have taken their Christian perspectives into the very den of the lions—the American philosophical establishment. Thinkers like Montgomery and Van Til may be called theologians with philosophical interests. Other Evangelicals can better be described as philosophers with theological interests. The work of someone like Calvin College's Alvin Plantinga can be very complex and profound. His arguments to show the rational plausibility of belief in God or to reveal the unexamined presuppostions of atheism are not meant to excite a Sunday school class or even most evangelical pastors. But they are the kind of contentions that Evangelicals interested in intellectual things have longed to see competing in the rough and tumble world of American academic life. The books of evangelical philosophers often carry imposing titles: Plantinga's *God, Freedom, and*

Evil; Reason Within the Bounds of Religion by Nicholas Wolterstorff (also from Calvin); *Faith Seeks Understanding: A Christian Approach to Knowledge* by Arthur Holmes (Wheaton); *The Possibility of Religious Knowledge* by Jerry Gill (Eastern); or *Belief in God: A Study in the Epistemology of Religion* by George I. Mavrodes (University of Michigan). Together, however, they provide convincing evidence that Christian belief can be as fully satisfying for the most learned professor as for the humblest layperson.

Recent Evangelicals have, in sum, been quite successful in reestablishing the self-respect of traditional orthodoxy and in providing ways to contest modern unbelief. There has not been such notable success in what could be called creative theology. No Jonathan Edwards has appeared in recent times to infuse evangelical thought with startling new insights or to make the Lord's truth strikingly more compelling to the modern mind. Yet significant work goes on in the effort to talk clearly and systematically about the ways of God among men.

THEOLOGICAL GAINS

The Holy Spirit

The widespread growth of the Charismatic movement has led to serious study of the person and the work of the Holy Spirit. No American Charismatic has presented the normal Pentecostal blend of theological and practical concern as well as South African David J. du Plessis' *The Spirit Bade Me Go* (1963). But American Charismatics outside the Pentecostal churches such as Episcopalian Dennis J. Bennett and Lutheran Larry Christenson have presented charismatic beliefs on the Holy Spirit's work calmly, clearly, and reasonably. The most significant noncharismatic study on the Holy Spirit in recent years is that of Frederick Dale Bruner, *A Theology of the Holy Spirit* (1970). Bruner, a missionary educator in the Philippines, had had extensive contact with Pentecostalism before writing his carefully thought out volume. In spite of genuine sympathies with the Pentecostal experience, he concludes that the New Testament simply does not back the Pentecostal picture of the Holy Spirit's use of extraordinary "sign" gifts.

God

Carl Henry has long studied the doctrine of God (see his *Notes on the Doctrine of God*, 1948), and he is now publishing a four-volume treatise entitled *God, Revelation, and Authority*. The first two volumes of this work make a strong argument for the fact that God's revelation to mankind is fundamentally rational—that is, it can be summarized in true statements. American Evangelicals have often shied away from tackling the doctrine of God, this cornerstone of Christian theology. Whether Henry's volumes will be the definitive evangelical treatment or not, they should influence other evangelical theologians to expend greater time and effort in wrestling with this all-important topic.

A Theology of Society

Henry is important in another arena as well. In 1947 he attacked evangelical social apathy in his book, *The Uneasy Conscience of Modern Fundamentalism*, and by so doing set in motion an effort to discover an evangelical theology for society. Since 1947 Henry has continued to call for a more profound evangelical response to modern life. Others have heeded this call and have provided striking theological statements of Christian responsibility for the world today. Mennonite John Howard Yoder's study of *The Politics of Jesus* (1972) provides a penetrating challenge to evangelical acceptance of American cultural standards. Yoder studies the texts of the New Testament intensely and concludes that pacifism and nonviolence form the proper way for Christians to respond to the world. Yoder's point of view has inspired other Evangelicals, such as the publishers of *The Sojourners* and Senator Mark O. Hatfield, to take more seriously the radical challenge that Christianity poses to the secular order.

Richard Mouw of Calvin College takes a different slant on the Christian's responsibility in the world. His books, such as *Politics and the Biblical Drama* (1976), argue that Christian faith carries with it a necessity to be involved politically. More optimistic than Yoder about the possibility of influencing culture in a Christian direction, Mouw shares with Yoder an ability to bring systematic Christian thinking to bear on political and social reality. Authors writing for more popular audiences—for example, Paul Henry *(Politics for Evangelicals)*, Robert Linder and Richard Pierard *(Politics: A Case for Christian Action)*, and Stephen Monsma *(The Unraveling of America)*—have tried to show how evangelical perspectives need to be broadened to see the potential for Christian influence in the political sphere. Public meetings like the 1973 Thanksgiving Workshop on Evangelicals and Social Concern have had much the same goal.

The Evangelicals mentioned to this point as being concerned about a theology for political life usually ally themselves with the center and left of American politics. But there are evangelical thinkers who see ties between Christian thought and the political right as well. Theologian Harold O. J. Brown *(The Restitution of the Republic)* and scholar

Gary North *(An Introduction to Christian Economics)* argue that the biblical views of man and of property demand freedom from governmental restraint in the economy but a return to publicly enforced ethics in society. As much as they differ from Yoder and Monsma, evangelical political conservatives have also been actively concerned about thinking in comprehensive theological terms about the problems of modern life. No one evangelical approach to society has become dominant in recent years. But since 1947 and Carl Henry's appeal to the conscience of Fundamentalism, Evangelicals have once again begun to think theologically about the needs of men in this world as well as in the life to come.

The Church

Innovative theology of a more practical sort has come from Donald McGavran of Fuller Seminary's School of World Mission. McGavran's books (such as *Understanding Church Growth*, 1969) and a growing literature from Americans serving on foreign mission fields (see McGavran, ed., *Eye of the Storm: The Great Debate in Mission*, 1972) have focused attention on the doctrine of the church. McGavran's thesis that it should be the normal expectation for a church to grow spiritually and numerically has provided a new outlook for the nurture of churches not only overseas but also in the United States.

Systematics

Evangelical theologians have made good strides in such specific doctrines as the Holy Spirit, God, society and the church. There has been, however, no flourishing of systematic thought as we observed in the period 1870 to 1930. The most successful evangelical systematics in recent years has probably been the two-volume work of James Oliver Buswell, Jr. His *Systematic Theology of the Christian Religion* (1962-1963) excels in providing detailed summaries of the Bible's own statements on a given theme. The weaknesses of the work include its preoccupation with the older Liberalism as its principal theologial opponent and its failure to use the insights of earlier Christian theologies. In spite of these weaknesses, a recent commentator has praised Buswell's work for "the unique way he preserved intact all of the fundamentals of traditional and thoroughly conservative protestantism without a distinctly 'Fundamentalist' or reactionary frame of mind."[1] Buswell, we could say, provided an example of a comprehensive theology on a return from exile but still not all the way home.

Other evangelical systematics in recent years have commanded respect but have not captured the imagination of Evangelicals at large.

Henry Clarence Thiessen's *Introductory Lectures in Systematic Theology* (1949) was used for many years as a standard text at evangelical schools. Thiessen was a moderate Calvinist of premillennial orientation who, like Buswell, exerted his greatest energies in combating American theological liberalism. His work drew heavily on the systematic theology of A. H. Strong. The Nazarene scholar and educator, Henry Orton Wiley, produced a three-volume *Christian Theology* (1940-1943) as a service to his denomination and the general Arminian-Holiness movement. Its roots lay in the revivalistic traditions of the nineteenth century and the distinctive Holiness teachings that grew out of Methodism. As could be expected, it is distinguished by a very full and judicious section on "Christian Perfection or Entire Sanctification."

The hard days for evangelical life in general after the 1920s have made it difficult to produce distinguished systematic theology. None of the evangelical traditions in recent days has possessed the stability, or the community of scholarship, which, for example, nineteenth-century Presbyterianism offered to Charles Hodge or early twentieth-century German Lutheranism gave to Franz Pieper. If evangelical competence continues to grow in the biblical areas, if evangelical cooperation succeeds in fashioning a living network of scholars, if serious concern for the language of contemporary life can be deepened—then we have cause to expect that systematic theology will again be written that nourishes the believer and provides a statement of comprehensive Christian thought to the world.

The Mainstream

We would be remiss in this survey if we restricted our attention to theologians in the strictly evangelical groups. While liberal theology has made great inroads into mainline denominations throughout the twentieth century, it has never been entirely successful in obliterating an evangelical voice. The two-volume *History of Christian Thought* (1946) by J. L. Neve of the Lutheran Church of America is one example of serious evangelical scholarship coming from a mainline church. Others have been offered by the president emeritus of Princeton Seminary, John Mackay, the Presbyterian church historians Robert Paul and John Leith, and the Canadian theologian Kenneth Hamilton to mention only a few. More conservative Evangelicals might see too much influence from neoorthodoxy in these thinkers, but they can still appreciate the efforts of these individuals to present biblical teaching systematically and intelligibly.

The most notable evangelical theology coming from the mainline churches is probably that of Donald G. Bloesch, a minister in the United Church of Christ and a theology professor at a United Presbyterian seminary. Bloesch, who calls himself "both evangelical and ecumenical," has produced a number of significant works in recent years. He has offered sensitive treatments of Christian living *(The Crisis of Piety, The Christian Life and Salvation)*. He has argued for the "conversion and transformation" of modern theology by the light of the Bible *(The Ground of Certainty)*. And he has offered a penetrating reassessment of Karl Barth *(Jesus Is Victor)*, which praises Barth for affirming the lordship of Christ over the whole world but criticizes him for denying the reality of the battle between Christ and Satan in the present age. Somewhat unexpectedly to many Evangelicals, Bloesch's voice from a mainline denomination is providing some of the theological maturity and biblical comprehension absent in the more strictly evangelical bodies.

Elton Trueblood

Finally, mention must be made of the theological work of Quaker Elton Trueblood. Although not tied closely to mainline evangelical organizations, Trueblood nevertheless has provided creative evangelical theology in traditionaly neglected areas. His works on the church *(The Company of the Committed*, 1961; *The Incendiary Fellowship*, 1967) have held up the vision of an active community where God is at work to heal the world in contrast to the more individualistic ideas of the church that have marked evangelical theology. Trueblood has written provocatively on the place of family life in Christian thought and life (see *The Recovery of Family Life*, 1953, written with his wife). This is an area where Evangelicals have not normally concentrated theological effort. In general, Trueblood stood valiantly as a spokesman for Christian verities in the years after World War II. While other evangelicals were putting their theological houses in order, he had already left home to argue an unbelieving world into the household of faith.

Words that Carl Henry spoke in 1950 still ring true as a contemporary assessment of evangelical theology: "the living and the dead alike doubtless would insist that only a beginning has been made in the theological task of evangelicals."[2] Yet by comparison to theology in 1930, evangelical theology in 1978 is relatively healthy. It can draw on widespread popular support. It has the backing of sound biblical scholarship. It has recovered an encouraging measure of self-confidence. It is meeting challenges from liberalism and secularism. It is producing a few works of genuinely creative insight. The pluralistic character of American Evangelicalism does lead to duplication and needless strife in theology, but the general picture is encouraging. If evangelical theology constitutes more a restatement of traditional Christian beliefs than a powerful breakthrough in the discussion of God, and if evangelical thought still is more influenced by practice than influencing it, American Christians can nonetheless be grateful that God has given evangelical theology a measure of health in the modern world.

FROM OVERSEAS

The story of modern evangelical theology does not end, however, when we have finished speaking of American theologians. As throughout American history, foreign influences have continued to shape native evangelical thought. From Germany, Helmut Thielicke has provided an example of pastoral theology at its best: biblical, relevant to the needs of his culture, and faithful to the divinity of Christ and his work. Another German, Peter Beyerhaus, has stimulated the American discussion of missions theology by his insistence upon the primacy of evangelism in the missionary task. From South America René Padilla has encouraged American Evangelicals to discover a genuine theology of liberation. Padilla's efforts to combine evangelism, nurture for Christians, and active concern for South America's oppressed masses have given evangelical theologians in the United States an example of new applications for old truths.

A major impact on American Evangelicalism has come from the work of Francis and Edith Schaeffer, expatriate Americans living in Switzerland. Beginning with *The God Who Is There* (1968) through *How Should We Then Live?* (1976), the Schaeffers have articulated an effective popularization of sound evangelical theology. Their books point to the utter despair that lies at the end of the road for modern humanism. They call the evangelical church back to high standards of interpersonal nurture and intellectual integrity (as in F. Schaeffer's *The Church Before the Watching World*, 1971). And they describe their own experience in which God has worked faithfully to fulfill his scriptural promises to believers (E. Schaeffer, *L'Abri*, 1969). The Schaeffers's work has not conclusively tied down all questions it has addressed, but it has shown Evangelicals what is possible if the revelation of God in Scripture is studied carefully and applied fearlessly.

Other major evangelical influences have come from France, Holland, and England. The French sociologist, jurist, and biblical student, Jacques Ellul, has produced searching critiques of modern secular life and offered believers far-ranging insights into the nature of Christian life. The Dutch legal philosopher Herman Dooyeweerd has inspired American Evangelicals, mostly from the Dutch Reformed denominations, to develop systematic Christian attitudes toward every aspect of life. Dooyeweerd's scholastic style makes difficult reading. His disciples' innovative discussion of "the Word of God" troubles some Evangelicals. And the Dooyeweerdian discussion of "sphere sovereignty" has not as yet succeeded in disentangling the various parts of existence or stating the exact Christian principles governing life in these spheres. Dooyeweerd's thought, nevertheless, has encouraged many young evangelical thinkers to persevere in the effort to understand the will of the Lord for the entirety of human existence in the world.

From Holland comes also the most effective systematic theology being published in America. G. C. Berkouwer's *Studies in Dogmatics* have been appearing in English translation at a rate of one every other year or so since 1952. From the first volume, *The Providence of God*, to the most recent, *The Church*, Berkouwer has treated the great themes of the faith with skill and sanity. If on rare occasions he accepts too much of modern European theology for American evangelical comfort, and if his consistently Reformed perspective leaves America's Arminians unimpressed, his works are still the closest thing to a definitive evangelical theology in the twentieth century. American Evangelicals who read Berkouwer come away stimulated, refreshed, and enlightened.

From the time of the Puritans, through John Wesley and J. N. Darby, the impress of British Evangelicalism has never left the American scene. In modern times it could even be argued that British orthodoxy sustained vital Christianity in the English-speaking world during America's "religious depression." The conversion of a young literature professor at Oxford University in 1931 would hardly seem to have been a momentous event in American evangelical history. Yet the works of C. S. Lewis (1898-1963) have given encouragement beyond comprehension to American evangelical theology. The delightful *Screwtape Letters* (1941), the sturdy defense of *Miracles* (1947), the forthright presentation of *Mere Christianity* (1952), and many other profound yet lucid works have done wonders for popular and scholarly theological interest in the United States. Above all, the winsome spirit and crystal-clear prose made his works a treasure trove for believers this side of the Atlantic. American Evangelicals could not always understand his pipe smoking and claret drinking, his indifference to eschatology and to a carefully defined doctrine of Scripture, but they recognized wholesome theology when they saw it and gave thanks to God.

In more recent times biblical scholarship by F. F. Bruce and other well-trained Englishmen have contributed to the fertile stock from which theology in America has drawn. The clearly written popular expositions of Anglicans John Stott and James I. Packer have also boosted the American theological enterprise. Stott's *Basic Christianity* presents the gospel clearly and forthrightly. Packer's *Knowing God*, a book on the doctrine of God, is rare in being as moving as it is informative.

No account of American theology would be adequate without acknowledging the contributions of these theologians from overseas. Only slightly less than the founders of Protestantism, they have continued to offer American Evangelicals timely and biblical insights. Particularly in the last forty years they have shared the solid meat of the Word with Americans who otherwise might have been forced to get by on spiritual milk.

Evangelical contributions from outside the United States offer another important lesson that goes well beyond theology. By heeding them, we gain a perspective on some of our own strengths and weaknesses that would not be possible if we restricted our vision to our own country. Russian believers who do not complain about the socialism of the Soviet Union, clear-minded Englishmen like C. S. Lewis who proclaim the faith forthrightly but who do not hold the same view of biblical inerrancy as most American Evangelicals, German state-church Lutherans like Helmut Thielicke who regard baptism and the Lord's Supper as real means of grace, South American Pentecostals whose zeal would look like fanaticism in most of our evangelical churches—all of these aid us in getting a better view of our own beliefs and practices.

Such voices from beyond our borders help us see how closely entwined we are with our American culture. They show us that our commitments to free enterprise, to our formulation of inerrancy, to our "low" view of the Lord's Supper and baptism, and to our standards of what is proper in worship are sometimes shaped by our peculiarly American experience. It is not the case that our convictions and practices are exclusively a product of that experience. But it is true that what we believe and what we do is often influenced by our environment. Evangelicals not caught up in this environment, but functioning as Christians in different contexts, such as Christians of the Third

World, often provide the best help in showing us the bedrock substratum of the faith that underlies Christian life in America and around the globe.

A LOOK AHEAD

It is entirely proper that the story of evangelical theology in America not be divorced from evangelical theology around the world. American believers have no corner on the truth and indeed have frequently needed correction and instruction from abroad. The practical character of American life has made Evangelicals better suited to give the world missionaries, evangelists, and relief agencies than creative theology. We do have our Jonathan Edwards and a whole host of solid lesser lights. But we have not produced rivals to the definitive Protestant theologians—Luther, Calvin, and Wesley—or a great theologian for all Christians like St. Augustine.

The achievement of American evangelical theology lies much more in asking questions that have immediate practical importance. This can be seen most clearly in attitudes toward God's saving work, taken in its fullest extent. The early Puritans, the revivalists of the eighteenth century, and the Reformed tradition in general have been concerned about upholding God's sovereignty in regeneration. They have hence worked toward a theology of the grace of God in the world. Nineteenth-century theologians like Nathaniel Taylor and revivalists like Charles Finney, the Methodists, as well as Holiness and Pentecostal strains within American Evangelicalism, have shown particular creativity in discussing the process of sanctification. In neither theory nor practice have these groups slighted conversion, but their most serious work has gone into the construction of a theology for Christian life in the world. More modern movements, such as dispensationalism, focus on the last days, a concern which leads to a theology for the end of the world. Evangelical bodies such as Lutherans, Reformed, or Mennonites, who retain closer ties to European origins, often place more emphasis on Christian values infusing the day to day structuring of existence. It could be said of them that they seek a theology for life in God's world.

The common theme which binds these groups together is a concern for God's providential work among men. It is precisely here, one could hope, that evangelical theology will exert itself in the days ahead to provide guidance amidst the pressing problems of the present day. What, theologically considered, is the best way of presenting the life-changing challenge of the gospel? What is the best way to describe and encourage a Christian's growth in grace? What is the best way to depict the 'blessed hope' of the Savior's eternal reign? What is the best way to bring the Bible's teaching on sin and salvation into a world of institutions and forces that often seem to run wild beyond the control of the individuals who set them in motion? It is very unlikely that a single evangelical answer will arise for any of these questions. Yet diligent effort to struggle with them is necessary if we desire the light from God's Word to be a lamp unto our feet in the last quarter of the twentieth century.

The tasks ahead for the evangelical life of the mind are no less demanding than for the somewhat narrower concerns of theology. At least some Evangelicals need to winnow the harvests of twentieth-century knowledge for the benefit of the Christian community at large. What in modern science, for example, do we need to embrace as the further revelation of God's truth in nature? Of which underlying assumptions in this same science do we need to beware? What are the things that a believer, acting consciously as God's servant, can do in modern art and literature, in modern politics, in modern business, in the age-old responsibilities of raising children and managing a household? These, and similar issues, lie before all Evangelicals. They pose particularly urgent problems for those who have been called to labor with their intellects for the sake of the kingdom of God.

The failures of evangelical theology and the weaknesses of our thought loom large in retrospective analysis. National concerns have unduly influenced the way we think. Too much time has been spent in unseemly bickering. Too much weight has been given to individualistic and quirky theological labor. Too many assaults on Christianity by its opponents and false friends have gone unanswered. Yet the theological labor of American Evangelicalism has not been in vain. As Charles Hodge once put it in describing the failure of Evangelicals to meet the attacks of Christianity's critics: "We can afford to acknowledge our incompetence . . . : and yet our faith remains unshaken."[3] Theology is the systematic study of God in his actions. Through all of its blunders, evangelical theology in America has been given grace to see that it is God who insures our knowledge of himself. The task of relating God's will to the contemporary world and of bringing the systematic truth of Scripture to believers goes on. The task is not easy. But it is one which cannot completely fail so long as God continues to draw people, even fallible American Evangelicals, unto himself.

4

"Holy Bible, Book Divine"

Evangelicals and the Bible

In Bergen, Norway, the rain poured down again like cats and dogs. A few tourists from the United States (one of the present authors and his wife) and from Belgium sat around a table in a restaurant. Through streaked windows they watched sheets of water pelt the gray-green landscape. Their conversation drifted from one topic to another until it fixed on the Watergate affair. After a few minutes of probing questioning, the gentleman from Belgium could not restrain himself and blurted out: "You Americans . . . are so moral. You get upset over trifling matters, little slips. The Nixon broil was nothing compared to the intrigues of our politicians in Belgium. I have heard that your presidents even take their oaths of office upon a Bible! This is incomprehensible to me, a European."

Certainly this Belgian gentleman thought the Bible was a notable piece of literature. Undoubtedly he knew that it had played a significant role in his own nation's history. But he, like so many other Europeans, could not understand how numbers of Americans in the last third of the twentieth century, an age of science and technology, still honored the Bible, an ancient piece of literature. How could many Americans still take its standards of morality seriously? In his mind the outrage over Watergate had a strange and yet sure connection with reverence for the Bible in the United States.

The European's belief that the outrage at Watergate was somehow related to a high regard for Scripture could be debated. His perception that the Bible continues to be highly respected by large segments of

American society is, however, quite true. *Time* magazine considered news about the Bible to be of such wide interest that a Christmas issue (Dec. 30, 1974) featured a lengthy article noting the ways in which recent archeological and linguistic studies have bolstered the authority of the Bible. The flood of commentary over Harold Lindsell's book, *The Battle for the Bible* (1976), is another indication of American sensitivity to the issue of biblical authority *(Time,* May 10, 1976). A comparable effort by a European to defend biblical inerrancy so forthrightly would have been ignored as outdated and irrelevant to modern concerns. But Americans, by the millions, take the Bible very seriously. A Gallup Poll in 1976 revealed that four out of ten Americans believed this very conservative formulation about the Bible, that it "is to be taken literally, word for word." Whether or not this many Americans follow the teachings of the Bible can be questioned. Without a doubt, however, the Bible remains the ultimate written authority for large numbers of them. Equally clear is the fact that many Americans actively resist attempts to lessen its authority.

What explains this continued fascination and reverence for the Scripture in America? To answer that question we must go back in history. We must consider first the central role the Bible played for European colonists who shaped early American culture. Then we will be in a position to analyze how attitudes toward Scripture began to change. Finally, it will be appropriate to look at the debate over the nature of biblical authority in our own day.

EUROPEANS AND THE BIBLE

When the first European colonists arrived in the New World, they brought along the attitudes toward the Bible that they had had in their homelands. Until late in the 1600s, most Protestant theologians and laypeople believed that the Bible was divinely inspired by the Holy Spirit. It was the revealed Word of God, utterly trustworthy not only for its doctrine, but for its history, its geography, and its ethics as well. In 1614 an Englishman, Robert Brerewood, made a list of the "principall Articles of Faith" believed by all European Protestants. One of its cardinal "Articles," or beliefs, was "the infallible verity and full sufficiency of the Scriptures." A current of scepticism about the Christian religion and the Bible's authority did exist in certain quarters; but sceptics and atheists were by far more the exception than the rule even in the most indulgent segments of European society.

Protestants on the continent differed over some theological issues with a passion, but they generally agreed that the original texts of the

Bible were without error. The German Lutheran, Quenstedt (1617-1688), spelled out his position like this:

> The holy canonical Scriptures in their original text are the infallible truth and free from every error . . . . Every single word which is handed down in the Scriptures is most true, whether it pertains to doctrine, ethics, history, chronology, typography or onomastics.[1]

François Turretini (1623-1687), a Reformed theologian from Switzerland, held just about the same view. He declared that the Holy Spirit inspired the writers of the Scripture so that the words they wrote were "free from all error." The Dutch theologian, Johannes Hoornbeek (1617-1666), noted that "nothing whatsoever was in fact able to be in error" in the Scriptures. So conservative were some Reformed and Lutheran theologians that they affirmed the pointing of vowels in the Hebrew Old Testament was inspired by God. Some theologians went so far as to argue that the Holy Spirit had guarded the biblical documents since their writing so the texts of the Bible available at that time were without error. Other Christians, Quenstedt among them, disagreed and argued that only the original copies penned by the biblical authors were without error. The student of the Bible had the task of working back to the original text by eliminating the errors that had crept in during the copying process. Regardless of their stance on this point, Lutheran and Reformed theologians were united in a very high view of Scripture.

In Britain the Puritans who had hoped to "purify" the English state church from within broke with some of their fellow churchmen over the question of the Bible's sole authority. The Elizabethan Settlement of 1559 enshrined the Bible and the Prayer Book of 1549 as the standards for public worship. The Puritans thought the Bible alone was enough. A Puritan spokeman, Thomas Cartwright (1535?-1603), put his position like this:

> The Word of God containeth the direction of all things pertaining to the church, yea, of whatsoever things can fall into any part of man's life . . . In making orders and ceremonies of the church, it is not lawful to do what men list, but they are bound to follow the general rules of the Scriptures.[2]

In the 1640s the Westminster Confession of Faith would repeat these sentiments for another age.

Anglicans did not challenge the authority of Scripture as such. As Bishop John Whitgift (1503-1604) stated the Anglican position, the applicability, rather than the authority, of Scripture was the issue:

> The Scriptures do contain all things necessary to be believed and to salvation. . . . Yet I do deny that the Scriptures do express particularly everything that is to be done in the church. . . .[3]

Colonists who came from the ranks of English church people brought the perspectives of their party to North America. Although not all of the Puritans or the Anglicans were fervent Christians in practice, they did acknowledge the authority of Scripture in principle.

In this respect the Protestant position on Scripture resembled certain aspects of the Roman Catholic position. The Council of Trent (1545-1563) affirmed the authority of Scripture, but also ruled that "Tradition" must have an equal place alongside it. Moreover it declared that St. Jerome's Vulgate was the only "authentic" version of the Bible.

In their use of the Bible, Roman Catholics of this period, as well as Protestants, sometimes indulged in fanciful interpretations of the biblical text. These frequently allegorical ways of treating the Bible did little for either group in living up to the authority which they claimed for Scripture.

THE FIRST BIBLES IN AMERICA

The first Bibles in North America were undoubtedly brought by Roman Catholics. In 1542, Fray Juan de Padilla, a Spanish missionary, lost his life on the plains of Kansas—put to death by the very Indians he had come to evangelize. When the Pilgrims arrived in 1620, a large community of Indians in the American Southwest had already been "Christianized" by Spanish Franciscans. The French Catholics, Marquette and Jolliet, explored the Mississippi Valley in the 1600s. These Europeans carried with them either the Latin Vulgate or vernacular translations of the Bible.

The earliest English explorers were Anglicans. Quite possibly the Bible which accompanied Sir Walter Raleigh's abortive attempt to settle the Carolinas in the late sixteenth century was the Anglican-sponsored Bishops' Bible. This version and the Geneva Bible were the most frequently used editions during the early days of the Virginia colony [South]. The Puritans of New England favored the Geneva Bible overwhelmingly. French and German settlers brought translations in their own languages to North America. Ultimately, however, the King James Bible of 1611 published in England became the most popular version in colonial America. Robert Aitken, a Scottish-born publisher, was authorized by Congress in 1782 to publish the first American edition, and other printers quickly followed suit.

The King James Bible shaped the language and thinking of many English colonists and their descendants in the United States. Its rendition of Psalm 23 ("The Lord is my shepherd; I shall not want . . . . Yea, though I walk through the valley of the shadow of death. . . .") remains today a source of comfort even among those who know little of the rest of Scripture. The influence of the King James Version can be further noted by the use of its "Thee, thou, and thine" forms in the prayers of many Christians today.

The first Bible published in the colonies was not, however, printed in a European language. Years before English Bibles appeared, John Elliot, "the apostle to the Indians," translated the Bible into Algonquin. Fifteen hundred copies of the New Testament in this Indian language were printed in 1661. Two years later they were joined by 1,000 copies of the Old Testament to complete the first Bible printed in North America. The work Elliot began was taken up in the 1800s by the American Bible Society (founded in 1816), which published Bibles in several Indian languages.

A PEOPLE OF THE BOOK

The New England Puritans, before all else, were a people of "The Book." Many motives, political, cultural, and economic, had led them to New England. Yet the chief motive had been the desire to create a society molded by the Bible's teachings. Hampered by strictures on the practice of their religion in England, they viewed the New World as a place reserved by God in which they could build their "City upon a Hill." Puritan efforts to translate the teaching of the Bible into practice were not always crowned with success. Nonetheless, the intensity of their desire was a moving tribute to the Bible.

In the early days of New England many preachers were anxious to expound the Word, "their tongues untied from the Prelates' [Bishops] injunctions." Now they had the long-awaited opportunity to expound freely the whole counsel of God for which they had been waiting. The Bible was their infallible guidebook for life. Its lessons must be made clear for all.

The Puritan view of Scripture was much the same as that of their contemporaries in Europe. Samuel Willard (1640-1707), a New England pastor, provides a good example of their high view of Scripture:

> Their very holiness declares (God's) authorship. They breathe nothing but purity. They call upon and direct men to glorify him that is the Author of them. On this fact of divine *authority* our surety

> of the coherence of Scripture rests, since it is inconceivable that there should be contradictions in the Word of God.[4]

Little wonder that the American Puritans debated hotly the way in which the Bible was to be interpreted: they were dealing with *eternal* truths.

The Puritans used the Bible not only in the creation of their political and religious institutions and as a basis for their theological works, but it was also a book for meditation and inspiration. Old Testament stories sustained them as they compared their own wilderness experience with that of the ancient Israelites. The Bible assured them that God was faithful to his chosen people if they obeyed His Word, but that He punished the disobedient without fail. We may question the Puritans' interpretations (particularly those identifying Israel's history with their own), but we cannot but admire their desire to place all of life under the authority of the written Word of God.

It is no secret that New England's literature focused on biblical themes. The *Bay Psalm Book* (a hymn book) was first printed in 1640 and went through at least twenty-seven editions. The *New England Primer* taught many a boy and girl in the elements of reading. It also gave them simple theology and Bible stories, from *A* ("In Adam's fall, We sinned all") to *Z* ("Zaccheus he did climb the tree, Our Lord to see").

The whole educational structure of New England was saturated with biblical learning. Harvard College students were encouraged "to lay Christ in the bottom, as the only foundation of all knowledge and learning." The Massachusetts Order of 1647 and the Connecticut Code of 1650 established public schools in great part to teach knowledge of the Bible, since it was "one chief project of that old deluder Satan to keep men from the knowledge of the Scriptures." As historian Bernard Bailyn has pointed out, some Puritans feared that their form of civilization would be "buried in the grave of our fathers" if the young did not receive a correct form of Christian education.

Dedication to the Bible had other effects as well. In the 1790s 85 percent of New England men could read compared to only 60 percent in the former colonies of Pennsylvania and Virginia. Professor Kenneth Lockridge argues that the Puritans' stress upon the reading of the Bible and other Christian literature helps explain this difference. The New England Puritans were indeed a people of "The Book," which in turn helped them become people of other books.

It would be false to leave the impression that all literature in seventeenth-century America arose from reflection upon the Bible. The well-educated avidly pursued classical studies and natural philosophy; others read books more directly applicable to their vocations. Yet the Puritans did press the imprint of the Bible, particularly Old Testament themes and values, deep into American culture. Their conviction that in New England lived a new chosen people became a particularly important bequest from the Puritans to later Americans. Writing in the nineteenth century, Harriet Beecher Stowe (author of *Uncle Tom's Cabin)* could affirm: "I think that no New Englander brought up under the regime established by the Puritans could really estimate how much of himself had actually been formed by this constant face-to-face intimacy with Hebrew Literature."[5] From the cradle, New Englanders were nurtured on tales of Abraham, Lot's wife, Noah, and David. New England parents named their children after Old Testament figures, a practice which continued well into the nineteenth century. The impress of the Bible, particularly of the Old Testament, left an indelible mark.

THE BIBLE IN OTHER COLONIES

In the past, historians have played off the "religious" Puritans of New England against the "irreligious" colonists of the Middle and Southern colonies. The Puritans were the godly founders of the nation while the Middle and Southern colonists were their apathetic Anglican and Catholic cousins. Within recent decades, scholars have presented a different picture. We have been shown that Puritans were not as strait-laced as their detractors imagined. For example, although they condemned drunkenness, some of them imbibed large quantities of alcohol. Nor were they the heavenly saints flitting through the New England woods whom their admirers picture. We also see more clearly now that many middle and southern colonists were resolute in their church life. Among these William Penn and the Quakers, the Scotch-Irish, and pious Mennonites and Moravians joined many establishment Anglicans in holding sincere religious convictions.

Nonetheless, even with all the historical revisionism, it still appears that an untamed spirit of irreligion characterized large segments of the Middle and Southern Colonies in the 1600s and 1700s. The American historian Carl Bridenbaugh speaks of many of these settlers as living in a "starved Spiritual condition" that was not fed until the Great Awakening of the eighteenth century. Certainly some Christians took their religion seriously, but as late as the 1760s there were colonists in the Back Settlement who had never even heard of the Lord's Prayer. Many lived together without marrying. The Bible and Christian morality were of no concern to such ones.

A missionary parson who preached to some backwoodsmen in 1768 told how trifling the results of a Christian ministry could be: "After the service, they went out to Revelling, Drinking, Singing, Dancing, and Whoring and most of the company were drunk before I quitted the Spott."[6] Perhaps the parson's account was sensationalized. But there are too many similar accounts for us to ignore a deep strain of godlessness running through colonial culture. We would do well to recall this when we are tempted to be too optimistic about the impact of Scripture in early America, whether in New England or in the southern colonies.

FIRST CHALLENGE TO THE BIBLE

The first revolt in America against biblical authority occurred in the last quarter of the eighteenth century. After the American Revolution the writings of Thomas Paine, Thomas Jefferson, and Ethan Allen brought to the attention of a good number of Americans a popular form of biblical criticism that derided the Bible's authority. These and others were caught up in the American Enlightenment—a movement which found its inspiration in the older European counterpart, the *Siècle des Lumières* (Age of Lights).

As we noted earlier, most European theologians in the seventeenth century, whether Protestant or Catholic, had believed the Bible to be the authoritative Word of God. In the 1680s, however, the Roman Catholic Richard Simon (1638-1712), author of the controversial *Critical History of the Old Testament* (1678), and the Protestant Jean Le Clerc (1657-1736), a young Arminian church historian from Amsterdam, entered into a sharp debate concerning the inspiration of the Scripture and particularly the Mosaic authorship of the Pentateuch. Each claimed to be defending the Scripture against "atheists" like Thomas Hobbes *(The Leviathan,* 1661) and Baruch Spinoza *(Tractatus-theologico-politico,* 1670).

During their tedious debate (two volumes each), Simon and Le Clerc advanced a number of arguments that undermined traditional beliefs in the Bible's inspiration. This debate (conducted in French instead of scholarly Latin) led many influential Europeans to modify or abandon traditional views of biblical inspiration. This "Battle of the Bible," during a period labeled by Paul Hazard as "The Crisis of the European Mind," eroded belief in the Bible's authority. Later in the eighteenth century the deistic or atheistic leaders of the Enlightenment, the *philosophes,* denied the miraculous accounts recorded in Scripture. They believed the "laws" of nature made miracles impossible. They denied that Old Testament prophecies had been fulfilled in Israel's history or in Christ's life. They argued that the Bible was filled with errors and that the Old Testament was ethically vulgar. For them, the Bible was a human literary production pasted together by credulous Jews and Christians.

In America, Thomas Paine (1737-1809) and Thomas Jefferson (1743-1826) popularized a shallow form of biblical criticism—elements of which came from their "philosophic" friends in England and France. Paine declared that the Old Testament consisted of Israelite myths. Jefferson on one occasion made his own copy of the New Testament by cutting out the miracle stories of the Gospels. Particularly in the 1790s it was evident that scriptural authority was under attack and that the attack was being led by some of the young nation's greatest Revolutionary heroes. Americans who had been spared European controversies over the Bible had to face up to some of the same issues which had led to the self-conscious abandonment of the Bible by Europe's *philosophes*.

Events at Yale College in the 1790s provide us with an intriguing illustration of how a skillful evangelical response was able to repel this first major attack against biblical authority. By that decade students at Yale were so enamored with the French intellectuals Voltaire (1694-1778) and Rousseau (1712-1778) that some called each other by the names of these Enlightenment leaders. Like their heroes, they had turned their backs on Scripture as the authoritative Word of God.

Into this situation came a new president of Yale, Timothy Dwight (1752-1817). One of Dwight's first biographers describes how he dealt with the problem:

> Until this time [1795], through a mistaken policy, the students had not been allowed to discuss any questions which involved the Inspiration of the Scriptures; from an apprehension, that the examination of these points would expose them to the contagion of scepticism . . . . It had led them to believe, that their instructors were afraid to meet the question fairly; and that Christianity was supported by authority and not by argument.[7]

Dwight met the situation head on. He chose to debate the students on this question: Are the Scriptures of the Old and New Testament the Word of God? The godly scholar was successful in his head-to-head encounters. His biographer dramatically describes the results of Dwight's efforts:

> The effect upon the students was electrical. From that moment Infidelity was not only without a stronghold, but without a lurking

> place . . . . Unable to endure the exposure of argument, she fled from the retreats of learning ashamed and disgraced.[8]

Nor did Dwight defend a middling view of Scripture. He taught rather that "each inspired man [among the Apostles] was, as to his preaching or his writing, absolutely preserved from error."[9]

President Dwight by himself did not shut down the floodgates on sceptical biblical criticism in the United States. More generally, the Second Great Awakening stifled the deistic movement and rebuffed the shallow form of biblical criticism that was popular in the 1790s and the early nineteenth century. Nonetheless, Dwight's painstaking efforts to listen to his students and to answer their arguments with care should serve as an instructive lesson: Flight from intellectual problems is not a Christian virtue.

Another lesson from this early period in our nation's history is that allegiance to the Bible does not by itself guarantee good theology. A contemporary of Dwight, Elhanan Winchester (1751-1797), pastored a Baptist church in Philadelphia until he came to the unorthodox conclusion that all people everywhere were, or would be, saved. Surprisingly enough, Winchester professed to discover this "universalism" in his study of the Bible. He wrote of his "conversion" to this point of view: "I shut myself up chiefly in my chamber and read the Scriptures, and prayed to God to lead me into all truth . . . . I became so well persuaded of the truth of Universal Restoration that I was determined never to deny it."[10]

From Timothy Dwight we learn how necessary it is to protect the authority of Scripture. From Elhanan Winchester we learn how important it is not to carry personalistic interpretations of Scripture beyond the boundaries of orthodoxy.

BIBLICAL CRITICISM BEFORE THE CIVIL WAR (1800-1861)

In the years before the Civil War the results of the Second Great Awakening acted as a buffer to keep American Evangelicals sheltered from a more corrosive form of biblical criticism. American seminary professors who kept abreast of the latest European scholarship knew, however, that uneasiness about the Bible was not a thing of the past.

New England, long the bulwark of Protestant orthodoxy, was ironically the area where liberal biblical criticism first took hold. A chair at Harvard College was endowed in 1810 for the promotion of "a critical knowledge of the holy Scriptures." At Andover Seminary the conservative Moses Stuart (1810-1891) took exception to the liberalizing trend at Harvard. Yet his career gave a foretaste of difficulties to come within orthodox Evangelicalism. When he attempted to incorporate some of the newest findings of biblical scholarship from Europe without giving up his orthodox view of Scripture, some of his friends became uneasy. "No sooner had I begun to speak of some of the varieties of German criticism, than some of my best friends began to feel a degree of alarm. It was not long before this became a matter of serious concern to them."[11] Later evangelical Bible scholars would also discover that suspicion of heresy frequently accompanied any attempt to use modern scholarship to attain a better understanding of the Bible.

On the whole, however, liberal biblical criticism in New England before the Civil War had little effect on evangelical churches. Pastors and laypeople alike were too caught up in revivalism, in winning the West for Christ, in worrying about slavery and other social ills to learn much about, or take seriously, the tiny knot of Harvard professors and their allies. It was the optimistic heyday of the evangelical movement when nearly all Protestants were considered "Evangelicals." Why bother about intellectual defenses of the faith, or about orthodox ways to employ the new scholarship, when it looked as if American Evangelicalism was about to conquer the world in the wake of a surging missionary movement? Evangelical prosperity bred intellectual complacency. Evangelical religion depended on warm "spiritual feelings" and saw little need to take account of new ideas.

A SERIOUS NEW CHALLENGE TO THE BIBLE'S AUTHORITY

During the "Gilded Age" (an expression coined by Mark Twain), 1865-1900, commitment of the nation's Protestants to the authority of Scripture was severely shaken. With but a few exceptions, evangelical churchmen were caught off guard. They were intellectually unprepared to handle a new wave of biblical criticism which swept into the land from Europe. The impact of this wave was heightened because it coincided with the mounting influence of an evolutionary philosophy of life extracted from Charles Darwin's scientific work.

Uneasiness could be noted even before the publication of Darwin's *Origin of Species* (1859). Geological studies had led some Bible students to wonder whether Bishop Ussher's dating of the creation of the world in 4004 B.C. was tenable. In 1852 the first issue of the *Presbyterian Quarterly Review* contained an article entitled, "Is the Science of Geology True?" The author of the piece argued that geology had proved the following points: 1. "That the Earth, instead of originating six thousand years ago had existed through an indefinite period, safely expressed by millions of ages." 2. "That creation, taken in its largest sense, instead of being accomplished in one of our weeks, was a gradual work through countless ages." He went on to point out that the Bible was not a book of science and that it should not be read for insights about "telescopes and steamboats."[12]

Other evangelical commentators argued that science should be studied but that it should not be allowed to challenge the Scripture. "Grant one grain of error in the Sacred Book and its authority is gone," wrote another Presbyterian in 1857.[13] Evangelicals were tiptoeing gingerly around an explosive possibility, that the findings of modern science might contradict the Bible, or at least some firmly established interpretations of the Bible. It was frequently difficult for these Evangelicals to know when modern science was offering better ways to interpret the biblical text or when it was questioning the Bible itself.

By the mid-1870s evolutionary thought had made great headway at the nation's leading colleges. One sign of its growing acceptance was the fact that James McCosh (1811-1894), president of that bastion of Presbyterianism, Princeton College, had adopted the principle of natural selection. McCosh, however, did hasten to assure worried Christians that natural selection was part of *God's way* of working in nature.

Many evangelical clergymen were genuinely baffled by these developments. Should they adopt McCosh's attitude and try to make an accommodation between "Christian" and "Darwinistic" approaches to science? Or should they espouse the attitude of Charles Hodge (1797-1878) of Princeton Seminary who argued strenuously that evolutionary natural selection was synonymous with atheism? Or was there some other stance to take? Should one quite simply judge the Scriptures by "science" and let the chips fall where they may? What, if any, was the difference between abandoning traditional interpretations of the Bible and abandoning essential Christian doctrines?

To complicate matters the American debate over the higher criticism of the Bible opened in earnest during the 1880s. Charles A. Briggs (1841-1913), who became a major participant in the debate, noted that Americans had been spared a major controversy over "higher criticism" until that decade:

> We have thus far been, at the best, spectators of the battle that has raged on the continent of Europe over the biblical books. The Providence of God now calls us to take part in the conflict. Our Anglo-American scholars are but poorly equipped for the struggle. We should prepare ourselves at once.[14]

Briggs's debate with A. A. Hodge and B. B. Warfield in the *Presbyterian Review* (1881) and his publication, *Biblical Study: Its Principles, Methods, and History* (1883) did much to precipitate the controversy. He argued that "the scientific study of the Word of God should be combined with a devout use of it."[15] Most evangelicals agreed with Briggs in principle. But they were dismayed when the term "scientific study" was equated with the use of the higher criticism of Scripture that had developed in Germany.

Since at least the 1820s American theological students had regularly traveled to Germany to finish off their theological education. In Germany biblical critics known as "Neologians" had been doing controversial studies on the Scriptures for quite some time. Charles Hodge, who had gone to Europe in the 1820s, learned of the newer biblical criticism but did not adopt it himself. Later in the century, however, other Americans returned from their studies in Germany as proponents of the higher critical views they had studied. They joined Briggs in attacking traditionally orthodox ways of viewing the Scriptures.

What did the orthodox believe about the Bible that the innovators, following German leads, challenged? The respected church historian, William Warren Sweet, gives us some clues about their beliefs when he writes, "Most Christian people in the United States were literalists as far as the Scriptures were concerned. . . ."[16] Mainstream American Evangelicals—whether Methodist, Presbyterian, Baptist, Lutheran, or among the smaller groups—believed that the Scriptures were the inspired Word of God. They believed the Bible was totally reliable in all that the Holy Spirit intended to teach through inspired authors. They used such expressions as "infallible" or "without error" in describing it. They did not question the authorship of the books: Moses really did write the books of the Pentateuch; the prophet Isaiah really did write the entire book bearing his name.

Some Evangelicals had developed careful theories of inspiration. Early in the 1800s, Archibald Alexander (1772-1851) of Princeton Seminary insisted that infallibility belonged to the original documents of the Bible: "We have the best evidence that the Scriptures which were in use when Christ was upon earth, were entire and uncorrupted, and were an infallible rule."[17] More commonly, though possessing high views of the Bible's authority, Evangelicals had not exerted much thought in constructing careful theories of inspiration. Until the 1880s that had not seemed necessary.

Correspondence between two Baptist leaders underscores the imprecise views which some Evangelicals had of Scripture. In December of 1867, Henry G. Weston, a future president of Crozer Theological Seminary, wrote to President Alvah Hovey of Newton Theological Institution, about the nature of the Bible:

> My dear Hovey: . . . that subject [is] one in which I am all at sea, except so far as a dogged belief in inspiration goes, without being able to define what "Inspiration" is . . . . I want you to give me what ideas you can conveniently put on two pages of note-paper. I'll fight for them to the death, for I shall heartily believe just what you say.[18]

Hovey, whom some called respectfully "the Baptist pope of New England," replied in a fourteen-page letter setting forth his conservative views on the Scriptures. Hovey's detailed knowledge of the subject was somewhat exceptional. Although most Baptist professors at the time believed with Hovey that the Scriptures were without error, they were like Weston in not having formulated their beliefs with care.

Higher critics found the orthodox view of Scripture, expressed learnedly by a Hovey or haltingly by simple believers, naive and not "scientifically" verifiable. The higher critics were interested in when and how the books of the Bible were written. These were questions the orthodox had not seriously posed. If Christ said Moses wrote the books of the Law, then Moses did in fact write the books of the Law.

Impressed by the Graf-Wellhausen hypothesis, many of the higher critics argued that the Pentateuch actually consisted of documents that sometimes treated imaginary or mythical events and were written very late in Israel's history. This was a more serious sort of criticism than American Evangelicals had previously faced. It was more sophisticated than the outlandish jibes of the eighteenth-century deists. It went well beyond the perennial challenges of the supposed "contradictions" in the Bible, challenges that the orthodox felt they had successfully answered with the tools of lower criticism (i.e., the efforts to find the correct original text).

Charles Briggs, who had studied in Germany between 1866-1869, was the focus of controversy. His inaugural address in 1891 on the occasion of his appointment to a new professorship at Union Theological Seminary denied the inerrancy of the Bible, the Mosaic authorship of the Pentateuch, and the unity of the book of Isaiah. He declared: "all a priori definition of inspiration is not only unscientific but irreverent, presumptuous, lacking in the humility with which we should approach a divine, supernatural fact."[19] In response, the 1893 General Assembly of the Presbyterian Church condemned Briggs and suspended him from the ministry. Other advocates of biblical higher criticism had previously been forced out of their teaching positions. Fourteen years before (1879), the Baptist Crawford Toy (1836-1919), had been pressured out of Baptist Seminary in Louisville, Kentucky. He then assumed a post at Harvard where he continued to champion the new critical perspective.

Despite these setbacks, higher criticism continued to gain ground. In 1892, William Rainey Harper (1856-1906) became the first president of the University of Chicago. A distinguished Hebraist in his own right, Harper, who admired Briggs's work, helped the university become a center for Near Eastern studies. Faculty members, more liberally inclined than Harper himself, were hired. Within a few years Chicago also became well known as a bulwark of higher criticism. Union Theological Seminary separated itself from the Presbyterian church after the Briggs controversy, as its professors increasingly adopted higher critical viewpoints.

The popular press gave large play to the new views, and seemed not as interested in traditional viewpoints. In 1891 the evangelist L. W. Munhall complained: "Just now a great deal is being said by these papers favorable to the 'Higher Criticism'. They publish little or nothing on the other side."[20] The newer views were brought to lay readers in still other ways. Washington Gladden's *Who Wrote the Bible?* (1891) became a best seller in the 1890s and was adopted as a manual for Bible classes in many YMCAs. Gladden proposed that the Bible should be studied like any other piece of literature. He played down its supernatural origins. It can be argued that Gladden's book contributed to the sapping of evangelical vitality in the American YMCA movement. Robert Ingersoll, the famous agnostic, spread the ideas of higher criticism in yet another way—heated debates with frequently inept defenders of orthodox Christianity.

By the 1890s, in sum, higher criticial views of the Bible had spread well beyond the lecture rooms of the theologians. Many Evangelicals observed this process with growing uneasiness. They were not entirely silent.

EVANGELICALS SHORE UP THE DEFENSES

For some Americans the findings of higher criticism (the term itself did not become really popular until the 1880s) may have possessed the kind of fascination that Mark Twain in his *Autobiography* ascribed to swimming holes—"which were forbidden to us and therefore much frequented by us. For we were little Christian children and had early been taught the value of forbidden fruit." The desire to "kick up heels" theologically may have led some into higher criticism. For other Americans—particularly Southern Baptists, Lutherans still close to their European origins, and blacks in diverse churches—higher criticism had little attraction. Occupied with other matters, they remained firmly convinced that the Bible was the Word of God.

At the seminary level, however, Bible-believing professors could not bury their heads in the sand and hope against hope that higher criticism would disappear. They saw that a good number of their fellow professors, clergymen, and some laymen were in a flutter about the "findings" of science and higher criticism. "Progressive" theology was winning converts in the northeastern states among Baptists, Presbyterians, Congregationalists, and Methodists. Consequently, in the 1870s, 1880s, and 1890s these men began to write on questions of biblical inspiration and higher criticism. Methodist, Baptist, Lutheran, and Presbyterian theological journals saw a growing amount of literature devoted to these concerns.

In the early 1880s A. A. Hodge of Princeton Theological Seminary and B. B. Warfield of Western Theological Seminary (he joined the Princeton staff in 1887) proposed a tightly knit defense of biblical inspiration and inerrancy. They did so in their famous debate with Briggs. In a collaborative article, "Inspiration," for the *Presbyterian Review* (April, 1881) they argued that the Scripture contained no errors. As Warfield put it: "A proved error in Scripture contradicts not only doctrine, but the Scripture claims and therefore, its inspiration making these claims." Where theologians earlier in the century had made more use of external proofs (science and philosophy) to substantiate the authority of the Bible, Hodge and Warfield emphasized once again the Bible's testimony about itself. New views in science and philosophy were calling into question the proofs, contained in such works as William Paley's *View on the Evidences of Christianity* (1794), which American Protestants had long relied on. Nevertheless, as Warfield particularly would make clear in other writings, the testimony of Jesus authenticated Scripture; Scripture spoke of itself as fully inspired; and that should settle the matter for Christians.

Although this was a strong defense of the Bible's authority, Hodge and Warfield did not treat as carefully the issue of how an inerrant Bible should be interpreted. Their clear response to the naturalistic thrust of higher criticism did not provide a comprehensive response to the scholarship of their day. How much reinterpretation of the Bible could go on to bring traditional orthodoxy into harmony with the new science? What weight could be given to the extensive linguistic and archeological studies trying to obtain a more precise view of the Bible's historical, geographical, and metaphorical language? A. A. Hodge's father, Charles, had sketched a promising way of answering these questions in his *Systematic Theology* (1871): "The words of Scripture are to be taken in their plain historical sense. That is, they must be taken in the sense attached to them in the age and by the people to whom they were addressed."[21] Unfortunately for later evangelicals, efforts at this time at defending Scripture itself far outstripped efforts to understand the "plain historical sense" of the book that was being defended so commendably.

A. A. Hodge and Warfield went on in their 1881 article to claim inerrancy only for the "original autographs" of Scripture, an expression Hodge had employed in the 1879 revision of his *Outlines of Theology*. Here he had written: "The Church has asserted absolute infallibility only of the original autograph copies of the Scriptures as they came from the hands of their inspired writers." He was happy to report that a "believing criticism" was "constantly advancing the Church to the possession of a more perfect text of the original Scriptures than she had enjoyed since the apostolic age."[22] Hodge contended that critics must demonstrate that an alleged inaccuracy existed in the original documents (as opposed to copies or translations) before Evangelicals would take their charges seriously.

Charles Briggs, as might be expected, took offense at this. He was particularly upset by the claim that biblical critics had to show that alleged errors existed in the "original autographs" rather than in the copied texts at hand in the late nineteenth century. To Briggs, this was a strategy designed to avoid the brunt of the higher criticism.

In his book, *Whither? A Theological Question for the Times* (1889) he wrote:

> It is admitted that there are errors in the present text of Scripture, but it is claimed that there could have been no errors in the original documents. But how do we know this? We have not the originals and can never get at them . . . . It is sheer assumption to claim that the original documents were inerrant.[23]

Hodge and Warfield did not budge before Briggs's rejoinder. They knew that their argument preserved the force of such passages as 2 Timothy 3:16, and they simply had found no claims in the Bible that the Holy Spirit preserved copies of the Bible from errors. Passages in the Bible about its own inspiration applied only to the original autographs. In addition, as they looked back to American Evangelicals before them and to European theologians of past centuries, they found themselves merely clarifying what had been assumed as a given truth.

The number of those who agreed with their position was impressive. Alexander Carson had made a similar argument in 1853 in his book, *The Inspiration of the Scriptures*: "We may indeed believe that inspiration of the Original, and deny the inspiration of every translation that exists."[24] Princetonians Archibald Alexander and Charles Hodge, the Congregationalist Timothy Dwight, the Baptist Alvah Hovey, the New School Presbyterian Henry B. Smith had earlier in the century all made a distinction between the original autographs and later copies of Scripture. And of course this was a common distinction for some European theologians of centuries past.

Evangelicals from other denominations besides Presbyterianism recognized a fleshing out of their own views in the Princetonian position that the Bible was "inerrant in the original autographs." The Lutheran Franz Pieper, in the *Christian Dogmatics*, was only one of the many who thanked A. A. Hodge and Warfield for this statement of the doctrine. Among Presbyterians themselves, the phrase "inerrancy in the original autographs" became the badge of orthodoxy. It was not indeed a new expression as such, but one encapsulating a long and widely recognized belief in response to the special problems of the late nineteenth century.

The struggle over Scripture, along with the older momentous debates of the time, was splintering the nineteenth-century Protestant monolith. Now there were Evangelicals and "Evangelicals." Disputes over how Scripture should best be interpreted continued, but the authority of the Bible itself was also becoming a divisive issue.

Evangelicals maintaining traditional orthodoxy allowed differing degrees of modern thought a place in their theologies. But all in this group held to the absolute veracity and authority of the Scriptures whether they used the expression "inerrancy in the original autographs" or some other formulation. A second group of Evangelicals tried more organically to join higher criticism or the apparent results of modern science with a high view of Scripture. Such a one was Asa Gray, a world-famous botanist at Harvard and a Christian since his youth, who struggled to unite his scientific studies and his faith. His conclusion: the stream of Scripture "brings down precious gold; but the water—the vehicle of transportation—is not gold."[25] Yet Gray held firmly to the belief that Christianity was constituted by "the advent of a Divine Person, who, being made man, manifested the Divine Nature in union with the human."[26] The leading Methodist theologian of the late nineteenth century, John Miley, was even closer to traditional orthodoxy. The second volume of his *Systematic Theology* (1894) affirmed the Holy Spirit's work of illuminating, communicating, and publishing divine revelation, but said the work was more important "with respect to [Scripture's] higher truths" than to its details. Still a third kind of "Evangelicals" cast off former beliefs and allowed the dictates of higher criticism and "science" to tell them what in the Bible was true and what was mythical or false. All too frequently, unfortunately, the mythical or false was thought to include the miraculous events in the Bible.

Some thoughtful observers in the closing decade of the Gilded Age saw one thing with increasing clarity: the general theological unity of American Protestantism was beginning to fragment. Groups of Protestants were gathering around different world views that could not for long be reconciled to each other.

THE ISSUE IN THEOLOGICAL CONTEXT

Before considering the Bible in twentieth-century America, it would be wise to pause in order to put the dispute that we have just described into proper theological perspective. We can do this best by noting first what debate over the Bible's character did *not* signify. The defense of the Bible, first of all, was not the paramount issue for all Evangelicals. In the 1880s and 1890s Lutherans spent much more time discussing the role of human ability in salvation. Methodists were being torn by disagreements concerning 'holiness' and 'the second blessing'. Spiritual descendents of Alexander Campbell and Barton Stone were in the painful process of dividing into "Disciples of Christ" and "Churches of Christ."

Secondly, even those most concerned about inerrancy among the Baptists and Presbyterians were not fighting just to establish the doctrine itself. Orthodox believers knew that heretics such as the Jehovah's Witnesses also believed in biblical inerrancy. They knew also that some acknowledged Christians thought the Bible contained mistakes. Their great concern, therefore, was to clarify how the Bible nourished Christian life and behavior when it was properly put to use. Charles Hodge yielded to no man in defense of the Bible; yet he saw clearly that Scripture was far more important for what it did than for what it was. This is why Hodge ended his section on the Bible in his *Systematic Theology* by emphasizing that the Bible makes plain "all things necessary to salvation" and that "all the true people of God in every age and in every part of the Church . . . agree as to the meaning of Scripture in all things necessary either in faith or practice."[27]

Nor, thirdly, did the Bible's defenders think that affirming inerrancy solved longstanding disputes within Protestantism. The same

Lutheran, Franz Pieper, who could praise the Presbyterians of Princeton for their statement on inerrancy could also say this: a high view of Scripture "has little practical value when . . . the more recent Calvinists (Hodge . . .) teach Verbal Inspiration and at the same time teach the doctrine peculiar to Calvinism."[28]

The defenders of infallibility did not even argue that an inerrant Bible was the foundation for Christian doctrine. B. B. Warfield, while noting the damage done when inerrancy is abandoned, did not make it the key to doctrine:

> Let it not be said that . . . we found the whole Christian system upon the doctrine of plenary inspiration. We found the whole Christian system on the doctrine of plenary inspiration as little as we found it upon the doctrine of angelic existences . . . . We do not think that the doctrine of plenary inspiration is the ground of Christian faith, but if it was held and taught by the New Testament writers we think it an element in the Christian faith; a very important and valuable element . . . which cannot be rejected without logically undermining our trust in all the other elements of distinctive Christianity by undermining the evidence on which this truth rests.[29]

Finally, the Bible's supporters did not defend it with the conscious intent to make a more Christian response to American society. Some defenders of the Bible did much to alleviate the difficult conditions brought about by the growth of industry and the rise of the cities in the late 1800s. But some who defended the Bible were as callous to these needs, or even more so, than those who called Scripture into question.

No, the primary reason that people like Hodge, Warfield, Hovey, and Pieper defended the inerrancy of the Bible was because they felt it was *a true Christian doctrine.* It was a true Christian doctrine, moreover, that was the sensitive point *at that time* for many Americans, Christian and non-Christian alike. All things being equal, defenders of inerrancy would probably have preferred to spend their time in evangelism with D. L. Moody or in clarifying God's gracious provision of salvation. But the shock of evolution to traditional interpretations of the Bible, the atheistic implications of "Darwinism" as a universal system of thought, the blatant affront to supernatural religion from German higher criticism—all of these made it necessary to rise in defense of this particular doctrine at this particular time.

PROTESTANT CHURCHMEN AND A BALANCING ACT

Early in the twentieth century a number of Protestants believed they could have it both ways: they could abandon a belief in the inerrancy of Scripture yet still maintain belief in basic tenets of the Christian faith such as the deity of Christ. For them, it did not follow that the ongoing health of the church depended on a concept of biblical inerrancy. Some even felt that higher criticism could clarify the Bible.

As the 1920s approached, however, some of these men began to have second thoughts as they saw colleagues who tried to walk this tightrope topple into the abyss of unbelief. A case in point is the experience of Augustus Strong, the noted Northern Baptist theologian. In 1904, Strong, an orthodox Christian, declared:

> We cannot . . . escape or ignore the results of modern criticism. . . . It may be, and it often is, constructive and illuminating, and in that measure it is only a new means by which Christ himself is throwing light upon the record of past revelations and enabling us to understand them.[30]

Strong subsequently incorporated some of the findings of higher criticism into his theology. Later editions of his well-known *Systematic Theology* (particularly the eighth edition) revealed a movement away from strict biblical infallibility. By 1918, however, Strong was taking a new look at the effects of higher criticism on the church. He agonized particularly over those training for the ministry:

> What is the effect of this method upon our theological seminaries? It is to deprive the gospel message of all definiteness, and to make professors and students disseminators of doubts . . . . The result of such teaching in our seminaries is that the student, . . . has no longer any positive message to deliver, loses the ardor of his love for Christ . . . . The theological seminaries of almost all our denominations are becoming so infected with this grievous error . . . . This accounts for the rise, all over the land, of Bible schools, to take the place of seminaries . . . . We are losing our faith in the Bible, and our determination to stand for its teachings . . . . We are ceasing to be evangelistic as well as evangelical, and if this downward progress continues, we shall in due time cease to exist. This is the fate of Unitarianism today. We Baptists must reform or die.[31]

With Strong we too can ask: what had gone wrong? Professor Norman Maring suggests that many Northern Baptists, after reluctantly abandoning the authority of an infallible Bible, established "vital religious experience" as the new authority. To their dismay, however, this new "authority" could not keep some Northern Baptists from moving toward a liberal form of Protestantism based on naturalistic assumptions. The higher criticism directly undermined the gospel message which A. H. Strong and other "moderates" held so dear.

By the time of Strong's critique in 1918, higher criticism and the naturalism of which it was a part were deeply implanted at the older Northern Baptist seminaries. Theological conservatives within the denomination had already founded a new seminary in 1913, Northern Baptist in Chicago. They hoped the new school would provide a training ground for an educated clergy faithful to traditional doctrine, and that it would counter the influence of schools such as the neighboring University of Chicago Divinity School. Astute Northern Baptists sensed that their denomination was splintering on a massive iceberg, the tip of which was the issue of biblical authority.

How did the laity in the Northern Baptist churches react to these unsettling developments? Our evidence here is both incomplete and conflicting. A comment made in 1907 by a contemporary historian, A. H. Newman, does give us an indication concerning life beyond seminary walls:

> The great mass of Baptist people, even in the States that have come most under the influence of the new theology, are conservative. . . . It is probable that even in New England and Middle States not one Baptist member in ten is conscious of any important change in theology or departure from the Old Baptist orthodoxy. In the western and southeastern States probably not one Baptist in twenty has been seriously affected by the "New Theology."[32]

Newman implied that a sizeable number of Baptist laymen maintained the "Old Baptist Orthodoxy" with its high view of Scripture despite the changing attitudes of Northern Baptist seminary professors (Southern Baptist seminaries were not much affected by the teaching of higher criticism in those days save for the earlier Crawford Toy affair).

A similar gap appeared in other denominations between the beliefs of local church people and seminary professors during this transitional period. It would be wrong to imply that orthodoxy had no voice then, however; for in such major publishing efforts as *The Fundamentals*, Evangelicals holding to the Bible's trustworthiness received strong support.

THE FUNDAMENTALS (1910-1915)

A major goal of the editors of *The Fundamentals* was to bolster the commitment of Evangelicals to the authority of an inerrant Bible. Of the ninety articles in the publication, one-third were concerned with the issue of biblical authority. These included six which dealt with the doctrine of inspiration and seventeen that treated issues raised by higher criticism.

James M. Gray (1851-1935), the president of Moody Bible Institute and a dispensationalist, set forth perhaps the clearest explanation of the doctrine of inspiration. His presentation coincided closely with that of the three Princeton Presbyterians who also wrote in the publication. Following the Princeton argument, Gray distinguished between 'revelation' and 'inspiration'. He denied a rigid dictation theory of inspiration, but he argued for inerrancy:

> Inspiration is not a mechanical, crass, bold compulsion of the sacred writers, but rather a dynamic, divine influence over their freely-acting faculties in order that the latter in relation to the subject matter then in hand may be kept inerrant, i.e., without mistake or fault.[33]

Everything in the Bible, Gray held, was infallibly and inerrantly recorded.

Quite perceptively, some of the authors in *The Fundamentals* accused higher critics of not being truly scientific. It was argued that higher critics who approached the Scripture with an unwillingness to allow the possibility of supernatural events could not be objective in their study of the miraculous in Scripture. True open-mindedness, true science, would demand that the evidence for each miraculous account be studied on its own merits. A truly open-minded critic could not help but be impressed by the recent findings of archeologists and historians that confirmed the accuracy of many biblical stories.

Some of the authors in *The Fundamentals* obviously believed that their articles, written painstakingly and politely, would show practitioners of higher criticism the weakness of their postion. A historian, Timothy Weber, has written: "The evangelicals thought they could beat the higher critics at their own game."[34] There was no defeatism here. They held that a Protestant who thought the matter through would naturally possess a high view of Scripture. What other conclusion could there be when considering the Founder of the faith and his statement that "Scripture cannot be broken"?

Some of the writers in *The Fundamentals* made use of their specialized knowledge of Greek and Hebrew and of criticial methodologies. But they insisted that laymen could also read modern translations of the Bible with real understanding. "The intelligent reader of the Bible in the English tongue, especially when illuminated by the Holy Spirit, is abundantly able to decide upon these questions for himself . . ."[35] This emphasis upon the ability of laypeople to read Scripture intelligently was helpful in a day when certain well-known pastors and seminary professors had lost their standing as faithful expositors of the Word of God. In some denominations laymen and local pastors increasingly had to rely on their own study of Scripture. Many turned to the notes of the Scofield Bible for guidance (see chapter 2). Then again, *The Fundamentals* gave the "common man" sane and well-argued assurance that faith in scriptural authority was not ill founded.

A number of observers saw clearly in the period 1900 to 1918 that cracks of division were emerging in the edifice of Protestant unity. They saw that many theological conservatives had little confidence in a number of seminaries where, by 1914, liberal colors flew openly. For example, pastors were steering young men and women away from "progressive seminaries" to Bible schools or training schools. But few commentators reckoned on the extent of the structural damage to the building. After all, the writers of *The Fundamentals* had not sounded a shrill note of alarm, but had offered calm, well-argued support for a conservative view of Scripture. For that matter, many seminary professors who had studied higher criticism still held basic Christian beliefs. And large swaths of Protestant America had not even been touched by the anguished debates.

Could not the edifice of Protestant unity be shored up with a little conciliatory effort by men of good will? After the "Great War" (1914-1918), the naiveté of this hope became very evident. In the twenties, the Fundamentalist-Modernist controversy wracked the house that sheltered Protestant unity and left it in rubble.

THE TWENTIES AND AFTER

Speakeasies, shoot-outs, and Scopes trial. These *s*'s too frequently sum up the 1920s in our imagination. Focusing on the spectacular events of the decade, we could be led to believe that in the twenties the Bible lost its place in American life.

Moreover, can anyone deny that some of the most popular writers and intellectuals stalked evangelical values during the Roaring Twenties? Do not the scandalous innuendoes in Sinclair Lewis's *Elmer Gantry* (1927) along with H. L. Mencken's satirical slaps at the Bible Belt make this clear? Professor James D. Hart has observed that "there was no best selling American novel that could be called religious in theme or attitude" during the decade. The conclusion could be drawn that only in the cultural backwaters of the nation was it possible for some holdouts to take the Bible seriously.

There is a good amount of truth mixed with error in this kind of evaluation. It is true that the twenties witnessed a visible loosening of the nation's morals. It is true that Fundamentalists lost face when

William Jennings Bryan appeared unable to withstand Clarence Darrow at the Scopes trial. It is true that many Evangelicals left the mainline Protestant denominations in reaction to Modernism. It is also true that a good number of Christians, often with bad grace, turned their back on attempts to influence American culture.

It is nonetheless false to assume that since Evangelicals lost places of leadership in the twenties that they ceased to exist save in the Bible Belt. In the early 1960s sociologists of religion were surprised to discover that conservative Christians constituted a large part of American Protestantism.

The fact of the matter is that theological conservatives had been there all along. The fact is that, for some thirty years or more, a popular press and the nation's educational establishment had tended to ignore them. The fact is that, after the twenties, the Bible was still cherished by millions of Americans in all parts of the country who admittedly had lost their ability, and sometimes their desire, to mold the culture of the nation.

Moreover, it is too simplistic to write off the Fundamentalists of the twenties merely as churlish, backward people who were unable to adapt to the rapid societal changes that the nation underwent during the decade. That would be unjust to them and would miss the point of many of their concerns. For some, undoubtedly, the issues were hazy. They had only a vague knowledge of "city slickers" and "scientists" who said we all came from monkeys and who somehow mocked the "old-time religion." But for others such as J. Gresham Machen at Princeton Seminary (who only reluctantly accepted the name of Fundamentalist) the issues were all too clear. After World War I, Protestant Liberals were publicly and aggressively challenging the basic tenets of the faith. For these people, biblical criticism, "science," and comparative religion made issues such as the Bible's inerrancy and infallibility passé. More disasterously, orthodox Christianity was passé for them as well. The Fundamentalists were not battling imaginary foes in the twenties.

Certainly the excesses of the Fundamentalists cannot be defended. Their writings were often too polemical and their verbal pronouncements too caustic. But, when all is said and done, their desire to defend the authority of the Scriptures and the truthfulness of the Christian religion is praiseworthy.

We all know that the twenties ended with an economic thud. But if one had listened attentively during the decade, another thud might have been heard when the house of Protestant unity collapsed. In the sorting-out process after the the collapse, Protestant Liberals gained control of most mainline denominations. Radio commentators and newspaper reporters went to liberal spokesmen when they wanted to sample Protestant opinions. Evangelicals, on the other hand, emerged from the twenties disheartened and disorganized. They bore a double burden: with everyone else they had to fight their way through the economic depression. Additionally, they often had to suffer the snide taunt of being culturally backward. Nonetheless, by the millions they remained unshaken in their belief that the Bible was the very Word of God, and that despite their experiences in the decade of speakeasies, shoot-outs, and the Scopes trial.

The evangelical "exile" following the twenties has been described in chapter 3. But were "Bible believers" really an insignificant force in the 1930s and 1940s? Statistics are hard to come by, but we do have a Gallup poll of 1952 whose results probably tell us something about the preceding decades. The Gallup poll asked this question: "Do you believe the Bible is really the revealed Word of God, or do you think it is only a great piece of literature?" The results: 85% of Protestants said the Bible was the revealed Word of God (Roman Catholics registered 88%; Protestant responses ranged from 72% for Episcopalians to 93% for Baptists). Figures can be made to do anything, particularly those generated by public polling. Nonetheless, the Gallup poll of 1952 gives us good reason to believe that "Bible believers" constituted a larger share of American Protestants than the liberal domination of the mainline denominations would have suggested.

Until the early 1960s or so Evangelicals generally worked out of the consensus that the Bible was not only the "revealed Word of God" (the Gallup poll formula) but that it was inerrant in the original autographs. The Evangelical Theological Society (founded in 1949), which brought together scholars from the Reformed, Arminian, and dispensational quarters of the evangelical community, affirmed this position categorically: "The Bible alone, and the Bible in its entirety, is the Word of God written, and therefore inerrant in the autographs." Southern Baptists, many Lutherans, Holiness and Pentecostal churchmen, and a host of other Evangelicals who did not use this formula generally held to similar views. Nonetheless very honest differences often existed among these groups concerning the way the inerrant Bible should be interpreted. The defenders of inerrancy also were not able to apply the Bible's teachings in American society as forcefully as they upheld its authority, and, in many cases, this left them open to criticism.

After the dust began to settle from the Fundamentalist-Modernist controversy, former allies in the defense of Scripture began to grasp the fact that they did not always read the Scriptures in the same way. The Bible Presbyterians and other members of Carl McIntire's American Council of Christian Churches shunned the National Association of Evangelicals after its founding in 1943 because of a difference in scriptural interpretation. They could not accept as biblical the tongues speaking of several NAE groups and hence refused to join.

After World War II it became particularly evident that the dispensational interpretation of Scripture differed dramatically from Lutheran, Reformed, and Methodist patterns. Eschatological teachings, a particular fascination for dispensationalists, often became the take-off point for testy debates over the best way to read the Bible. Who, really, was interpreting the Bible "literally"? Was there one dispensation of God's grace, or two, or seven, or more? Were there two people of God (Israel and the church) or just one?

For outsiders looking in and for Evangelicals who had remained in the mainstream churches, these debates possessed a touch of the unreal. Why were separatistic Evangelicals stirred up about the cloudy issues of biblical prophecy to the neglect of the clear issue of church unity—the particular fascination of some in the mainline Protestant churches during the 1940s and 1950s. For many theological conservatives the answer to this question was simple. The creation of the state of Israel—to dispensationalists a direct fulfillment of biblical prophecy—signaled the beginning of the "last days." Who would not be interested in prophecy if he or she saw it unfolding in the stories covered in the morning newspaper? As for the ecumenical movement, despite the participation of some genuine Evangelicals, might it not represent the beginnings of an apostasized World Church—itself a herald of the "last days"? Interest in prophetic teachings continued to make many Bible-believing Christians, particularly dispensationalists, suspicious of mainline Protestants.

Understanding this context, we can better appreciate how the publication of the Revised Standard Version of the Bible (1952) touched a raw nerve in large segments of the evangelical community. Even though this translation was based on Greek and Hebrew texts that were more accurate than the ones upon which the King James Version was based, many Evangelicals treated it with suspicion. For one thing, the National Council of Churches sponsored its creation. On separatistic principles, many theological conservatives boycotted any production from that suspect organization. Then again, some Evangelicals saw in the RSV's rendering of Isaiah 7:14 ("Young woman" where the King James Version had "virgin") a liberal slap at a treasured prophecy of Christ's Virgin Birth.

Evangelicals by the score remained steadfastly attached to the King James Version. They did this in spite of the fact that, for some, its beautiful but ancient English tended to obscure the very message of the Bible that they had fought so hard to protect. Later, however, large numbers of these same Evangelicals rushed to buy copies of the new translations that appeared in the 1960s and 1970s. Sales of Ken Taylor's *Living Bible* paraphrase were particularly strong. With other Americans, Evangelicals wanted Bibles that were easier to understand. The fact that many of the new versions bore "seals of approval" from trusted evangelical leaders and were published by evangelical presses helped overcome reluctance to use newer versions.

As the trauma of "exile" gradually wore off, renewed evangelical openness to scholarship and to American culture created concern among some defenders of the Bible. Christian colleges stressed liberal arts more and more. Evangelical seminaries hired academically well-qualified faculty. Billy Graham's ecumenical crusades were increasingly successful. Worldly-wise Evangelicals were increasingly visible. Seeing all this, some in the late 1950s wondered if Evangelicals were opening themselves to the same influences that had led to an attack on the Bible's authority earlier in the century.

THE SIXTIES: THINGS OUT OF WHACK

The 1960s constituted a traumatic decade for many Americans. The Cuban Missile Crisis, the assasinations of John and Robert Kennedy and Martin Luther King, the war in Viet Nam, the Free Speech Movement at Berkeley, the Chicago Democratic Convention of 1968, heightened racial strife, the well-publicized generation gap—all of these bore down hard upon the nation's "Silent Majority," itself a phrase of the sixties. A few articulate theologians caused a sensation in the popular press by proclaiming the "death of God." Other clergymen took to the streets in quest of social justice, an action which greatly alarmed those church people who were used to a separation of politics from religious belief. For whatever reason, Americans increasingly declared that "religion is losing its influence" (1957: 14% of a Gallup national sampling, 1962: 31%, 1965: 45%, 1967: 57%).

But had American Protestants at large actually come to believe that God was dead? Had they given up earlier commitments to the Bible's authority? Once again a great gap yawned between the statements of denominational leaders and radical theologians and the apparent beliefs of the general Protestant community. The Gallup poll of 1965 revealed a deep reservoir of orthodox religious belief in the nation: 85% of Protestants were "absolutely certain" that God existed; 73% said that Jesus Christ was God; and 85% affirmed that the Bible was the "revealed Word of God" (exactly the same percentage of the 1952 Gallup poll). As far as the pollsters could tell, American Protestants had budged relatively little in their professed beliefs since 1952. The conviction that "religion was losing its influence" perhaps reflected the frustration of a large number of Protestants who felt helpless to arrest developments in modern life they did not like.

At the beginning of the 1960s, Evangelicals faced another division focusing on the Bible. In 1960, the well-known evangelical spokesman, Harold Ockenga (b. 1905), called for a "New Evangelicalism" that would be theologically orthodox, open to scholarship, and sensitive to the social and political problems of the nation. Many Evangelicals agreed with the thrust of this appeal. For them the days of exile were over.

Another section of the evangelical community, the modern Fundamentalists, had grave doubts about this development. Stressing a militant separatism, they accused the "Neo-Evangelicals" of making dangerous compromises with liberalism and neoorthodoxy. They argued that compromise would inevitably lead to the abandonment of—first—biblical inerrancy and —finally—of the Bible itself. History, they feared, was about to repeat itself.

By 1960 they were convinced that they had evidence for their concerns. They could cite the Billy Graham New York City Crusade of 1957. How could Graham, America's foremost Evangelical, allow "decision cards" to go to liberal churches, or Protestant Liberals to share the speaker's platform? Moreover, rumors began to circulate in the late 1950s that certain faculty members at the highly respected Fuller Theological Seminary [Pasadena, California] no longer believed in biblical inerrancy, even though the school retained a credal statement to that effect.

The division that resulted pained many Evangelicals deeply. Godly men and women on both sides of the debate felt personally wounded by the harsh rhetoric issuing from both camps. Fortunately, the vast majority of the laity escaped the agony of families and churches being ripped apart in the wake of judgmental vendettas. Evangelicals who had remained within the mainline denominations looked at this struggle with a different kind of fear. Would the side effects of this evangelical skirmishing compromise the long efforts of those who had stayed in mainstream churches to revitalize an evangelical presence in these groups?

From whatever perspective it was viewed, the situation was disquieting. Whether this was the first phase in what Harold Lindsell has called a "Battle for the Bible" can be questioned. It cannot be questioned that hard choices faced American Evangelicals on the issue of the Bible's character and its proper use.

BATTLE FOR THE BIBLE (1960s AND 1970s)

If there has been a "Battle for the Bible" in the 1960s and 1970s, it has not been so much a struggle of Evangelicals against Protestant Liberals as Evangelicals against themselves. In that lies great heartbreak.

One of the first signs of difficulty emerged in 1962 when Fuller Theological Seminary began to rethink part of its statement of faith on the Bible. Eventually a new statement read this way: "All the books of the Old and New Testament, given by divine inspiration, are the written Word of God, the only infallible rule of faith and practice." Where, many Evangelicals wondered, was an affirmation that the Bible was without error? Did the Fuller people really mean that the Bible contained historical or geographical mistakes? For some this was the proof of the pudding: "New Evangelicalism" led *inevitably* to the compromising of biblical authority.

Fuller representatives hastened to assure the evangelical community that no slight was intended to the Bible's trustworthiness, or to its determinative place for Christians. They contended that Fuller's new position was in fact a faithful reflection of the Bible's own view of itself. The Bible, it was argued, did not intend to speak with modern standards of accuracy in mind. It existed to communicate the message of salvation.

A few Evangelicals were convinced. Others, who retained serious doubts, felt their lingering fears were justified when Fuller professor Paul King Jewett's book, *Man as Male and Female,* appeared in 1975. In this volume Jewett argued that the Apostle Paul had actually erred in his discussion of male-female hierarchy by violating his more basic teaching on the equality of all people in Christ. In the minds of many Evangelicals the long efforts by Fuller spokesmen to reassure the evangelical public about their "soundness" on Scripture was dealt a serious defeat.

In the 1970s an even broader division over Scripture troubled the

Lutheran Church—Missouri Synod. According to *A Study of Generations* (1970), 40 percent of Missourians were prepared to say that those who did not believe in inerrancy "are not true to the Christian faith." Another 40 percent leaned toward the position of those who held this strong belief in inerrancy. A storm that had been brewing for some time unleashed its full force at the governing convention of the church held in New Orleans in 1973. President Jacob A. O. Preus and a majority of the LCMS went on record supporting a high view of biblical inerrancy. More than forty years earlier a Missouri convention had accepted the "Brief Statement" that declared "Since the Holy Scriptures are the Word of God, it goes without saying that they contain no errors or contradictions"—a position well in accord with that of theologian Franz Pieper who dominated the church's life between 1880-1932.

The greatest cause of concern among conservatives at New Orleans was the denominational seminary in St. Louis (Concordia) where, it was feared, in Preus's words, that "theological liberalism and the use of the historical-critical method" were undermining belief in the Bible. A majority of the 1050 voting delegates (58 percent) at New Orleans approved a resolution which brought about the resignation of the seminary's president, John H. Tietjen, whom many suspected of compromise on the inerrancy question. In protest to this removal a large number of the school's faculty and students left to found a "Seminary in Exile." As Tietjen saw the controversy in the Missouri Synod, "the authority of the Bible" was not the chief issue. Rather, "interpreting the Bible is an issue. There is a disagreement over what is legitimate and what is illegitimate in biblical interpretation. The rule of tradition in biblical interpretation is an issue."[36]

The minority, more liberal group had wanted to use the tools, and some of the assumptions, of critical biblical scholarship. The majority, more conservative faction wanted to retain the infallibility and the inerrancy of the Bible. Were these positions entirely at odds? Some outside observers, such as James E. Adams (who has written a biography of Jacob Preus), do not think so, but the forces in Missouri found no common ground. The majority, with enough troubling evidence to support their case, believed the minority's use of the Bible led to the rejection of the Bible's plain teachings (that a literal Adam existed, that the Red Sea parted miraculously). The minority feared that their idea of a "proper Christian scholarship" would be sacrificed to an imposition of "wooden literalism" on Scripture.

For Jacob Preus, himself, the stakes in the controversy over the Bible were very high. In the pamphlet "It is Written" (1971) he had let this be known in no uncertain terms: "It seems unbelievable that there should be controversy in the Christian church regarding the doctrine of Scripture. For when all is said and done, there would be no Christian religion, no Christian church, no knowledge whatsoever about Christ without the Scripture."

Other less spectacular debates over Scripture were also taking place among Southern Baptists, Presbyterians in the South, the Disciples of Christ, and other groups. It is difficult to say exactly why more liberal views of Scripture have appeared in evangelical circles in recent years, or why some theological conservatives have frequently seen every new interpretation of Scripture as an attack on Scriptural inspiration or inerrancy. A number of factors can, however, be adduced.

The renewed openness by Evangelicals to higher education has certainly played a role. President Preus of the Missouri Synod, for example, lays much of the blame for the liberalizing attitude toward the Bible at Concordia Seminary to "other ideas" picked up "at non-Missouri graduate schools." Beyond question, a certain number of young scholars (from evangelical backgrounds), and to a lesser extent pastors, who have taken graduate work at Yale, the University of Chicago, or other leading universities, have reformulated their religious beliefs while at these institutions. In doing so, they have not always maintained their attachment to evangelical views on the Bible. Seminaries in particular often must make difficult choices in the hiring of faculty from among these well-trained men and women. Spiritual harm can result when someone is hired who retains the name of Evangelical without Evangelicalism's fidelity to an infallible or inerrant Bible.

A second source of difficulty involves a historical argument. In the 1970s a few Protestant scholars have argued that the concept of biblical inerrancy was a recent innovation, dating from the work of A. A. Hodge and B. B. Warfield in the 1870s and 1880s. Professor Ernest Sandeen's *The Roots of Fundamentalism: British and American Millenarianism 1800-1930* (1970) did much to advance this argument. Earlier he had written that a belief in the inerrancy of the original documents of Scripture "did not exist in either Europe or America prior to its formulation in the last half of the nineteenth century."[37] In the 1970s some "young evangelicals" have accepted Sandeen's position. They use this reading of history as one source to justify formulations for a doctrine of the Bible that does not affirm inerrancy or an equivalent concept.

Those who take this postion are indeed correct that the English word *inerrancy* appears to have been a new coinage in the late nineteenth century. They are also correct that many who have held to Biblical inerrancy have not always followed out the Bible's own mandates for Christian life, particularly in social and intellectual areas. Yet earlier evidence in this chapter has shown that a view of scriptural "inerrancy" (if by other expressions—"infallible," "without error" . . .) was well grounded in Protestantism since the Reformation. In 1881, Charles Elliott of the Chicago Theological Seminary put the case this way, and without undue exaggeration:

> The first of these theories was brought out in the controversy occasioned by the work of Le Clerc (born at Geneva 1657, died 1736), which impugned the strict infallibility of the Scriptures and asserted the existence of more or less error in them. From the Reformation until that time [the Le Clerc-Simon debate, 1685-1687; see above, this chapter] distinct theories of inspiration were scarcely known in the church. The assertion of the absolute infallibility of the Holy Scriptures and the denial of all error in them rendered any theory except that of plenary inspiration unnecessary.[38]

For that matter, "Inerrancy" (or an equivalent concept) has been a common belief of many Christians since New Testament days. Most Evangelicals are more concerned about presenting the gospel to a needy world than in debating theological matters. But most are also determined that a historical argument with some valid points not be used to undermine a very long tradition of evangelical faithfulness to Scripture.

A third source of current evangelical difficulty with the Bible has not received much attention. During the last two decades evangelical scholars have frequently devoted their energies to producing new translations of the Bible or new works of biblical reference. Such projects have consumed much of the time and energy of many professors and pastors. Consequently, they have often not had the time to produce the well-crafted journal articles and books in which critical matters receive calm and convincing evangelical attention. The result is that younger Christians have sometimes looked in vain for first rate responses to the issues which nonbelieving, liberal, and neoorthodox thinkers probe in textbooks and the scholarly literature. Evangelical scholars were, for example, largely caught off guard when the thorny issues of women's roles in the church or the church's witness in society appeared in the 1960s. It proved much easier to criticize political activism or to lash out at unacceptable treatments of the woman's question (as Jewett's *Man as Male and Female* was for most Evangelicals) than to construct careful postions of their own.

One of the great tasks, therefore, to which Evangelicals serious about the Bible's authority need to set themselves is a renewed commitment to sound exegetical and theological study of the *whole* Bible, and not just to certain favorite passages on biblical prophecy. Moreover, evangelical scholars need to propose their points of view more frequently and with resolution and scholarship in the general marketplace of biblical study. They have the data in hand and the skill with which to make their positions compelling. The times are opportune for advances of this sort; even the nonevangelical scholar, John A. T. Robinson, is now arguing for an early dating of the New Testament books (see *Time*, "The New Testament Dating Game," March 21, 1977).

Evangelicalism's sometimes bitter controversies over the Bible in recent years have not apparently affected the majority of Bible-believing Christians. A Gallup poll of 1976 reveals that four out of ten Americans believe that the Bible "is to be taken literally, word for word"—a very conservative formulation. Without doubt, nowhere near this number of Americans live out this belief in the Bible's authority day by day in their lives. Yet once again pastors and laymen by the score appear unwilling to water down their conviction about Scripture.

It could even be argued that the growing popularity of Evangelicalism in the 1970s rests on a firm confidence in an utterly reliable and authoritative Bible. The traumas of the 1960s had distressed some Americans. Familiar props were shaken. Casting about for *a sure word*, many turned to churches and organizations making no bones about the Bible's authority. There they sensed that the gospel message of Christ Jesus was taken very seriously. Pentecostal churches, among the most intense Bible believers, experienced a particularly striking growth. That pollster George Gallup called 1976, "The Year of the Evangelical" was no fluke, nor a mystery.

Evangelical churches—whether independent, in separatistic denominations, or in mainline settings—should be well staffed in years to come. A number of evangelical seminaries are graduating each year hundreds of future pastors, Christian workers, and teachers who are committed to a well-considered belief in biblical authority. These persons understand that belief in the living Word and obedience to the written Word cannot be separated.

SUMMING UP

We have come to the end of our all too rapid historical survey. What, in sum, can explain the fact that millions of Americans in the last third of the twentieth century still profess belief in the Bible as God's revealed Word? Several suggestions might be entertained.

First, the Europeans who came to North American shores were frequently very serious about religious matters. They generally held a high view of Scripture. The impress of that commitment could still be felt by Harriet Beecher Stowe in the middle of the nineteenth century. It continues today, at least in part because of that earlier reverence for the Bible.

Second, the periodic revivals in America have provided a reservoir of belief in Scripture and a defense against negative criticism of the Bible. Not until the late nineteenth century, some two hundred years after the crucial battles for the Bible in Europe, did the American populace at large experience widespread attacks on Scripture.

Third, American Evangelicals have developed the fluid habit of creating new institutions when established ones seemed to compromise Christian orthodoxy, including an orthodox position on the Bible. By the 1970s many of these institutions had passed away or changed their original posture, but an extensive network of churches and schools faithful to evangelical orthodoxy remained and showed remarkable vitality.

Fourth, the confident rejection of the Bible that characterized an earlier day has given way to a general impression that the Bible is much more accurate and trustworthy than some had previously suspected. To cite just one example, *Time* magazine (October 18, 1976) quoted Professor David Noel Freedman of the University of Michigan on the recent discovery of the ancient Eblan Kingdom in the Middle East (e.g., compare the reference to Eber with the same name in Gen. 11:14 and Num. 24:24). Freedman admitted that this new finding confirmed the veracity of a set of biblical passages that liberal scholars had long regarded as mythical. Then he confessed:

> We always thought of ancestors like Eber (the great-great-great-grandfather of Abraham) as symbolic. Nobody ever regarded them as historic—at least not until these tablets were found. Fundamentalists could have a field day on this one.[39]

One final source of the Bible's continuing influence is extremely important. It cannot be underscored enough. Americans by the millions have found that the Bible speaks to the heart. Many who care nothing about theories of interpretation or inspiration care deeply about Jesus Christ, the Son of God, and about the salvation he brings. They care, as did many American colonists three hundred years ago, about the words of comfort in the Psalms for life's moments of tragedy.

They care about the ministry of the Holy Spirit as explained in Scripture. They care about the Bible's discussion of the "end times." For these Christians the Bible remains the *sure word* for yesterday, today, and tomorrow. It is God's *Word.*

* * *

Tucked away on a winding side street of the Left Bank of Paris is a little secondhand book shop. Its shelves are crammed with leather-bound volumes from the sixteenth, seventeenth, and eighteenth centuries on Scripture, theology, and church history. One day an American ventured into the shop to look at some seventeenth century books on biblical criticism. The proprietor said to him: "You know, I service a very small clientele. Europeans are just no longer interested in questions about the Bible and theology." Then the American recalled a conversation which he had had one rainy day in Bergen, Norway, about the Bible and the Watergate Affair. He thanked God that many people in his own land still took the Bible very seriously indeed.

PART II: EVANGELICALS AND THE CHURCH

5

"Revive Us Again"

The Revival of the Church

Above the church door the lights from a neon sign glowed a hazy red through the early dusk: "Revival Services Every Sunday Night." At 7:45 P.M. lively piano music began to drift from the open doors of the modest church. The tune was partially drowned out by the din of traffic passing through the streets of this southern town.

Farther north, in Chicago, blue and white buses rolled into the sprawling parking lots of McCormick Place. Members of Sunday school classes and other church groups climbed out of them and walked with hurried steps into plush facilities where they would hear America's most popular evangelist, Billy Graham.

Both meetings, that summer evening, lie in the long tradition of revivals and evangelistic campaigns which have touched this land. The impact of this tradition upon the way Americans think about Christianity has been great. Jonathan Edwards believed that the First Great Awakening (1740-1744) was a sign that God had chosen North America as the beachhead for His millennial kingdom. During the on-again off-again days of the Second Great Awakening, the church historian Robert Baird noted in 1843 that any churchman antagonistic to revivals certainly could not be evangelical. In the twentieth century, Billy Sunday and Billy Graham talked the language of revivalism, and Americans ranked them among their most honored men.

From Jonathan Edwards to Billy Graham, from itinerant Methodist preachers to television evangelists, the awakening tradition has had a long career. To tell briefly the story of this tradition—with its many changes of emphasis, with its many changes in methods, and with its many changes of expectations—is our purpose. By relating this story, we hope to cast some light on the otherwise bewildering combinations of "revival" campaigns that move through the nation each year. The revival tradition still flourishes in the United States after her two hundredth birthday; it still pumps new lifeblood into the nation's evangelical churches.

* * *

Throughout history the individual Christian has found that his or her love for the things of God sometimes grows weak. Enthusiasm for praying alone and with others, for reading the Scriptures, and for helping in the life of the church diminishes. The cares and the attractions of the world hang heavy upon the mind. To combat such "spiritual depression," the Christian needs spiritual cleansing and renewed love for Christ. As the Holy Spirit works in the believer's heart, spiritual health returns.

In a similar fashion, the Christian community at large has moved from periods of vitality to periods of spiritual dullness. The life of the church reflects the lives of its members. So it should not be surprising that the story of awakenings in American is the story of alternating renewal and decline.

SPIRITUAL UPS AND DOWNS IN EARLY AMERICA

Even the early settlers of the Massachusetts Bay Colony experienced chronic difficulties in maintaining the disciplined commitment and righteousness of the "elect." Initially, the faith of the Puritans seemed quite vibrant. In the 1630s, they delighted in hearing the Word of God preached freely by the approximately ninety ministers who had come with them in that decade. Certainly, the Puritans had their squabbles. Certainly, they were not so hallowed that they were able to withstand all temptations. But in general, they sought to be obedient to the God who had led them to their own "Promised Land."

By the 1650s however, a few pastors—particularly the older ones—believed they saw signs of rebellion and apostasy among the young. Increasingly, Puritan pastors warned their flocks that God's wrath would come upon the entire community for the callousness of individuals to sin. Their warnings became so commonplace that it is difficult to know precisely when primitive Puritanism began to decline in the seventeenth century.

During King Phillip's War (1675-1678) with the Indians, perhaps one man out of every sixteen of New England's white population lost his life. This gave irrefutable proof to some Puritans that God was angry with them for having violated their societal covenant with him. By the time of the Reforming Synod of Boston in 1679, the catalogue of alleged Puritan "sins" was quite lengthy. The list ranged from impropriety of dress to putting "the bottle" to the lips of Indians.

In the next years Solomon Stoddard (1643-1729), the grandfather of Jonathan Edwards, witnessed a series of "harvests" at his Congregational church in Northampton, Massachusetts (1679, 1683, 1692, 1712, 1718). But more generally, the spiritual situation in New England did not improve. By 1700, some observers believed that the affairs of the land were dominated more by tavern life than by church life. Most people did not bother to seek church membership. In 1702, Increase Mather moaned: "Oh New England, New England! tremble, for the glory is going: it is gradually departing."[1]

The situation in the Middle and Southern Colonies was if anything worse. Religion, never a major concern for many of the colonists here, was not prospering. Anglican clergymen, for example, lacked bishops to counsel them. On occasions, parishioners conveniently forgot to pay their parsons. The Reverend Thomas Bacon sadly complained: "Religion among us seems to wear the face of the country, partly moderately cultivated, the greater part wild and savage."[2]

American religion had entered into a period of sluggishness. This spiritual state paralleled the situation in England before the time of John Wesley, where gin addiction, rowdiness, and religious indifference were eating away at society.

STIRRINGS

By the 1720s, there were signs in North America that religious interest might be on the rise. In the Raritan Valley of New Jersey, Theodore Frelinghuysen (1691-1748) and Gilbert Tennent (1703-1764) witnessed, in their Reformed congregations, a renewal of concern for godly things, for prayer meetings, and for the preaching of God's Word. Then some years later in 1734 and 1735, Jonathan Edwards, who was pastor of the Congregational church in Northampton, saw approximately three hundred souls added to his church as an awakening surged through it and others in neighboring towns. According to Edwards two unusual events helped create the new concern for religion. The first was the sudden death of two people in nearby Pascommuck, which startled the community and which was followed by growing interest in spiritual matters. The dramatic conversion of a woman known as the "greatest company-keeper in the whole town" was the second. Another factor that Edwards underplayed was his own preaching on justification by faith, which certainly abetted the Awakening as well.

Intrigued by what was going on in Northampton, Edwards wrote a detailed account of the proceedings: *A Faithful Narrative of the Surprising Work of God . . .* (1737). This volume was one of the first "manuals" on revival in American history. It alerted many pastors to what they might expect when an awakening came their way. After reading it during a walk from London to Oxford in England, John Wesley (1703-1791) wrote in his *Journal:* "Surely this is the Lord's doing and it is marvelous in our eye."

Edwards affirmed that God alone determines when such awakenings take place. They are God's miracles. Men can pray and prepare their hearts, but God alone in his sovereign will determines the timing of his "seasons of mercy."

THE FIRST GREAT AWAKENING

One such "season" dawned in 1740. In the fall of that year the English evangelist, George Whitefield (1714-1770), made a remarkable tour (73 days; 800 miles; 130 sermons) through New England. Preaching wherever he could attract a crowd, Whitefield aroused the interest of a large range of people—from farmers to Harvard students. Quite simply, he was a marvelous speaker. Someone joked that Whitefield, merely by pronouncing the word "Mesopotamia," could bring an audience to tears. When Benjamin Franklin heard the evangelist speak in Philadelphia, he was duly impressed—particularly by Whitefield's ability to project his voice so that it could be heard by a large crowd. Although Franklin's interest in the evangelist was apparently based on mere curiosity, others who heard Whitefield had their "old foundations broken up" and turned to Christ by the score.

The rains of the First Great Awakening had begun, and its flood waters would soon sweep through the colonies. As the historian Edwin Gaustad has noted, "nearly everyone got wet" in 1741-42. All social classes were touched by the excitement. Great agony of soul affected individuals as they considered their personal sin. People anxiously desired to be one of the "elect." Numbing spiritual lethargy was giving way before spiritual renewal. "Religion" now meant much more than a routine and paltry assent to orthodox creeds. It became a heartfelt commitment to Christ.

Unfortunately, some of the promoters of the Awakening (the New

Lights and New Sides) employed flamboyant and excessive tactics. This often provoked sharp, antagonistic feelings among those who opposed the Awakening as an emotional contagion (the Old Lights and Old Sides). Of particular irritation to the pastors of established churches was the itinerant preaching of some New Lights whose messages often included dramatic denunciations of the Old Light preachers. Gilbert Tennent's sermon, *The Danger of an Unconverted Ministry* (1740), particularly incensed them. Whitefield described some of the opponents of the revival as "dead men speaking to dead congregations." Not surprisingly, Old Light and Old Sides pastors often closed their church doors to the New Light itinerants.

By 1743-1744, controversy over the authenticity of the Awakening and over the methods used by its adherents apparently stifled the revival in New England. And yet its effects on education (the founding of several schools for New Lights) and its effects on the practice of American religion were felt for many decades. Moreover, in corners of the South the results of the Awakening continued for years and kept the spiritual temperature high for thousands of colonists.

In light of what would come later, it is especially important to note the general Calvinistic cast of the Awakening. According to Jonathan Edwards and George Whitefield, God alone in His good pleasure awakens Christians from their spiritual slumbers; He alone leads sinners to turn to Him in faith. The preacher is merely an instrument in God's hands; he does not cause the awakening to come upon his audience. God Himself is responsible for reviving saints and converting sinners.

THE GOSPEL UNDER ATTACK

By 1760 Ezra Stiles, a future president of Yale College, looked back upon the Great Awakening as a time when people were "seriously, soberly, and solemnly out of their wits." Public attention directed to the French and Indian War (1754-1763) began to shift the interests of Americans away from religion to politics. Even preachers began to load their religious vocabulary with political connotations (see chapter 8).

Anti-Christian ideas, inherent within strains of French Enlightenment thought, began to influence some colonists during the Revolution, particularly after the signing of the French-American alliance (1778). Ethan Allen (1738-1789), Elihu Palmer (1764-1806), and Thomas Paine (1737-1809) propagated their own home-grown varieties of deism. During the early 1790s, even some pastors were known to be enthusiastic about the books of these men.

At Yale in 1800, only one of the students in the graduating class admitted church membership. On the national scene, church membership dipped to between 5 and 10 percent (although it should be noted that church membership requirements were more demanding then than they are now).

In brief, evangelical health did not characterize the decades during which the Founding Fathers established our government. But once again spiritual lethargy was broken up by an awakening—a second one of national proportions. In the 1790s local revivals in New England gave evidence of its coming in the East. But its most famous origins were in the West.

SECOND GREAT AWAKENING—IN THE WEST

In 1797, James McGready (1758?-1817), a high-powered and fearless gospel preacher in Logan County, Kentucky, made a covenant with his parishioners to persevere in prayer for an outpouring of the Holy Spirit:

> When we consider the word and promises of a compassionate God, to the poor lost family of Adam, we find the strongest encouragement for Christians to pray in faith; to ask in the name of Jesus for the conversion of their fellow men . . . With these promises before us we feel encouraged to unite our supplications to a prayer-hearing God, for the outpouring of his spirit, that his people may be quickened and comforted, and that our children, and sinners generally, may be converted. Therefore we bind ourselves to observe the third Saturday of each month, for one year, as a day of fasting and prayer, for the conversion of sinners in Logan County, and throughout the world. We also engage to spend one-half hour every Saturday evening, beginning at the setting of the sun, and one half hour every Sabbath morning, at the rising of the sun, in pleading with God to revive his work.[3]

It appears that their prayers were in time answered. By 1800, McGready was able to write in the *New York Missionary Magazine* that a revival was beginning in Kentucky like a "few scattering floods of salvation."

Indeed, the western phase (1797-1805) of the Second Great Awakening did see large numbers of frontiersmen turning to the Lord. The emotional excitement and the physical "exercises" that touched both the saved and the unsaved have made the character of the Awakening difficult to assess. However, its impact in pulling the nation out of spiritual doldrums cannot be doubted.

In the first years of the new century Barton Stone (1772-1844), James McGready, and others organized camp meetings in Kentucky. Thousands of rough frontiersmen camped together for several days in order to hear the gospel and to socialize, though sometimes the latter was done a little too freely.

The most spectacular of the meetings was at Cane Ridge. It occurred in August of 1801. Estimates vary as to the number in attendance, from 10,000 to 25,000 persons. A few contemporaries called the events at this assemblage, "the greatest outpouring of the Spirit of God since Pentecost." Ministers were scattered about the grounds and preached simultaneously. Participants could wander about and choose the speakers (both black and white) they wanted to hear. A preacher, James B. Finley, reported that at one session the noise was like that of Niagara; multitudes were "swept down in a moment, as if a battery of a thousand guns had been opened upon them, and then immediately followed shrieks and shouts that rent the very heavens." Even he was affected by a "peculiarly-strange sensation" that came over him: "My heart beat tumultuously, my knees trembled, my lip quivered, and I felt as though I must fall to the ground."[4] He fled to the woods on two occasions and finally wished he had stayed at home.

Some commentators have suggested that the physical phenomena (the jerks, the dancing exercise, the singing exercise . . .) that emerged during the western Awakening can be explained in psychological terms—perhaps the coarse frontiersmen were finding a gut release for their pent-up emotions in religious excitement. Others have proposed that these phenomena resulted from very real spiritual struggles between demonic forces and God himself. At any rate, by 1803 the "heavenly fire" which touched sinners and converted them, had spread into Tennessee, Ohio, Georgia, North and South Carolina and was eventually matched by flames of revival up the East Coast.

Helping consolidate the gains from the camp meetings, Methodist circuit riders (who had been active since the late eighteenth century) organized a network of small groups of believers (societies) throughout the western landscape. These rawboned Pauls and Peters ventured out in any weather to preach the good news. It was not merely a joke that on the coldest days only crows and Methodist preachers could be found out of doors. In fact the Methodists profited so much from the Second Great Awakening that by the 1840s, they had become the largest denomination in America (along with the Baptists they had overtaken the Congregationalists, Episcopalians, and Presbyterians in church membership).

SECOND GREAT AWAKENING—IN THE EAST

In 1787, "revivals" broke out at two small Presbyterian colleges in Virginia, now known as Hampden-Sydney and Washington and Lee. These were the first signs on the Eastern Seaboard of the Second Great Awakening. A good number of students, including Barton Stone, became enthused about the gospel. Several of them later became leading pastors in the western phase of the Awakening.

The grandson of Jonathan Edwards, Timothy Dwight (1752-1817), became president of Yale College in 1795. At the time religious "infidelity" was much in vogue with the students. But those who had formerly scoffed at the Bible met their debating match in Dwight, who argued persuasively for its trustworthy character (see chapter 4).

In 1802 a student revival at Yale witnessed the conversion of one-third of the student body (75 out of 225 students). It touched off a series of awakenings which revived eastern colleges periodically during the next fifty years. These revivals helped furnish trained manpower to lead the evangelistic surge in the nineteenth century. Newly converted graduates from eastern colleges frequently went west to shepherd the enthusiastic but uneducated congregations.

Other forces also pushed the gospel westwards. Organizations such as the American Bible Society (1816), the American Tract Society (1825), and the American Home Missionary Society (1826) spent thousands on gospel literature and on subsidies for pastors in the hinterlands of the West and South. Hudson states:

> . . . the whole voluntary society apparatus launched a great "saturation" campaign to save the Mississippi valley and thus to save the nation. The goal was a Bible for every family, a Sunday school in every neighborhood, a pastor in every locality, and tracts in abundance . . . The statistics tell an incredible story of Bibles shipped, tracts distributed, Sunday schools organized, and churches established.[5]

Evangelical religion began to mushroom in the West as well as in the East. The Second Great Awakening fed its growth.

By the 1830s not only were Evangelicals growing rapidly in numbers, but revivals had become one of the most important features of their church life. In fact some commentators again believed that a world-wide revival was right around the corner. The editor of a new edition of Jonathan Edwards's writings on revival wrote in 1832: "Never before has the Holy Spirit been poured out in so many places at once: never before has the Lord Jesus gathered so many into his churches, in the same space of time, 'of such as shall be saved.' There is reason to believe, that these displays of divine grace will continue to increase, till one general revival shall extend over the habitable globe."[6]

REVIVALS—CHARLES FINNEY STYLE

Probably more than any other person, Charles Grandison Finney (1792-1875) molded the way people perceived revivalism in the middle third of the nineteenth century.

In his *Memoirs,* Finney recalled how as a young convert he had become troubled by the Calvinistic or "Edwardian model" for awakenings. He did not agree with Edwards that Christians needed to wait upon God to choose the time and the means to save sinners and to revive the "saints." In *Lectures on Revival* (1835), he summarized a new approach. He contended that, as God has established laws in the natural world, He has done so in the spiritual world as well. If we obey God's rules for revival, we *will have* revival: "The connection between the right use of means for a revival and a revival is as philosophically sure [scientific] as between the right use of means to raise grain and a crop of wheat."[7] To his way of thinking, revivals were not miracles (as Edwards had said); they could be promoted by following certain steps. Did not the Bible (2 Chron. 7:14) read: "If my people, which are called by my name, shall humble themselves, and pray, and seek my face, and turn from their wicked ways; then will I hear from heaven, and will forgive their sin, and will heal their land"?

Finney's new ideas about revival bore fruit in "New Measures"—such as "protracted" meetings, the "anxious seat" (where sinners under conviction could go to be counseled), and an extensive use of itinerant preaching. These "New Measures" became the building blocks upon which less well-known evangelists (such as the Methodist [Holiness] evangelists, Phoebe and Walter Palmer) constructed their campaigns. They would eventually become popular among Christians of various denominations, including some Calvinistic bodies.

Finney's theology influenced the way he and other evangelists preached the gospel. Finney argued that, as a man can choose to sin, so he can choose to commit his life to Christ. The preacher's task was to persuade the individual to make the right choice, to turn from a life of sin to a life of discipleship. Certainly, the Holy Spirit works to convince the sinner of the truths of Christ, but ultimately the individual must decide for himself to forsake his sin and follow the Lord. It was Finney's belief, as well, that conversion might take place at any time. It did not depend on a decree of election by God, nor on a "season of mercy."

Finney also insisted that backslidden Christians could be similarly persuaded to return to their original commitments to Christ. In fact the principal concern of the revivalist was to "revive" Christians from their spiritual lethargy. Christians once revived would then attract sinners to a hearing of the gospel. Revivals were to be part and parcel of normal church life; they could solve most church problems. They were not extraordinary happenings, as Edwards had suggested. Itinerating professional revivalists could bring them to most any town if they followed the "New Measures" with care.

Not everyone agreed with Finney. Calvinists like Charles Hodge (1797-1878) of Princeton Theological Seminary and the Rev. Albert B. Dod of Princeton College roared their disapproval at his analysis of revivals in general and conversions in particular. They accused him of Pelagianism (the belief that man begins salvation on his own). Scholars today still debate the accuracy of their charge. In any case, Finney's thinking strengthened the movement by many Christians away from Calvinism to Arminianism. Under Finney's influence others more comfortably mixed the two views.

Finney's style as an evangelist—his direct appeals to men and women to come forward to the anxious seat where they could be counseled, his plain talk, his layman's clothes—gave a common touch to evangelistic campaigns. He emphasized the necessity of reaching the urban poor with the gospel. Particularly from 1840 to 1857 Finney encouraged evangelists to take their campaigns into urban areas. Evangelical religion should leaven the life of the cities; it should not be limited to colleges and frontier regions.

With Finney's obvious success and with the substantial benefits for society which followed in the wake of his type of revival, it appeared that the "Edwardian model" for awakenings would soon fall from evangelical horizons. Americans were caught up in a society of "democratic temper." It was the age of Andrew Jackson. The idea of "eternal caste" divisions based on the decrees of election did not much appeal to the "common man" of Jackson's era. Finney's concepts of revival fit his age well. Some would argue that they fit too well and had in fact been forged by the heady individualism of the day.

THE BUSINESSMEN'S AWAKENING

In 1857-1858 another major Awakening touched the land. For some commentators this Businessmen's Awakening, as it was called, defied preconceptions of what an awakening should be like. As contemporaries noted, it was neither frenzied nor raucous, neither precipitated by the preaching of any outstanding revivalist nor provoked by any special calamity.

This was a revival prompted by prayer. Undoubtedly, the financial crisis of 1857 shook some New York businessmen from their trust in material things and thereby created receptive hearts for the gospel. But calm prayer and testimony meetings across the land were more characteristic of it than a religious excitement spawned by panic.

Jeremiah Lamphier began the Fulton Street prayer meetings (Fall 1857 - Spring 1858) in New York City with only a few businessmen coming together at noontime to pray. A bell would ring if an individual prayed or testified more than five minutes in these one hour gatherings. The growth of this type of meeting was startling and others soon began throughout the city. This phenomenon was heralded across the nation by newspaper articles and by the telegraph system. In fact the telegraph companies allowed "saints" to send free telegrams to "sinner" friends urging them to be converted.

Whether through emulation of the New York meetings or through spontaneous local initiatives, prayer meetings sprang up in many other states. In Boston Charles Finney received this report about the popularity of prayer meetings from a Midwesterner: "I am from Omaha in Nebraska. On my journey East I have found a continuous prayer meeting all the way. We call it two thousand miles from Omaha to Boston; and here was a prayer meeting about two thousands miles in extent."[8]

The prayer meetings were soon followed by evangelistic campaigns that heightened the impact of this Awakening. Probably some six hundred thousand American turned to Christ as Savior at this time. A great many Christians were also renewed in their faith. Unfortunately, the South was largely unaffected by this revival.

THE CIVIL WAR AND AFTER: REVIVALISM UNDER SCRUTINY

The ship of evangelical unity faltered upon the rough seas of the American Civil War (1861-1865). It had been badly shaken by the divisions over slavery among Baptists and Methodists, during the previous decades. It was rocked as well by theological divisions over the nature of Calvinism. Yet it was the war which ultimately swamped the ship.

During the war, revivals moved through the ranks of both Billy

Yank and Johnny Reb. But these revivals did not restore either national or evangelical unity. The fratricidal bloodshed which kept the country together physically drove it apart spiritually.

Immediately following the war (1865-1867), a sound of revival was heard from one border of the South to the other. Throughout the country, the entire evangelical community moved to right itself, only to be battered by a new series of challenges.

America was rapidly becoming a pluralistic religious society. The dominant role of white Anglo-Saxon Protestants in American culture was placed in jeopardy as Catholic, Jewish, and unchurched immigrants poured into American ports, particularly in the last decades of the century. Earlier, some Protestants called Nativists fought unseemly battles to arrest the growth of Catholic influence. In addition, the fragile theological concord of American Evangelicals began to disintegrate in debates over the findings of biblical criticism, comparative religion, scientific research, and new philosophies. Both of these important challenges deserve a closer look.

The increasingly pluralistic character of American religion was to have a profound effect upon the history of revivals. Each of the three major awakenings up to this time had been cast in the terms of traditional Protestantism. The individuals who were "revived" or converted generally understood the language of the preachers or evangelists. Both convert and preacher usually shared the same givens—vocabulary and values—of a Protestant nation.

An example from Civil War annals illustrates this point. The *Christian Commission* was an organization that ministered to both the physical and spiritual needs of Union troops. According to personal workers, nearly all the young men who made professions of faith in Christ had received prior religious education as youngsters. The message of the gospel was familiar to them. Commission workers noted that in the aftermath of a battle, they would often find the wounded of both sides lying together where they had fallen. These soldiers could frequently be heard singing hymns to their common Lord and Savior. In song, they shared an evangelical faith with their enemies.

After the tragic War, the nation continued to drift away from its Protestant moorings. As the American people became more numerous and more religiously diversified, some observers felt that another national awakening was very unlikely. More and more Americans, whether Roman Catholics, Jews, or the unchurched, found the language of Protestant revivalists alien to their experience. For example, Roman Catholics in ethnic neighborhoods of the cities could live their lives without having much contact with Protestants (for many Protestants had moved to the suburbs). Robert Handy, the historian, has suggested that by the 1920s or so, Anglo-Saxon Protestants finally gave up on their hope of making other Americans into their own image.

Moreover, the new intellectual challenges to the Christian faith tended to dampen the enthusiasm for revivals among some Protestants. In his *Manual of Revivals* (1884), G. W. Hervey took note of this shift in attitude:

> It is too late in the day to apologize for revivals or to attempt to establish their importance. We are indeed well aware that there is a certain class of pastors who take but a languid interest in this subject. They consider that their call is not to say to men, "Be ye reconciled to God," but rather to say to the sacred Scriptures, "Be ye reconciled to science, to reason, to intuition, to consciousness."[9]

Liberally inclined Evangelicals began to turn their back on the revival tradition—that tradition which had so dominated American Protestantism before the Civil War. Instead, following the lead of Horace Bushnell's *Christian Nurture* (1847), they elevated Christian education in the local church over gospel preaching as the means to bring individuals to a "Christian world view." This trend continued into the twentieth century.

Conservative Evangelicals, on the other hand, still hoped for national awakenings. In practice however they tended to see as one thing revival in the churches and mass evangelism in the cities and towns. In their programs of evangelistic outreach, they continued to build up the role of the itinerant preacher. Nor were the warnings of staunch Calvinists about the "cheap conversions" served up by itinerant evangelists generally heeded. In fact, G. W. Hervey noted in 1884 that professional evangelists now found growing acceptance among theological conservatives in the mainline denominations: "It is but fair to add that some of these friends of pastoral evangelism favor professional revivalists, and would not hesitate, upon an emergency, to invite their co-operation."[10] Of course for Methodists and others, this was no new development. They had relied on itinerant evangelists, both men and women, for some time.

DWIGHT L. MOODY

Dwight Lyman Moody (1837-1899), that famous former shoe salesman, was a pivotal figure in reshaping the revival tradition in America during the last third of the nineteenth century. Charles Finney had stressed revivalism as a force to keep the local church healthy; he wanted to see the faith of believers strengthened, believing that the conversion of sinners would follow. Moody, on the other hand, stressed evangelism—the conversion of the sinner. Reviving the sagging commitment of the saint was very important but still secondary. This shift of emphasis led many Americans to equate revivalism with evangelistic campaigns.

Moody borrowed, and then modified significantly, several of Finney's "New Measures." Moody did hold his own "protracted services"—in a particular town. He called inquirers forward to "seats of decision"—a reworked edition of the Methodists' "anxious seat" that Finney, though not a Methodist, had used so effectively. Moody was well aware of the fact that he had moved away from Methodist vocabulary. Someone once asked him: "Do you advocate anxious seats?" Mr. Moody replied: "I would rather call it seats of decision; but in union meetings you know we have to lay aside a good many of the different denominational peculiarities. The anxious seat is known to the Methodists, but if we would call it that the Presbyterians would be afraid and the Episcopalians would be so shocked they would leave. . . ."[11]

The way Moody urged sinners to "come forward" solidified that practice in mass evangelism meetings. He declared: "It makes no difference how you get a man to God provided you get him there."[12] The church historian, James Johnson, describes Moody (who did not write a formal theology text as had Finney) as "an Arminian up to the cross but Calvinist beyond it." Moody did pioneer a new procedure by inviting persons under conviction to move to an inquiry room where they could be counseled in a more private setting.

As much as he resembled Finney in some matters, Moody went far beyond him in the way the revivals (or evangelistic campaigns) were organized. In the early years of Moody's ministry, committees comprised of local pastors and laymen would invite the evangelist to come to their town. The committees assumed total responsibility for organizing the meetings. Moody and Sankey, his soloist, would arrive only a day before the campaign to make certain that all was in order.

As Moody's operations became larger, particularly after 1875, he felt obliged to involve himself more in the planning of the campaigns. He attempted to standardize the procedures to be followed. Handbills were sent out in order to "make possible the surface excitement of mass revivalism," as J. F. Findley has written. Directives on the duties of ushers and choir members became more uniform. The financing of campaigns was to follow special guidelines.

In the school of practical experience Moody, a big-hearted evangelical stalwart, hammered out the techniques which modern day mass evangelism also uses. The success which greeted his efforts guaranteed that twentieth-century evangelists would take a long, hard look at how Moody had run his revivals or evangelistic campaigns.

Although Moody continued to hold large meetings almost until his death in 1899, he gradually came to the conviction that the day of the hippodrome service might be drawing to a close. No longer was he convinced that inquirers received adequate Christian instruction even in his own inquiry rooms. He found that his personal workers were often ill prepared to handle counseling responsibilities. Perhaps for this reason, Moody began in the 1880s to devote much of his valuable time to founding schools where he hoped children and young people might be grounded in the Christian life and where they might learn the skills of a lay evangelist. These institutions included Northfield Seminary for Girls (1879), Mount Herman School for Boys (1891), and the Bible Institute of Chicago (1889), now Moody Bible Institute. By stressing Christian nurture, Moody showed himself to be a sensitive and wise evangelist.

R. A. TORREY AND THE TURN OF THE CENTURY

A good number of lesser known revivalists did not concur with Moody's judgment that the days of revivals and mass evangelism were coming to an end. In the closing decades of the nineteenth century, Sam Jones, Charles Alexander, and especially Reuben A. Torrey continued to hold large revival services. Torrey's thoughts on revivals are significant, not only because he was an evangelist of international reputation, but because he believed that Moody's mantle had fallen on his shoulders.

Torrey (1856-1928), had been converted at Yale University during a visit by Moody to that institution. In 1901 Torrey edited a volume entitled *How to Promote and Conduct a Successful Revival With Suggestive Outlines*. In it, he clearly affirmed his belief that America stood on the brink of another national revival as the twentieth century dawned:

> Revival is in the air. Thoughtful ministers and Christians everywhere are talking about a revival, expecting a revival, and best of all, praying for a revival. There seems to be little doubt that a revival of some kind is coming, but the important question is, What kind of a revival will it be? Will it be a true revival, sent of God because His people have met the conditions that make it possible for God to work with power, or will it be a spurious revival gotten up by the arts and devices of man?[13]

Torrey sounded much like Finney when he stated that men could meet God's conditions and thereafter have revival. Indeed Torrey admired Finney's *Lectures on Revival* very much. On the other hand, he roundly condemned his contemporary revivalists who thought they could program revivals *per se:*

> In many a so-called revival men feel that they are themselves quite sufficient for the work at hand. They think that if they can only have the right plans, and the right machinery, and the right advertising, and the right sort of singing and preaching, the desired results will follow.
>
> For some years in our country, we have been trying these machine-made revivals, and the result is a sorry and sickening failure. We must feel our utter helplessness and dependence upon the Holy Ghost.[14]

Paradoxically enough, Torrey himself became the target of criticism for allegedly using "commercial tactics" in organizing his own campaigns in England.

As to the likelihood of another national awakening, the Democratic populist William Jennings Bryan (1860-1925) had his doubts. As he saw it, Americans at the beginning of the twentieth century were becoming so caught up in pursuing material gain and the good life that only with difficulty could they be persuaded to fix their minds on spiritual things. Nonetheless, Bryan, who had been converted at a revival service in a local Presbyterian church, hoped that a great revival would come so as to "prevent monopolies from robbing the people and bring an end to wars for the purchase of trade."

A national awakening did not come. Many smaller revivals did in 1905 and 1906. A reporter for the *Los Angeles Times* wrote the following account of a very significant one which began during the spring of 1906:

> Meetings are held in a tumble-down shack on Azusa Street, near San Pedro Street, and the devotees of the weird doctrine practice the most fanatical rites, preach the wildest theories and work themselves into a state of mad excitement in their peculiar zeal. Colored people and a sprinkling of whites compose the congregation, and night is made hideous in the neighborhood by the howling of the worshippers, who spend hours swaying forth and back in a nerve-racking attitude of prayer and supplication. They claim to have the "gift of tongues" and to be able to comprehend the babble.[15]

Modern American Pentecostalism was born during the Azusa Street Revival. W. J. Seymour, a godly black Holiness preacher, was the principal leader. Seymour followed the teachings of Rev. Charles

Parham, who had earlier (1901) discovered students speaking in tongues at his "Bethel Healing School" in Topeka, Kansas. The key tenet of the movement became the belief that an individual could be assured of the baptism of the Holy Spirit if he or she spoke in tongues (see chapter 2).

For some three years both the sincere and the merely inquisitive came to witness the revival in Los Angeles. A good number got caught up in phenomena that resembled the "exercises" so closely associated with camp meetings in the early 1800s. Many looked to a Pentecostal experience as proof that they were indeed authentic believers. Moreover, this experience frequently renewed their desire to serve the Lord with enthusiasm.

Despite criticism from dispensational and Reformed Christians, who believed that the more spectacular gifts had ceased in the post-apostolic age, Pentecostal "apostles" carried their "revivalistic" message deep into the South. In addition, the message was particularly well received by the disenherited classes of America's burgeoning cities. Storefront churches that black novelist James Baldwin recalls so well in *Go Tell It on the Mountain* became the centers for "hot" gospel preaching. Both black and whites often found in Pentecostal churches a human and divine acceptance, unusual in harsh urban settings. It made life on earth a little easier. Hopes for a better life in heaven were strengthened as well.

* * *

As our own century began, the term *revival* had come to mean different things to different people. For some, it referred to an occasion when God in His good pleasure chose to awaken in believers a desire to be better disciples of Jesus Christ. Others concentrated on meeting God's conditions for the revival of the saints and the conversion of sinners, certain that God would honor these efforts. For Pentecostals, the term was associated with an outpouring of the Holy Spirit. "Spiritual gifts"—particularly the gift of tongues—were evidence of this grace. But for a larger number of Americans, the term had become virtually synonymous with evangelistic meetings during which sinners were "saved." Many American cities and towns still welcomed itinerant evangelists who held "revivals."

BILLY SUNDAY

William "Billy" Sunday (1862-1935), a Chicago White Stocking baseball player, was converted in 1886 outside the Pacific Garden Mission in Chicago. A few years later he turned his hand full-time to holding revivalistic campaigns. As a result, mass evangelism received a major boost. Unfortunately, it also received some unsightly blemishes.

Building on Finney's concept of conversion and on Moody's procedures for organizing meetings, Sunday employed hard-hitting rhetoric and acrobatic antics to entrance his large audiences. The statistical results from his appeals were impressive. Sunday's associates estimated that by 1914, some three hundred thousand individuals had hit the famous "sawdust trail." That is, they had walked the sawdust pathway to the front of one of Sunday's wooden tabernacles and there committed themselves publicly to Christ as "Savior and Master." Sunday's career crested between 1914 and 1919 with campaigns in Pittsburgh, Philadelphia, Boston, Los Angeles, Washington, and New York (a claim of 98,000 converts in the latter city).

Sunday considered himself to be a revivalist (evangelist). As such, he felt constrained to defend revivals in a day when their value was increasingly questioned. He frequently demonstrated their importance by polling his audience and noting that the vast majority of Christians in attendance had been converted in revival meetings.

Sunday also reacted strongly against the Edwardian model of awakenings. He declared: "I believe there is no doctrine more dangerous to the Church today than to convey the impression that a revival is something peculiar in itself and cannot be judged by the same rules of causes and effect as other things." In the tradition of Finney, he continued: ". . . I believe that when divinely appointed means are used spiritual blessing will accrue to the individuals and the community in greater numbers than temporal blessings."[16]

The evangelist reasserted the dual function of revivals: "First, it returns the Church from her backsliding and second, it causes the conversion of men and women. . . ."[17] He included the stirring of saints to new spiritual vitality as a major thrust of his revivals. But his emphasis on the number of souls saved made possible the continued identification of revivalism with evangelism in the public mind.

After World War I, America entered into a "religious depression" (1925-1935), as some have called it, even before the economic one signaled by the Great Crash of 1929. Contemporary observers were surprised that the financial calamities which befell the nation in the 1930s did not provoke an awakening of national dimensions. Such an awakening had followed the Wall Street crash of 1857. Sunday was one who believed that the economic depression had been ordained by God to shake America out of its doldrums. In the *Boston Herald* of March 2, 1931, he noted: "Sometimes I'm glad God knocked over the heavens to put America on her knees before she became too chesty. . . . Our great depression is not economic, it is spiritual and there won't be a particle of change in the economic depression until there is a wholesale revival of the old-time religion." The revival did not come, however. Indeed, a good number of itinerant revivalists settled down to pastor local churches and tabernacles.

Sunday became so pessimistic about the deteriorating situation in America and the rise of Hitler in Germany that he predicted that the end of the world would come in 1935. It appeared that the day of large-scale revival meetings was over, despite the fact that blacks and whites in Pentecostal, Baptist, Independent, and other churches, continued to experience local revivals as common fare.

WHY REVIVALISM APPEARED TO LOSE ITS APPEAL

It is difficult to ferret out the reasons why many Protestants became disenchanted with revivalism. After all, revivalism had been a successful force in pushing Evangelicalism to the forefront of American religion in the 1800s.

Why, then, by the 1930s did so many look upon it with mounting suspicion? Here we enter into the world of images. There is evidence that Billy Sunday's emotional preaching and bombastic speech reinforced a negative image of the revivalist in action. Even to this day, when the word *revivalist* is mentioned, some Americans see in their mind's eye a sweat-soaked evangelist, wildly thrashing his arms as he berates an emotionally charged crowd about the torments of hell and damnation. Sinclair Lewis's novel *Elmer Gantry,* published in 1927, added a few finishing touches to the image. The evangelist Gantry was a hypocrite whose chief purpose was to shake down the gullible faithful for their money. The picture of the scoundrel-revivalist, no matter how it made its way into the collective consciousness of Americans, probably played a significant role in disabusing them of their commitment to revivalism.

It is also significant that Protestantism no longer dominated Americans' religious loyalties. As we noted, revivals had generally been promoted by Protestant evangelists.

Then again, Protestant Modernists had their own reason for finding revivalism distasteful. Revivalism, they believed, had survived in the 1930s chiefly as a tool of "benighted" Fundamentalists. How could an "educated" man or woman accept any practice of those "biblical literalists" who had battled Modernists, monkeys, and moviehouses in the 1920s and 1930s? Was not Christian education

(Sunday school, YMCA, YWCA groups, etc.) rather than dramatic spiritual conversion a better means of "Christianizing" the populace?

In brief, a good number of Americans did not bemoan the apparent passing of revivalism as an essential characteristic of Protestantism. In 1946 Reverend William Sperry, the dean of Harvard Divinity School wrote: "We are tired of religious revivals as we have known them in the last half century. . . . Among all but the most backward churches it is now agreed that education ought to be, and probably is, the best way of interesting our people in religion and of identifying them with one or another of our many denominations."[18]

Yet obituaries for revivalism or mass evangelism after World War II were premature. Conservative Bible believers, Jack Wyrtzen and John R. Rice for example, held large rallies and campaigns where scores came forward to accept Christ. In fact, John R. Rice, aware of what he called "Defeatist Voices" concerning mass evangelism, published a volume in 1950, *We Can Have Revival Now,* in which the possibility of a nationwide awakening was envisioned. Neither the practice of holding revival meetings nor the hope of national awakenings had completely died out. Down South among the Southern Baptists, revival meetings moved along at their normal clip.

A POST WORLD WAR II AWAKENING?

Surprising as it may first appear, some historians now speak of a religious awakening of gigantic proportions that lasted from the end of World War II until at least 1958. They point to the fact that Americans joined churches in record number (1940—64.5 million church members; 1950—86.8 million; 1958—109.6 million) contributed large sums of moneys to religious causes, bought scores of books by Fulton Sheen, Norman Vincent Peale, and Billy Graham, professed a belief in God (97% of the population), and declared that the Bible was the "revealed Word of God" (85% according to the Gallup poll of 1952).

Yet for all the talk about God, this "awakening" lacked the evangelical underpinnings of the First, Second, and Businessmen's awakenings. That is, it most often lacked the gospel message associated with "old fashioned" revivalism (to use a term of Charles Fuller). Allegiance to a vague "God" dominated this religious resurgence rather than a commitment to the God of the Bible and to Christ as Savior and Lord. President Eisenhower's remarks in the 1950s make this point in a dramatic fashion: "Our government makes no sense unless it is founded in a deeply felt religious faith and I don't care what it is."[19]

For many, this contentless religion concerning "God" was very palatable. It made few demands on an individual and it was socially respectable. It was sometimes dressed up in patriotic terms. To be an American was, in the minds of many, to be a Christian.

BILLY GRAHAM

The emergence of Billy Graham (b. 1918) to national prominence during the early 1950s, particularly after his remarkable Los Angeles meetings, did bring a Bible-based revivalism to the general public's attention once again. Amplifying the campaign methods of Dwight L. Moody, Graham held "Crusades" that were the sophisticated counterparts of earlier revival meetings. Where Moody had called people to seats of decision, Graham appealed to them to make "decisions for Christ."

Graham insisted that God alone gives an individual the "new birth." He and his staff were nonetheless fairly confident that if prayer and good planning preceded the "Crusades," Graham's messages would stimulate at least some individuals to come forward to accept Christ as Savior. The large numbers of decisions for Christ registered, for example, in the New York City Crusade of 1957 seemed to bolster this analysis. Television coverage of the Crusades brought the spectacle of huge audiences and large choirs as well as the invitations to "accept" Christ into the homes of millions. Once again, for the general public, revivalism and mass evangelism appeared to be one and the same.

Many Americans responded to this more "respectable" form of revivalism with enthusiasm. To avoid even a hint of scandal, Graham took meticulous pains to keep his financial records in order. He avoided heated discussions with his critics. His messages were direct but not frantic. His famous statement "The Bible says" became familiar to even hardened non-Christians. He was consistently placed high on lists of Americans' "most admired" people. The end result was that Graham helped weaken the image of the revivalist as an Elmer Gantry charlatan. Unfortunately, some of his fellow revivalists continued to make that image a plausible one.

"REVIVAL"—DEFINITIONS ABOUND

In the mid-twentieth century, the term *revival* still had multiple meanings. In certain local settings during the 1950s, some commentators still applied the term *revival* to those occasions when Christians were stirred to renew their commitment to Christ. President V. R. Edman of Wheaton College, Illinois, described the moving of the Holy

Spirit upon his student body in 1950 as a revival. He believed that it followed the model for revivals set down by Finney. In the early 1960s President Edman frequently called upon students to pray for another revival of this sort.

John R. Rice, the editor of *The Sword of the Lord,* which calls itself "America's Outstanding Revival Weekly," defined revivals to include both the winning of the lost and the refreshment of the saints. In his 1950 book on revival he spelled out that definition clearly.

> Some would make a distinction between revival of the saints and evangelism, winning the unsaved. But all the great soul winners have used the word revival to include not only the stirring of Christians and winning them to a new consecration, . . . but the winning of the unconverted to Christ.[20]

Other evangelists in the 1950s (influenced frequently by general concern for the "deeper life") used the words *dedication* and *consecration* (see Rom. 12:1-2) to refer to meetings where Christians renewed their commitment to their Lord, but they preserved the word *revival* for evangelistic meetings. Thus, the term *revival* in the 1950s and 1960s meant for some Christians specifically the conversion of the lost. But for others, it was a general term that could be applied to any spiritual upturn among saints and sinners alike.

Nor have the 1970s brought about a consensus concerning any one meaning of the term. Those who have read Brian Vachon's *Look* magazine article, "The Jesus Movement Is Upon Us," (Feb. 9, 1971) may think of "Jesus Freaks" witnessing on street corners, Christian communes, and Pacific Ocean baptisms, as defining characteristics of revival. After describing them, Vachon wrote, "An old-time foot-stomping, hand-clapping religous revival is happening, and it's got California stamped all over it. Look out, you other 49 states. Jesus is coming." Other individuals look at revivalism very differently. They conjure up a picture of a small Southern church holding its weekly revival meeting on a Sunday night, or a Billy Graham Crusade at McCormick Place in Chicago, or a charismatic meeting where the Spirit of God stirs up participants to speak in tongues and receive healing mercies, or any one of a dozen other pictures. That the word *revival,* as it is popularly used, defies a simple definition is perhaps upsetting for the linguistic purist; but for others, this circumstance is a happy confirmation of the richness of the revivalistic tradition in America. Even those who decline to use the term because of its Elmer Gantry connotations are frequently engaged in ministries that borrow extensively from revivalistic practices of longstanding.

REVIVALISM TOMORROW

What of tomorrow? Will revivalism in any of its various formats continue to play a major role in the life of evangelical churches? Probably so. As the bicentennial year, 1976, drew to a close, several news magazines indicated that America might be on the brink of another national revival. Just like Nicodemus of old (John 3), many Americans wanted to know what it meant to be "born again" *(Time,* Sept. 27, 1976). News magazines also noted, however, that a competing phenomenon of another sort was in process: the disciples of diverse Eastern religions were moving throughout the land (particularly in California) and making scores of converts. Evangelical leaders became quite concerned that Bible believers not overlook the fact that Transcendental Meditation, for example, possesses certain Hindu ingredients (despite the claims of its propagandists that it is religiously neutral). Ironically, the spiritual battle for men's minds took a new and dangerous turn at the same time that Evangelicals began to rejoice about their much publicized success.

Speculation about what will happen in the future is just that, speculation. Nonetheless, it appears that a few suggestions about the future of Christian revivalism might be helpful. Some Christians will continue to hold large scale evangelistic campaigns—they may or may not use the term *revival* to describe them. Some will hold traditional "revival" meetings in their local churches. A number of Christians will continue to declare that only a national awakening or revival will halt this country's slide toward judgment. Still others will use the expression *revival* in a very broad fashion for any increase of spiritual vitality among saints or sinners. Canopying such diverse meanings, the word *revival* appears to have a future in the speech of Americans.

The actual practice of "old-fashioned revivalism" appears to have a future as well, even though some of the old methods may fade or disappear entirely. The Sunday evening service, for example, at one time provided many churches with a regular evangelistic thrust. Before the era of the car and the television set, the unconverted often welcomed an invitation to attend such a gathering on a slow moving Sunday evening; or they sometimes wandered in uninvited. This type of meeting seems to be less popular today, although there are notable exceptions.

Indeed, some evangelical churches no longer have recourse to "revival meetings" or Sunday night evangelistic meetings, which have often been replaced by biblical exposition. Pastor George Baybrook of

Hawaii recently surveyed six "thriving" churches in an attempt to discover their common features. He found that they had "little in the way of special speakers, special music, revival meetings, and the like." Rather they stressed Bible study, the use of members' spiritual gifts, and "body life" meetings.

Probably television will fill in the gap left by the reduced numbers of "revival" meetings in reaching America's non-Christian populations. The broadcasting of large scale "Crusades" of Billy Graham and other evangelists will bring the message of salvation into the homes of millions. The same can be said of the new type of Christian "talk show" featuring music, testimonies, the gospel message and an invitation to "call in" to be counseled. (Charismatics have often been in the forefront in gospel proclamation through the mass media.) Many Americans who do not darken the doors of a church will accept Christ as their Lord and Savior in the privacy of their own homes. Determining how to "follow-up" these new converts will be an increasingly critical problem. They will need to be put in contact with local Bible-believing churches.

Others will be converted after watching quality Christian films in the local cinema. Through Campus Crusade, Inter-Varsity, Campus Life, Young Life, and Word of Life, young people in high schools and universities will discover a new life in Christ. The times are changing and Evangelicals are making adjustments. "Old-fashioned revivalism" may be wrapped in new packages and it may bear new names, but some of its contents and practices will certainly survive.

In their desire to reach America with the gospel, Evangelicals will need to be careful to fend off internal dissensions that could compromise their mission.

It is yet to be decided how charismatic Christians and non-charismatic Christians will work together in their use of the rich revivalistic tradition. In that many of the new Charismatics are hesitant to claim that "speaking in tongues" is *the* evidence of the reception of the baptism of the Holy Spirit, there is hope that some accommodation can be made between the two groups.

Black and white Christians will also need to learn to work together better in joint evangelistic and church renewal efforts.

REVIVALISM: AN EVALUATION

From the days of Jonathan Edwards to Billy Graham, revivalism has helped shape the way Americans think about Christianity. Hundreds of black, brown, and white revivalists, or evangelists, have trekked this land, warning Americans of their "lost" or "backslidden" condition while at the same time preaching the gospel message of Christ's love and forgiveness. Evangelicals owe much to these men and women, who, often unheralded and poorly paid, helped create the revivalistic tradition as they served their Lord by proclaiming the good news of the gospel.

Yet, revivalism has not been an unmixed blessing for Christian churches. The demagoguery and showmanship of some "revivalists" antagonized a portion of the American population. There are people today who believe that "gospel preaching" necessarily involves simplistic religion and the emotional hype. Godly evangelists and preachers have encountered suspicion and hostility due to the reputation of some of their greedy and egomaniacal "colaborers." The movie *Marjoe* with its picture of a cynical child revivalist has not helped efface the hypocritical image.

Problems have also been created by the understandable stress of evangelists upon conversion. This emphasis has led many Americans to feel that being "born again" was the end of the Christian life rather than its important beginning. Once converted, new Christians were frequently left on their own. They were not "followed-up." Many never realized that the gospel is not only simple, but also profound and demanding. Many never learned that the creeds, Christian education, Bible study, and discipleship instruction, could aid them in their spiritual life.

Sometimes such endeavors were even condemned by the revivalist as "from the devil," or as "capable of making new converts lose their enthusiasm for witnessing." In brief, American revivalism on occasions contributed to the trivialization of the full counsel of God, to the minimization of worship in evangelical church services, and to the denial of certain forms of Christian education.

On the other hand, despite these sad concomitants, millions of Americans over the years have found true peace with God as they responded to the gospel message proclaimed by "revival" preachers. Others have renewed their dedication to Christ. Schools and churches, numbed by spiritual lethargy, have become spiritually alive after being touched by a revival. Revivals have encouraged individuals to flesh out their Christian commitment by meeting the social and personal needs of their neighbors. And then, in at least a few instances, the nation as a whole has been pulled out of a state of spiritual indifference by a Christian revival.

In sum, revivalism has awakened large segments of the American people to follow Christ as Lord and Savior. Its legacy to the evangelical churches of America has been tremendous. And its future does not appear to be dim either. In the last quarter of the twentieth century, Americans still pray and sing, "Lord, revive us again."

6

"I Love Thy Kingdom, Lord"

The Americanization of the Church

There is something distinctly American about the rawboned preacher Barton W. Stone (1772-1844). He was born in Maryland, and was raised in Virginia and became part of that first great surge across the Appalachians after the War for Independence. Not one to be tied down, Stone was converted in North Carolina, served a brief stint as a barnstorming evangelist in the new state of Tennessee, and finally moved on to Kentucky, where in August 1801 he was at the center of the famous Cane Ridge Revival.

Barton Stone was a restless spirit, not unlike the Andrew Jacksons, Davey Crocketts, and Sam Houstons that set out, each in his own way, to make a mark on the frontier. Moving out of settled communities to match their own wits and will against the rugged conditions of the West, each left his own characteristic imprint upon American history of what it meant to be a rugged individualist.

Barton Stone left his mark by bringing the church to the frontier, or more accurately, by carving out of the frontier a new concept of the church. Ordained to the Presbyterian ministry, Stone discovered, soon after arriving in Kentucky, that he could no longer live with Presbyterian doctrine or church organization. A year later he pushed this idea to a logical extreme and proclaimed that it was not just the Presbyterians that were wrong. All church structures were suspect. Signing the "last will and testament" of the group of churches to which he belonged, Stone vowed to acknowledge no name but Christian and no creed but the Bible.

What was striking about Stone's new religious movement, the Christians or Disciples, was not merely that a strong religious leader set out to organize a new church under his direction. That kind of separatist impulse was widespread in the nineteenth century, as chapter 7 will show. What was really striking about Stone's contribution was that he rejected lock, stock, and barrel traditional ideas about the function and significance of the institutional church. In particular, Stone emphasized two themes that would increasingly come to characterize the way many American Evangelicals thought about and participated in the church.

In the first place, Barton Stone exalted the role of the individual believer and resisted the authority of clergy over laity. "Everyman for himself, and God for us all!"—these were sentiments that the Christian movement wholeheartedly endorsed. Any Christian alone with his Bible had the privilege—indeed, was under the obligation—of dealing with God face to face. Americans for the last century and a half have liked this idea. Is this not what life is all about, one man facing up to his responsibility on his own two feet and not trying to hide in the crowd or permit another man to mediate between himself and God? Just as the ideal American of an earlier day stood alone in taming the frontier and in modern times achieves dignity and worth through individual endeavor in, say, industry or sports, so the American Christian must face God alone and come to terms with him on his own.

By encouraging Christians to be rugged individualists in their faith, Barton Stone also advised them to shake off the crusty traditions of the institutional church and return to the simplicity of the New Testament. In a conscious attempt to wipe clean the slate of church history, Stone declared that the creeds, confessions, ceremonies, and theologies hammered out by the church over its eighteen hundred year history should be "consigned to the rubbish heap of human invention on which Christ was crucified." In their place Christians should restore the life and faith of the primitive church. The quest for "New Testament Christianity" likewise has been a hallmark of Evangelicals in America from that day until this. Just as American culture in general has taken pride in shedding what many believed to be the corrupt sophistication of Europe, so American Christians have not worried about slighting the history of the church in order to concentrate on the supernatural activity of the God of the Bible in contemporary affairs. As one evangelical church proclaimed on its cornerstone: "The Church of Christ. Founded in Jerusalem in A.D. 33. Established in Sweetwater, Texas, A.D. 1928."

The recasting of traditional ideas about church authority and church history points up the pervasive influence of American culture upon the kind of ecclesiastical arrangements that have flourished in this country. In a nation that is one of the most "churched" in history, most Americans think they know very well what the church is—do they not, in fact, see one on every other street corner? But the question arises whether this familiarity has wrongly molded how we think about the church. American Christians, for instance, have had a difficult time understanding that God's primary goal in history involves more than the individual Christian and that God has chosen to work in history primarily through a corporate agent, the church. Given our heritage, we do not readily admit that the local church is a whole greater than the sum of its parts. In order to get a handle on some of the cultural assumptions that have shaped the way American Evangelicals view the church, it will be instructive first of all to examine the meaning of the church for some of America's earliest settlers, the Puritans, men and women who had little use for the kind of individualism that Barton W. Stone found so enchanting.

CHURCH AND SOCIETY IN EARLY AMERICA

It is very difficult for us in the twentieth century to understand the values and priorities of our forefathers three or four centuries removed. The seventeenth-century man would surely have answered the question "What is the ideal society?" by stressing unity, order, authority, hierarchy, and stability. From our way of thinking, which puts priority on diversity, mobility, independence, and progress, the mind-set of early modern Europe seems dull and stifling. But if we would know what the Reformers or the Puritans meant when they spoke of the church, it would be helpful to study how their society functioned. One of the hidden rewards in studying different cultures is to put our own in better perspective.

"Corporate" Society

Men in the time of John Winthrop and William Bradford, founding governors of Massachusetts and the Plymouth Colony, had a view of society that can best be called "corporate." Far more medieval than modern in scope, it stressed the welfare of the whole society before that of any individual. *Salus populi suprema lex* was the motto that was the foundation of this social attitude—"The welfare of the people is the supreme law." Accordingly, the Puritans did not come to the New World as a recent presidential Thanksgiving proclamation put it "to allow the individual to develop to his full potential." They would have denounced such an attitude in no uncertain terms. The vision that they had for establishing a society in the New World is expressed in the name they gave to Massachusetts, a "Commonwealth." The obvious meaning of the term is the welfare of the whole, the well-being of all of society together.

The Puritans claimed that Scripture taught that society should function as a living body. It was not a group of independently moving atoms that happened to be thrown together; instead it was a body politic. Because society was designed to be a unit, the welfare of the whole took precedence over individual considerations. To the settlers aboard the *Arbella,* John Winthrop in his famous speech, "A Modell of Christian Charity" (1630), outlined this view of commonwealth. He emphasized that each individual must take responsibility for the needs of his neighbor. "We must abridge ourselves of superfluities" in order to maintain the less fortunate, he said. "Particular estates cannot subsist in the ruin of the public"—that is, private wealth will do no one any good if the society as a whole fails.[1]

Other Puritans stated the same social philosophy. The Englishman William Perkins put it like this: "A man called to be a Christian should live a certain kind of life, ordained and imposed on man by God for the common good."[2] Thomas Hooker, the founder of Connecticut, expressed the same conviction in these terms: "For if each man does what is good in his own eyes, proceeds according to his own pleasure, so that none may cross him or control him by any power; there must of necessity follow the distraction and desolation of the whole."[3] The Puritan view of the calling is a good example of this attitude. In answer to the question of how a man should choose his profession, John Cotton said that a calling is not valid unless it is socially beneficial: "If thou hast no calling tending to public good," he said, "thou art an unclean beast."[4]

The organic structure of society in early Massachusetts reflected this social philosophy. The land system of the early villages was primarily the open field pattern, where each man held plots in various places around the town and everyone lived in the center. Decisions concerning what to grow and when to plant and harvest were made by the town rather than the individual. In early New England the government put a limit on prices according to the theory of just price—that a merchant should not be able to grow rich at the expense of the public. Several noted merchants of early Boston were censured for covetousness in this regard. Another example of commonwealth spirit was the support each village gave to its "worthy poor"—those who for some reason could not fend for themselves. The Puritans believed in a corporate society; the will of the individual was subordinate in many ways to the well-being of the whole.

The Benefits of Inequality

A second characteristic of society in the 1600s that will help us understand Puritan views about the church is the refusal to admit that all men are created equal. Stated positively, the Puritans believed that God has endowed men and women with different gifts and callings. Some have the ability to assume authority, for instance, others the grace to submit and pursue a more humble calling. In his speech, "A Modell of Christian Charity," which so greatly emphasized social community, Governor Winthrop also asserted: "God Almighty in his most holy and wide providence hath so disposed of the condition of mankind, as in all times some must be rich some poor, some high and eminent in power and dignity, others mean and in subjection."[5] The same analogy of the body was used to explain how some men were gifted with prominent positions in society, while others had to learn their place as "less comely parts."

The implications of this emphasis choked off ideas of social mobility. At every turn society informed the individual that he must determine the place God had given him in society and remain there. The foot could not complain because it was not an eye. Puritan culture implemented this social philosophy in a variety of ways. When land divisions were made for new towns, equality did not serve as the primary standard; the leaders of the society were given considerably more than the commoners. Similarly, leaders in a church enjoyed seats of prominence, and Harvard College ranked each entering class in order of social standing. This was a static view of society, one that stressed obedience to God-given authority.

It is true that early New England elected their leaders, but their society was not a democracy in the modern sense. The Puritans never admitted the equality of all men. Although they could have elected anyone governor of the colony, in fact they always chose a man who had obvious ability and social standing. And when elected, the governor did not bend his policies to reflect every whim of the public. The emphasis was on the fact that God had made him a ruler and he was first responsible to the Creator and not to the people. As the Puritans described it, this was a "speaking aristocracy in the face of a silent democracy."[6] Thus we see that the Puritans had a corporate and hierarchic view of the nature of society, assumptions that they shared with most Europeans in the early modern period.

The Puritan View of the Church

But what about the more basic question of the nature of the church in a corporate society? Protestants such as Luther, Calvin, and the Puritans held an extremely high view of the visible church. It was nothing less than the primary agent of God's meaningful activity in history. The same Luther who argued for the priesthood of all believers also said, "Whoever seeks Christ must find the church," and again, "I believe no one can be saved who is not part of this community and does not live in harmony with it in one faith, word, sacrament, hope, and love."[7] According to Calvin, God had deposited the treasure of the gospel in the church, which He ordained because of man's weakness. "Enclosed as we are," said Calvin, "in the prison house of flesh, having not attained to the rank of the angels, God accommodated himself to our weakness by establishing a means of our drawing near to him." Because of our ignorance, sloth, and fickle disposition, God ordained the church to be to us a "Mother." "For there is no other way to enter life," he continued, "unless this Mother conceive us in her womb, give us birth, nourish us at her breast, and lastly, keep us under her care and guidance until, putting off mortal flesh, we become like the angels. Our weakness does not allow us to be dismissed from her school until we have been pupils all our lives. Furthermore, away from her bosom one cannot hope for any forgiveness of sins or any salvation . . . . It is always disastrous to leave the church."[8]

The Puritans likewise had no place in their thinking for a solitary Christian. The church was the instrument that God had established to do his work in the world. From what we have said about their view of a corporate society, it is easy to see how they naturally would think in terms of the church—a group of people—as being of utmost importance. This is not to deny their considerable emphasis on the importance of individual salvation and commitment, but along with their stress on personal regeneration they would naturally understand the necessity of the individual functioning as a member of Christ's body. The Puritan's social experience confirmed his theological belief that man must not seek his own end, but must commit himself to the church to be nourished and brought to maturity in a social context. He would naturally grasp the idea of commitment and loyalty to something outside himself. The children who read in John Cotton's 1646 catechism about the church being a congregation of saints joined together to worship the Lord and to edify one another, knew from their day to day experience the reality of mutual commitment. Their whole culture impressed it upon them in a hundred different ways.

Similarly when the Puritans put great stress on the authority of those whom God had given the gifts of preaching and teaching, their audience would have no trouble realizing exactly what they meant. They deferred to others' authority in daily human relationships because they knew God had given some the abilities to rule. Likewise in the church, they would naturally respect those appointed as leaders over them.

A further aspect of this view of the church was its historic unity. Calvin calls detestable the attitude of some "who have a passion for splitting churches, in effect driving the sheep from their fold and casting them into the jaws of wolves."[9] Elsewhere, he says that we must not thoughtlessly forsake the church because of petty dissensions. The church was not something pragmatic to be used by the Christian when he needed spiritual aid, but it was primary. The Christian's commitment to it was demanded and assumed. The credal and confessional basis of Reformed churches in early modern society is the best example of their commitment to the historic unity of the church. The church was not something that men in the present formed for certain spiritual ends; instead, it was an objective institution based on creeds dating back to the early church. The basis of the church was a received system of teaching that it should pass on to its children.

The Reformers' view of the sacraments is another indication of their lofty view of the church. The emphasis of their teaching in this regard was that Christ actually does something objective in the sacrament. In communion the true Christian is actually given spiritual nourishment at the time when he physically eats the bread and drinks the wine. And in baptism God actually confers his blessing upon the recipient. In this way it is demonstrated again that God is present in the church and actively at work. The church was anything but a means to some individualistic end. Instead, God resided there, conferred his grace there, and from there initiated his meaningful activity in history. In claiming to be a Christian, a man or woman identified with this divine institution without question.

If we glance again at society in the sixteenth and seventeenth centuries, it is easy to see how such an exalted view of the church could prevail. Protestants, like their Catholic counterparts, believed in religious uniformity, that only one church could exist in any particular geographical area. Thus, the individual had little choice of which church he would join. Furthermore, the church was structured on a parish basis so that where a man lived determined the exact congregation to which he would belong. The individual's decisions were at a minimum; that which was stressed to him was the objective character of God's church, the necessity of involvement in it, and the authority with which it spoke to the individual.

In summary, then, we see that the Puritans saw the church as the primary agent of God's activity in history; and their social experience confirmed this teaching. No competing churches or other religious organizations cluttered the decision-making process. They knew that God acted only through one institution, the church. Secondly, we see that with their corporate view of society, the idea of the church as Christ's Body, the real communion of the saints had practical, down-to-earth meaning. It would be somewhat easier to relate effectively to a Christian brother with whom one worked together every day in the fields. Thirdly, the minister of the church was recognized as teaching with real authority. The Puritans stressed that in all of society God bestowed gifts of leadership, and the church was certainly no exception. Men easily accepted the concept that all did not have equal abilities. Finally, the church was not seen primarily as a voluntary association of the like-minded, but as an institution that had existed objectively throughout history. At any point in time, people belonged to the same church that the apostles had formed. The church was unified throughout history and this gave it a lofty, exalted place in their minds. The emphasis was not on their decision to join the church, but on their privilege of participating in a continuing temple where God dwells uniquely with his people.

"EVERYMAN FOR HIMSELF AND GOD FOR US ALL"

In 1840, the Frenchman Alexis de Tocqueville toured the United States and wrote his reflections on American culture. In trying to come to terms with how Americans differed from Europeans, he coined the word "individualism." "The Americans," he said, "demanded that they were free, masterless individuals; they sought absolute independence and equality of status. They imagine that their whole destiny is in their own hands." According to Tocqueville, Americans had reversed the corporate view of society that had reigned for a millennium and in its place adopted the social philosophy that all values, rights, and duties originate in the individual. He argued that in the past there had not been an individual who, in effect, "did not belong to a group and who could be considered absolutely alone." But nineteenth century

Americans were keenly aware that they lived in a new age; they prided themselves on that fact. It was an age of freedom, and men jubilantly praised their equality of status, their absolute independence, the realization that their destiny was in their own hands. The self-reliant individual objected to all kinds of restraints and accepted authorities.

What was taking place in politics is probably the best indication of this broader cultural pattern. This was the age when democracy first became the supreme political virtue. Any man's vote was as good as his neighbor's. In the sixteen years after 1824, the percentage of eligible voters who turned out for presidential elections jumped from less than 30 to over 80 percent. With this change went an alteration in the nature of political leadership. Andrew Jackson, a frontier Indian fighter and self-made man, stood in marked contrast to the sophisticated and genteel leaders of the early Republic: Washington, Jefferson, and Adams. Jackson openly embraced the spoils system under the philosophy that any citizen of the republic should be able to perform the work of government. This period also witnessed a major shift in campaign techniques. No longer did men aspiring for office debate issues in the context of political philosophy, as had been done throughout the period of the Revolution and Constitution. Now the emphasis shifted to the sensibilities of the common man. Jackson ran as the self-made man from the West. His coarse friends around him were a political asset rather than a liability. He spoke the language of the people. In this same vein, William Henry Harrison used the symbol of the log cabin and a jug of cider in the campaign of 1840, even though Harrison himself lived in a mansion. Politicians lowered their appeal to the common denominator of their culture. Indicative of this shift was the rise of the mass political meeting. Speeches at these affairs were based on images rather than issues. The common man was the standard to which politicians appealed. Democracy, the rule of the people, had come of age.

Economic attitudes were also a good picture in miniature of the broader cultural patterns. Before this time, the government had always assumed that it should control the economy for the best interest of the whole. Mercantilism, an economic philosophy devoted to the best interests of the nation, reflected this attitude clearly. But in the nineteenth century Adam Smith's new ideas of *laissez faire* were becoming economic law. They said essentially that government must withdraw from the economy and allow the individual to pursue his own interests. The assumption that followed was that as each atom in society went its own way, somehow the good of the whole would be met.

Both in theory and practice this philosophy bore fruit in the new American republic. In that age the myth of the self-made man became ingrained in the American consciousness—any man could make a fortune if he only had the drive and determination. The rags to riches story became the standard hope of parents for their children and for aspiring entrepreneurs. In practice, Americans at unprecedented rates organized their own enterprises and struggled to move up the social ladder.

Legal history is interesting during this period in its emphasis on contracts, business agreements between individuals that are binding by law. Whereas the leading English legal scholar of the seventeenth century devoted only forty pages to contracts, the foremost American legal authority in the early nineteenth century took two-thirds of his volume to explain the subject. Men wanted contracts simple and available to all. Americans thrust aside all barriers that blocked their goal of becoming self-reliant entrepreneurs. In this regard Tocqueville summed up his attitudes about the Americans and their economy: "I know of no country, indeed, where the love of money has taken a stronghold on the affections of men and where a profounder contempt is expressed for the theory of the permanent equality of property."[10] It is somewhat difficult to analyze exactly what happened to the church in this new atomistic society where self-reliance and self-improvement were the most cherished social values. But in attempting to do so, let us examine the effects upon the church of three dominant forces: revivalism, individualism, and denominationalism. These developments are woven intricately together and none can be considered independently of the entire fabric. But let us follow first the strand of revivalism.

Revivalism

The revivalism that blossomed in early nineteenth-century America raised acute problems for traditional conceptions of the church. Where people previously were taught that the church was the primary agent of God's activity in the world, they now were faced with the novel situation in which local congregations were no longer the center of action. Itinerant evangelists such as Charles Finney came into an area and demonstrated such spiritual power and effectiveness that the local church by contrast looked like the dead among the living. How could the nominal church member, who was brought to life at a revival camp meeting, return home and be excited by what was happening in the local church? Why should he be excited about something that had not previously awakened his own spiritual sensibilities?

In addition, the revivalistic spirit also coincided with a theological view of the church that also played down the importance of local assemblies. Cooperating as they did in revivals and reform movements, nineteenth-century Evangelicals naturally were aided by the concept of the invisible church, regarded as all people everywhere who truly loved the Lord. Although the idea of the visible church remained strong (particularly in some Baptist circles), attention paid to the idea of the invisible church was a way for Evangelicals from any denomination to rejoice over the progress of the Lord's work in all the others. Focus on this concept, however, may also have had the effect of loosening ties with local bodies of believers.

Individualism

If revivalism and the idea of the invisible church raised these kinds of questions about the church, the second area of consideration, individualism, gave answers that substantially altered how Christians thought about the church. In at least three important ways traditional conceptions of the church were changed by the new philosophy of individualism. First, many American Protestants began to consider the entire history of the church as one long tale of corruption. True enough, Luther and Calvin, Edwards and Wesley had all dismissed what they considered unbiblical about creeds and confessions, but they had also endorsed those parts that clarified the gospel. American Christians, by contrast, preferred to strive for primitive Christianity unsullied by the ceremonies and theological subtleties built up over the years. Barton W. Stone wanted to dump the entire history of the church upon "the rubbish heap of human invention." Charles G. Finney, the most powerful revivalist of his day and second president of Oberlin College, came to similar conclusions. In rejecting the creeds of the Presbyterian Church, Finney announced:

> I found myself utterly unable to accept doctrine on the ground of authority. . . . I had nowhere to go but directly to the Bible, and to the philosophy or workings of my own mind. I gradually formed a view of my own . . . which appeared to me to be unequivocally taught in the Bible.[11]

Another Presbyterian Albert Barnes found this kind of revolt against inherited authority sweeping America in the 1840s: "This is an age of freedom," he said, "and men *will* be free. The religion of forms is the stereotyped wisdom or folly of the past, and does not adapt itself to the free movements, the enlarged views, the varying plans of this age."[12] Along with other Americans intent on shaking off the sophistication of

Europe, American Evangelicals sought to ignore the confusing subtlety of abstract theology and return to the simplicity of the Bible.

One stout critic of this self-avowed primitivism was John W. Nevin, a graduate of Princeton Seminary and professor at the German Reformed seminary at Mercersburg. Nevin called the ahistorical attitude prevalent among American Christians a sect mentality. He said that its emphasis solely on private judgment and the Bible "involves of necessity, a protest against the authority of all previous history, except so far as it may seem to agree with what is thus found to be true; in which case, of course, the only real measure of truth is taken to be, not this authority of history at all, but the mind, simply, of the particular sect itself."[13] Without the backdrop of Christian history, a sect mentality could parade its own idiosyncracies as "self-sprung from the Bible, or through the Bible from the skies." What Nevin found so galling about this purported return to the simplicity of the New Testament was that American Protestants now considered it a virtue to reject the past without even bothering to see if they could learn anything from it.

A second way that individualism weakened the church as an objective institution was that it threatened to rob the officers in the local church of any authority. Barton Stone argued that the converted man guided by the Holy Spirit needed no guidance from theologically trained clergymen, no supervision by ecclesiastical authorities. "To deny this," wrote Stone, "is to degrade God. . . . By conversion man is restored to the image of God and made capable of hearing, understanding, and obeying his commands."[14] This kind of privatism and hostility to authority is an extreme example, but it certainly points in the direction where much of Evangelicalism was headed. If we would examine the Baptists and Methodists, we could note the same stress on spontaneous experience rather than institutional authority and the same focus on the assurance of private belief rather than on any authority in the church.

The obvious result of this stress on the assurance of private belief was a fundamental revision in the way church members conceived of the roles of their ministers—and in turn a real change in the minister's role. The Congregationalist leader Lyman Beecher noted this danger: "No minister can be forced upon his people without their suffrage and voluntary support. Each pastor stands upon his own character and deeds, without anything to break the force of his responsibility to his people."[15] The danger was that a minister was forced to cater to every whim of his church—that the laity would go far beyond just influencing their pastor and force him into a mold of their liking. A minister might no longer function as an authority in any real sense but merely a politician, a persuader, a charismatic figure, who attempted to convince his congregation of individualists to go along with his program. Tocqueville stated the point clearly when commenting on the nature of the evangelical clergy: "You meet a politician when you expect to find a priest."[16]

The third way that individualism changed the function of the church was in the relationship of saints one to the other within a local church body. In the early nineteenth century this change did not become apparent, because to a large degree evangelical churches continued to function as closely knit groups ministering to each other's needs. We find this particularly true on the frontier, where churches of the Methodists, Baptists, and Disciples often served as the only real centers of social cohesion. But what does take place at this time is an intellectual shift that did erode in great measure the interdependency that previous generations had found so natural. Starting with the priority of the individual, the church became a functional instrument to meet his needs and gain new converts. Although a community of Christians might find it helpful to continue their fellowship together, what happened when serious problems arose or some did not think their own needs were fulfilled? The answer was obvious: as the church became a means to one's private spiritual ends, it could not endure any real crisis. Furthermore, when Christians did not feel any great spiritual need, they were able to think of the church as relatively unimportant without violating their conscience. A subtle distinction now was made between saying the church is Christ's body apart from which a Christian cannot live and saying a Christian would find a church spiritually helpful.

In the nineteenth century, then, people adopted a new working definition of the church. Whereas Christians previously had seen the church as God's primary agent of activity in human history, the new view saw it as a voluntary association functioning to aid the individual Christian in practical goals such as spiritual growth and the gaining of converts. In the new perspective no institution had an inherited or traditional authority; instead, all human organizations found their basis in the uncoerced consent of the individual. In this context one can easily see how traditional views of the sacrament became meaningless. The will of the individual was the primary foundation for human organization, and the church was no exception. Because there was no authority inherent in the church, the idea that God could work objectively in the sacraments simply did not follow. When one defined the church as a product of human volition, he precluded it from possessing objective authority. Under this new way of thinking, God's presence in the church could be no more than the sum of his presence within each individual Christian. Similarly, as the church came into being only when Christians joined together, so the sacrament was only constituted when they remembered Christ's death, or when they pledged to fulfill their baptismal vows.

Denominationalism

We have looked at how revivalism and individualism have affected the American church. The final influence was denominationalism. If what we have already said made the church seem intellectually irrelevant to nineteenth-century Christians, what they saw all around them made the idea of the church much less important in a practical way. The establishment of religious freedom in the United States in the late eighteenth century created a unique historical situation. For the first time a predominantly Christian nation loosed the church from state control and allowed different and competing manifestations of the church to operate freely. The result was that Americans did not look to one church as God's agent in history, but to a vast array of different denominations competing with each other for converts and influence.

In a context of denominationalism, American Evangelicals confronted three trends that made the local church seem even more irrelevant. The first was the fact that no particular denomination had exclusive claim to the truth of the gospel. Denominations tended to look on each other as possessing the same truth but with each having a peculiar mission or a distinctive focus. "Each denomination," said a leading Evangelical, "is working out some problem in the Christian life, developing some portion of truth. Each has its part to perform, its particular work to do for the kingdom of Christ, which it, in the present condition of things, is better equipped to do than any other."[17] Despite the positive contributions of this cooperative mentality, it did raise an obvious psychological problem for the individual church member. Why was his or her local congregation significant at all? If the real core of the gospel was something that fifteen other churches in town possessed, why was one particular expression of the church of great importance?

Dietrich Bonhoeffer once stated that "it has been granted to the American less than any other nation on earth to realize the visible unity of the church of God." During the nineteenth century the splitting of old denominations and the forming of new ones accelerated to such an extent that the historian can hardly list the hundreds of groups claiming to be authentic churches. Charles Hodge said that the "unblessed ambition of restless individuals" had made schism a major problem in his day. And it is easy to see why such a proliferation would tend to breed a certain cynicism about the ultimate value of any particular congregation. This is the second problem of denominationalism: that in America the number of new groups continued to mushroom. This kind of separatism, which the next chapter will explore in detail, did present another real problem. How can one view the local church as of great importance, when anyone can put out a shingle and have their own new church? The lofty views of the church held by the Reformers and the Puritans arose in a period of uniformity when great stress continued to be placed on the historic continuity of the church despite the break with Rome. In contrast, Americans in the nineteenth century divided the body of Christ into so many pieces that it was no wonder that many became sceptical about the value of the church as an institution. Evangelical actions in taking the church lightly spoke much louder than evangelical arguments about the importance of the church.

A third facet of denominationalism that eroded a high view of the church was the growth of extrachurch agencies fully capable of performing the work of the church. No evidence is more telling of the shift in evangelical concepts of the church than the phenomenal growth of nondenominational organizations. If the church was simply one of the functional agencies to do God's work, then why not turn to a more effective tool if the church failed to fulfill her mission? In the first half of the century, Evangelicals created over 150 voluntary societies with concern for foreign and home missions, Bible and tract distribution, temperance, the welfare of the insane, prison reform, and scores of other worthy functions formerly assigned to the church. The striking thing about this situation was that the leaders of the church did not view the agencies as competitors; in fact, they sponsored many of them and looked to their activities to play a role as important as the work of any local parish ministry. The work of professional evangelists, missionaries, and social reformers, men and women without primary allegiance to any local church, far overshadowed that of the pastor.

The undeniable strength and vitality that this voluntarism brought to American Christianity did leave at least one bitter residue: the local church inheriting the task of caring for spiritual needs of the same people day in and day out lost much of its appeal. How could the church down the block compete with the dynamism of a Finney or Moody revival, of a campaign to change the course of history by saturating the West with Sunday schools, or of a call to leave all and take the gospel to Africa or India? The Christian in nineteenth-century America who was intent on serving God and leaving the world a different place after his sojourn found exciting opportunities everywhere, except perhaps within the four walls of the church he attended week by week.

We have seen that revivalism, individualism, and denominationalism have seriously hindered attempts in American Protestantism to understand the church as a significant institution. How could the church speak with a compelling voice, when the institution had been robbed of its authority, splintered into a thousand pieces, and replaced to a large extent by more functional agencies? The answer is that most Evangelicals of the last century could not think of the church as the unified, catholic, body of Christ that moved triumphantly through history and against which the gates of hell could not prevail. But they did continue to think in ultimate categories. What was the primary agent of God's meaningful purpose in history?

One possibility is that at the very time individual denominations failed to function as the church, Americans increasingly turned to the nation as the primary agent by which God works in history. Having the church lose its purposive functions, universal and catholic in scope, many Americans apparently transferred such loyalties to the nation. As G. K. Chesterton once wrote: "America is a nation with the soul of a church."[18] This theme will be developed fully in chapter 8, but it is important also in this context. To read very far in the writings of nineteenth-century Protestants is to be struck with the way they identified America with the growing kingdom of God. Lyman Beecher's attitude was typical: "Only America can provide the physical effort and moral power to evangelize the world."[19] From America the renovating power would go forth which would bring on the millennium. In Beecher as well as in a host of other ministers, one notes the union of American democracy and Christianity into a force that would not only renovate this land but also then spread to all mankind. That the nation became endowed with such lofty religious purpose follows in part from the fact that no competing denomination could any longer make that claim.

THE PROBLEM OF SUCCESS AND THE COMING OF "BODY LIFE"

The heritage of nineteenth-century attitudes about the church forms a backdrop for evangelical thinking even into our own day. Time has failed to kill off attitudes that place the individual at the center and the church on the periphery. The evangelical community has continued to define the church from an individualistic perspective, has continued to slight the deep interdependency that the communion of the saints implies, and has continued to be satisfied that God's work in the world is done by agencies other than the church. Yet in our own day a deeper crisis confronts the evangelical church, one which even more profoundly threatens the scriptural ideal of the church.

This new problem is so dangerous precisely because it is so subtle. It comes not in the form of a barrage from Madeline Murray O'Hare against the foundations of religion nor in the open attack of secularists proclaiming that the church should close its doors. No, this new problem comes as an angel of light and in fact is welcomed by most Evangelicals. The problem of which we are speaking is that of success. The biggest problem that Evangelicals face in America today is that the church has been an unexpected success in twentieth-century society. We can talk all we want about the secularization of society, but the fact remains that by 1960 two-thirds of the population of this country were church members of some sort. This is an astounding figure when one realizes that in 1900 only about one-third of Americans belonged to churches, and that in 1850 at the height of Protestant influence in this country only 15 percent of the population were church members.

In the 1970s, moreover, there has been something of an evangelical renaissance with seminaries bursting at the seams, publishing houses becoming truly big businesses, missions continuing to expand, and churches far outstripping the growth of mainline denominations. The campaign of Jimmy Carter in 1976 and his election as president riveted the attention of the news media upon these trends and led the pollster George Gallup to call 1976 "the year of the Evangelical."

Perils of Prosperity

Why might this success story be so detrimental to the true ideas of the church? The late sociologist Will Herberg was convinced that the paradox of contemporary America is that although we are growing secular at an unprecedented rate, at the same time we have become much more religious. According to Herberg, "the secularism that pervades the American consciousness is essentially of this kind: it is thinking and living in terms of a framework of reality remote from the religious beliefs simultaneously professed."[20] Put in other terms, we could say that religion is so popular today because it makes so few demands.

Other sociologists of religion have likewise concluded that the primary function of the church in American society is to confirm and sanctify the values of the individual, his community, and even of the way he views his whole society. For the individual the church can easily become an emotional service station to relieve worry. In the church God pats the individual on the back, assures him that he is important, and sends him back to the world the same as when he entered. The religion of the American church is often a "faith in faith," a "religion in general." It does not generate its own values but instead sanctifies the values present in the general community.

In light of this prevailing religiosity, the evangelical church must face the reality that almost everyone in American culture has grown up in some way related to a church and thus already may have compartmentalized his idea of what the church should be. The even more urgent danger is that Christians themselves relegate the role of the church to that given it by our society. The millions of Americans who belong to evangelical churches all too easily judge the depth of their own church commitment by the norms of society rather than those of God's Word.

Evangelicals could heave a great sigh of relief if the "Christianity" defined as peace of mind, emotional security, and a power to live by was associated only with churches that had clearly departed from the gospel. But the problem is closer to home. We live in a culture dominated by the quest for immediate self-fulfillment, the pursuit of the "good life," and the avoidance of pain at all costs. In the midst of this culture and lacking a deep sense of Christian history, Evangelicals have too often structured their churches to stroke rather than to ruffle these cherished assumptions. We have too easily tried to woo men to Christ by promising them a counselor to sooth all anxiety, a friend to give status and standing, and a guide to smooth any rough spots in the path ahead. Instead of calling men and women to reorient their lives to God, contemporary Evangelicals have too easily made the gospel the answer to a set of questions that are faulty in the extreme, as if Christ were nothing more than the key to personal self-fulfillment. There is enough truth in what *Newsweek* had to say about the evangelical message in its cover article of October 25, 1976, to cause us grave concern. There the evangelical message was labeled "not a call to Christian servanthood, but an upbeat stress on what God's power can do for you . . . a salvation-brings-success ethos."

This nurturing of what J. I. Packer has called a "self-absorbed breed of evangelical adults" has accelerated rather than impeded an unbiblical view of the church. Rather than challenging the individualism of American culture, many congregations, taken by an exclusive emphasis on evangelism and church growth, have actually encouraged their members to evaluate the church on the basis of what it can offer by way of inspiration, warm feelings, or entertainment. Members grow accustomed to looking at the church not as a center of interpersonal relationships under the Word of God but as sanctified emporiums competing with weekend camping trips, Little League baseball, and television for their free time. They are places of cooperation where people must be quite careful not to step on anyone's toes lest that person flee to the church down the block.

As a consequence, we usually do not get very involved with one another as church members, choosing rather to focus our church friendships on noncontroversial topics. The project-centered activities of "successful" churches, such as Vacation Bible School, missionary crusades, day camps, and fund drives, can usually be accomplished with a minimum of personal commitment to others. Indeed they sometimes even act as buffers to keep people from spending time and energy with one another. It is a constant wonder how little church members know of their fellow members even after years of attendance and participation. We will let the minister take care of the odd person or two who feels in need of a boost from spiritual counseling. Church has its place and so do our fellow believers, but these are not of utmost importance to us and must take a back seat to our individual dealing with God. The result of these attitudes is that evangelical churches have tended to be weak while extraecclesiastical efforts such as evangelistic crusades, which draw us into nonreflective action instead of personal interaction, have been prominent.

New Winds

Fortunately, our discussion of the church does not end here. In recent years there has been a small but growing movement among Evangelicals to take a new look at the church in light of America's individualistic culture. The result had been a new concern about the importance of the local church as a community of mutual sharing and concern. With a fresh exuberance and a whole new vocabulary, Christians throughout America had suddenly become "evangelical" about what was once called the fellowship of believers but is now called "body life," "koinonia," supportive fellowships, or Christian community. This rediscovery of the importance of the church is evident in a flurry of books—*Body Life*, *The Problem of Wineskins*, *The Church Is People*, *Building*

Up One Another, and *Community and Commitment*, in a growing movement to establish small support groups as a key element in the life of the local church, and in a variety of new or reorganized churches (often called fellowships) that have recast the function of the church with a heavy emphasis on mutual commitment, discipline, and the importance of spiritual gifts.

It is refreshing indeed to witness this emphasis on the church as a people who share a commitment to each other for better or worse. But this new concern does have an interesting twist. The wave of interest in community within the church followed a renewed concern for community that sprang up throughout America in the 1960s. Not only did Evangelicals not recognize this issue until awakened by the shouts of the broader culture (where was koinonia or body life in the 1950s?), but seemingly we still have not come to terms with those cultural forces that prompt us to rethink the church when we read passages such as Ephesians 4:1-16 and Romans 12:3-8. Conditioned to respond positively to openness and close interpersonal relationships by broad cultural forces, many Evangelicals, particularly those under forty, have become convinced that the institutional church needs a more human face.

The point to be made is not that these lessons are any less valuable or that these developments are any less a movement of the Holy Spirit. But what should also strike us is how difficult it is to think in patterns other than those given by the social experience that surrounds us. To a degree that few of us realize, we are all children of our times. A study of the church in America reveals the remarkable correlation between the social assumptions of a given culture and the way that Christians in that culture decide to structure the church. While we certainly cannot remove ourselves from our environment any more than could the Puritans or Barton W. Stone, we must at least struggle to understand that culture and its underlying assumptions. If Evangelicals, looking to the future, would not relegate the mission of the church to the whims of an evil world, we must strive to become culturally self-conscious. Then and only then can we begin to build a different model of human relationships that will reveal to a watching world what it means for disciples to love one another.

7

"Sound the Battle Cry"

The Division of the Church

As different as they are in other respects, the makers of alphabet soup and the leaders of American churches do have one thing in common: the ability to bring random letters of the alphabet into interesting combinations. Soup makers could perhaps learn a trick or two from the abbreviations of American church history—SBC, ABC, NBC, GARB, CBA, BBF, or BBU from the Baptists; UPUSA, PCUS, PCA, OPC, and RPCES from the Presbyterians; LCA, LCMS, ALC, and ELIM from the Lutherans; NCC, COCU, NAE, and ACCC from ecumenicists of every stripe. It is not the purpose of this chapter to discuss whether the alphabetizing of American Protestantism has left it "in the soup." What we want to do is look at one of the primary causes behind the multiplication of Protestant churches in America. This is the force of separatism. Although other reasons also help account for the number of church groups in America, few have been more important than the separatist's desire to break away from error in order to establish a purer church. The problem of separation is by no means an exlusively American one, but America has been the scene of more ecclesiastical separations for more different reasons than any other area in the world.

The principle of separation itself is as old as belief in the God of creation. God separated the offering of Abel from that of Cain. When God entered into covenant with Abraham, he set apart one man and his descendants as the means by which all mankind would be blessed. In Christ's teaching there was no mistaking virgins with lamps ready and those unprepared, the house built on rock from the one built on sand. The Lord himself likened the members of his kingdom to wheat and fruitful vines, those standing outside to weeds and barren branches. Later in the New Testament Paul urged Christians not to be "conformed to this world, but to be transformed by the renewal of your mind" (Rom. 12:2 RSV). And James contended that one of the marks of true religion was remaining "unspotted from the world" (James 1:27 RSV).

In light of this biblical evidence, Christians have always seen a clear difference between the children of God and the children of the world. But while Christians have agreed that believers are to be God's separate people, they have differed widely among themselves as to how proper biblical separation is to be put into practice. As a result, separation either from the sinful "world" or from erring fellow believers has taken many different shapes through the centuries.

From the time that the Roman empire accepted Christianity in the fourth century until the Reformation of the sixteenth century, only one major separation occurred, the division of Eastern and Western Christianity completed by the Great Schism of 1054. Early in the fifth century the great Augustine had taught that the visible church on earth was "a mixed body" in which both believers (the wheat) and unbelievers (the tares) existed. The ideal of purity was important to Augustine and the Christians of the Middle Ages, but it was an ideal that God himself would carry through at the last day. Until then it was necessary to tolerate a certain degree of impurity within the church.

THE REFORMATION AND SEPARATISM

One of the accomplishments of the sixteenth-century Reformation was to bring the theoretical ideal of separation more actively into practice. Martin Luther did not question Augustine's conviction that the visible church inevitably contained true and false believers. What he did question was that the visible church of his day was truly Christian. Luther broke with Rome because he felt the papal system of Christianity, in particular its doctrine of salvation by faith *and* works, gave true Christianity a mortal wound. With Luther we see a fundamental motive for separation that would often appear in American church history as well: the conviction that one's present church is destroying the essence of the Christian faith.

Luther was not the only Reformer who thought Roman Catholicism destroyed real Christianity. John Calvin, Menno Simons, and many other "protesting" Christians expanded his critique of the Catholic church. Yet, while agreeing with Luther that separation from Roman Catholicism was neccessary, these reformers were unable to establish a new "catholic" (i.e., united) church. Agreeing in principle that Roman Christianity needed drastic reforming, the reformers divided among themselves over the shape that Protestantism was to take. These separations *among* sixteenth-century Protestants arose from disagreements over both doctrine and practice. Such differences would appear also in America as two additional causes of separation in the church.

Separation over doctrine was illustrated best in the face-to-face confrontation between Luther and Zwingli in 1529. This meeting had been called in order to form a common Protestant doctrinal front against the Roman Catholics. The Protestants of Germany (Luther) and the Protestants of Switzerland (Zwingli) were able to agree on many important issues, but they came to a parting of ways over the question of the Lord's Supper. Luther held that the words, "this is my body," of Matthew 26:26 were to be understood literally; Zwingli stuck to a more figurative interpretation. The German and the Swiss, who both had separated from Rome in order to defend the heart of the gospel, now went their separate ways.

The Reformation in England provides an example of a separation over practice. The formal separation from Rome in the reign of Henry VIII (1509-1547) became, during the brief reign of his son, Edward VI (1547-1553), a genuinely spiritual one as well. Very soon in this reforming process, however, strains began to appear. One group of English reformers wanted practices in the church limited to what the Bible specifically demanded. The other party wanted to preserve traditional practices so long as the Bible did not specifically forbid them. The issue came to a head over the wearing of ceremonial robes—the first group called this practice sinful since it was not demanded by Scripture; the second approved since it was not expressly forbidden. Members of both groups became martyrs when the Catholic Queen Mary succeeded Edward VI in 1553. Yet their differences over practice came to the surface again during the Protestant reign of Elizabeth I (1558-1603). The stricter group came to be known as Puritans because of its desire to *purify* the church. Eventually, disagreements over the practices of the church led to separations. The Puritans and Pilgrims who came to America were representatives of the separating bodies. So from the earliest planting of Protestantism in America, separation had been a part of the church's life.

ROGER WILLIAMS, SEPARATING OVER SEPARATISM, THE ROLE OF PERSONALITIES

The career of Roger Williams in early New England shows us someone who separated for yet other reasons. Williams believed that Christians should be completely separate from impure Christianity. Williams's story also gives us a foretaste of another factor decisive for separations in America—the dynamic individual. He was only the first of many vigorous leaders who would form new denominations, groups, or associations when they found themselves unable to live with the older bodies.

The churches of early New England had tried very hard to establish a truly Christian system in the New World. To give just one example, the Church of England allowed people who could not profess to be regenerate Christians to join the church and participate in the Lord's Supper. In New England, however, the churches restricted membership to those who could give a credible profession of conversion. The Puritans of New England had not cut every tie with the official church in the old country, but they had made it clear that they desired a purified church and a purified Christian practice in the New World.

When Roger Williams arrived in New England in 1631, he rejoiced at finding such a pure expression of Christian faith and practice. He was troubled, however, at the reluctance of New Englanders to renounce the evil church in England. Williams was concerned lest the remaining ties between the purified churches of New England and the corrupt churches of England transmit religious corruption to the New World. In the words of historian Edmund S. Morgan, Williams "could not bring himself to soil his new purity by joining in worship with people who, though pure themselves, failed to renounce the impurities of England."[1] Or as Williams himself put it when refusing a ministerial call from the Boston church: "I durst not officiate to an unseparated people, as upon examination and conference, I found them to be."[2]

The governor of Massachusetts Bay, John Winthrop, replied to Williams that it was not necessary to be absolutely separate from corrupting influences in order to have a genuine church. When Williams disagreed, he left Massachusetts Bay for the stricter separatism of the Pilgrims at Plymouth Colony. Yet even here Williams was disappointed. He thought that the members of Plymouth churches who returned to England for visits should not worship in Anglican churches there. When the leaders of the Plymouth Colony failed to accept Williams's opinion, he left Plymouth and returned to Massachusetts.

Williams's ideas rapidly brought him into further difficulties, and in 1636 he left for good and established a new colony, Rhode Island. Williams's separatistic views later led him to argue that one should not pray in the company of nonbelievers. For a brief period he even restricted Christian fellowship to just his wife. Although Williams later relaxed his position on separatism, his career provides an early example of a fourth reason for separating. In his eyes, the failure of other believers to make a clean break with unbelief was a good reason for *him* to separate from them. Williams also showed the kind of power that a single, strong-minded individual could have. Later American separatists would be even more bold in setting up new organizations to compete with the ones left behind.

THE GREAT AWAKENING AND SEPARATION

Separatism was not a live issue in the colonies for nearly a century after Williams's departure from Massachusetts. With the great series of revivals beginning in the late 1720s and known to later students as the Great Awakening (see chapter 4), separatism again became a very important matter in American religious life. Some separations during the Great Awakening were quickly healed over. Others continue to this day.

Two influential books which appeared in 1743 signaled a coming separation over the essence of the faith. The first of these was by Jonathan Edwards, *Some Thoughts Concerning the Present Revival of Religion in New-England.* In it Edwards affirmed forthrightly "that the extraordinary work that had of late been going on in this land, is a glorious work of God."[3] Edwards pointed to the lives that had been changed by the revival's preaching. He did not deny that the revival led to spiritual pride in some of its supporters. He admitted that some had erroneously claimed special revelations from God while in the heat of the revival. But he also contended that the positive results of the revival far outweighed the negative. In short, Edwards was speaking up for the New Light point of view.

The second important book, containing the opposite or Old Light perspective, was written by the prominent Boston minister Charles Chauncy (1705-1787). His *Seasonable Thoughts on the State of Religion in New England* offered a point-by-point rebuttal to Edwards's approval of the revival. It was fanaticism that was sweeping the land, thought Chauncy. The revival was little more than an occasion for New Englanders to toss over the benefits of stable traditions for the untested fantasies ("freaks" he called them) of their own brains.

The battle lines drawn by Edwards and Chauncy hardened over the next decades until a very clear break appeared in American ecclesiastical history. From the tradition of Chauncy arose Unitarian and Universalist churches stressing the primacy of human reason, denying the supernatural work of Christ, and viewing the church as a creature of society. From Edwards flowed the evangelical revivalism of the nineteenth century, from which modern Evangelicalism in turn is derived. This strain defended the Bible as divine revelation, argued for a supernatural conversion by the Holy Spirit, and saw the church as a creature of the Word. This separation, spotlighted so clearly by the books of Edwards and Chauncy, took place over a fundamental disagreement in what it meant to be a Christian.

Charles Chauncy rejected the theology of the Great Awakening, and his rejection laid the groundwork for Unitarianism and Universalism. Unlike Chauncy, leaders of other separations arising from the Great Awakening accepted the basic theology of the major revivalists. Their separations arose over doctrinal and practical matters *within* awakened Protestantism. Where modern Evangelicals usually give Edwards a white hat and Chauncy a black one in their dispute, it is much harder to sort out the good guys from the bad guys in the other separations of this period.

Four basically evangelical groups emerged from the revival. The most "conservative" group, Old Calvinist Congregationalists in New England and Old Side Presbyterians in the middle colonies, affirmed traditional Reformed theology. But, placing great stock in the stability of traditional churches, it did not like revivalistic practices—itinerant preaching without the permission of regular ministers, encouragement of uneducated lay preachers, unseemly emotions. The second group, New Light Congregationalists and New Side Presbyterians, who shared Jonathan Edwards's general perspective, was the mainstay of the revival in its early years. Unlike the even more "Radical" groups, however, it had no serious objections to the way in which colonial churches were set up. The Separate or Strict Congregationalists, on the other hand, felt that the established church order was too corrupt to be salvaged. Although this third group was content with the Congregational polity and the Calvinistic theology of New England, it was definitely not content with the spiritual state of these churches. In order to see biblical teachings applied strictly, this group separated from the established churches to begin congregations of their own. Yet a fourth group, the Baptists, agreed with the revivalistic theology of the New Lights. Like the Separate Congregationalists, they thought that the traditional churches were not truly biblical. The Baptists and the Separates were not able to unite, however, because of a doctrinal difference. The Baptists, with a heightened commitment to personal conversion, could not understand how Separate Congregationalists could continue to baptize infants, even the infants of believers.

The presence of these four groups led to a great number of separations, some over matters of great moment and others over relatively petty concerns, some resulting in permanent schisms and others in merely temporary splits. Temporary separation usually involved differences in ecclesiastical practice and theological emphasis rather than overt disagreements over doctrine. In the middle colonies, for example, Presbyterians divided into separate New Side and Old Side denominations for a seventeen-year period from 1741 to 1758. New Side Presbyterians participated actively in itinerant preaching and did all that was possible to encourage godly living. The New Side men still thought Presbyterian structures were imporant but not nearly so important as the need to spread the gospel as widely and rapidly as possible. Their Old Side opponents, many of whom had recently arrived from Scotland, where doctrinal formalism was much more the order of the day, saw things differently. They cast a suspicious eye on itinerant evangelism, feared that emotionalism was overwhelming Christian stability, and thought that the structures of Presbyterianism should not be set aside in the revivalistic passion of the era. Because the conflicting points of view remained differences in emphasis rather than becoming a clean break over disputed doctrine, communications remained open between the two bodies. After the revival fires had cooled somewhat, reunion was achieved in 1758. A common fidelity to Scripture and to the principles of Presbyterianism, as well as a tolerance of minor differences in doctrine and practice, brought the two "sides" back together.

The career of Isaac Backus (1724-1806), an influential Baptist leader, shows how separations brought about by the revival could result in permanent divisions. Backus was converted in 1741 as revival swept through his hometown of Norwich, Connecticut. Backus joined the established Congregational church of Norwich in 1742, but then in 1747 he left his home church to help form a Separate body. He took this step because he believed that truly Christian churches must take greater care in admitting only converted people than did the Norwich church. When in 1748 Backus accepted the call to serve as pastor of a Separate Congregational church in North Middleborough, Massachusetts, he still had not advanced beyond the position of other

Separates who would one day return to New Light Congregationalism. In North Middleborough, however, Backus began to be increasingly troubled about the question of baptism. In 1751, after much soul-searching, he and his wife were rebaptized by immersion. For five years Backus tried to mediate between the Baptist and infant baptism viewpoints within his Strict Congregational church, but this proved to be an impossible task. In 1756 Backus became the founding pastor of a Baptist church that he would serve for the next half century. His theology retained its affinities with that of Jonathan Edwards, and his views on ecclesiastical fellowship continued to be distinctly New Light; but his attitude toward baptism separated him from the New Light Congregationalists with whom he otherwise shared so much in common. His last separation became a permanent one which neither time nor theological good will was ever able to close.

So long as differences arising from the Great Awakening remained disagreements of practical emphasis, the differences could be mediated. But when differences extended into doctrine, chances for reunion decreased. Although Christians still professed a desire to see a catholic (i.e., harmonious and unified) Christian witness in the colonies, by 1750 many colonial Protestants put more stock in differences separating themselves than in the ideal of unity.

The Awakening was also important in that it brought up many of the issues that would divide Evangelicals throughout American history. Differences over baptism continue to be a sore point. For instance, it has only been with great reluctance that the Disciples of Christ have recently accommodated their baptismal views to the standards of the Consultation on Church Union, COCU. And COCU is an organization that is suspect to many Evangelicals who would have even greater reluctance to "compromise" their views on baptism than do the Disciples of Christ in joining COCU. Other issues raised by the Awakening have been, perhaps, even more troubling: What is the proper style of Christian spirituality? Is it fervent, emotional, enthusiastic, and affective; or is it calm, rational, deliberative, and cognitive? And what about the revival's theology? Jonathan Edwards, Isaac Backus, and most of the other Awakeners preached a restored Calvinism that gave very little scope to the sinner's capacities. God, the revivalists thought, had not only provided salvation in Christ but had selected by the council of his own will those whom the Spirit would move to accept that salvation. In stating these ideas so crisply, the revivalists invited dissent not only from the Old Lights, who were moving away from traditional evangelical theology, but also from some supporters of awakened Christianity who questioned parts of Calvinistic theology. About the only prominent feature of later separation not present in the Great Awakening is the overarching role of dynamic leaders. Individuals like Edwards, Chauncy, and Backus were important as spokesmen for their groups' viewpoint. None of these, however, displayed the eagerness to form new church bodies that later leaders possessed.

SEPARATION IN THE DAWN OF THE NATION

The period from the Great Awakening to 1800, a period preoccupied with nation forming, set the stage for future church divisions in America. Ideological currents popular in that day gave a systematic and widely accepted rationale for separation. The ideals that had been fought for in the Revolution, or which lay embedded in the arguments for independence, very naturally came to be important for Christians as well.

From the Revolution, Americans took strong ideas about the sanctity of natural rights and the dangers of governmental interference in personal affairs. What could be a more natural right than the privilege of constructing a relationship with God on terms determined by oneself? In keeping with the implications of this concept of freedom, American Christians came gradually to assume that no denomination could be favored by law and that no law could interfere in the peaceable internal functions of the churches. This type of thinking strikes the twentieth-century American as commonplace, but in the eighteenth century where a unified, legally established church was still the norm throughout the Western world, the American argument was a novelty.

This new way of looking at religious freedom provided a sturdy theoretical basis for later ecclesiastical separations. Revolutionary thought took it for granted that the people were capable of constructing their own political and social institutions. Although it was actually a radical departure from earlier ecclesiastical patterns, American Christians under the influence of Revolutionary thought also acted as if the creation, organization, and maintenance of churches were as much human rights as the formation and direction of political institutions. In the Old World the church had been considered something given by God and regulated by his properly consecrated ministers. Except for a small dissenting fringe, European Christians into the nineteenth century did not entertain the idea that they were capable of creating churches and charting their courses. In America a different cast of mind prevailed. It was assumed that Christians had not only the right but the duty to create ecclesiastical institutions as their own consciences demanded. The hardy individualism of Revolutionary thought encouraged the bent toward ecclesiastical separatism. Modern historians have called the idea of the church developing in this time "voluntarism." By this is meant the belief that churches originate or are supported by the voluntary acts of their members.

SEPARATION IN THE NINETEENTH CENTURY

As the nineteenth century dawned, Christians in America possessed a history in which ecclesiastical separations had become commonplace. In the idea of voluntarism they had a ready-made warrant for further separations. The Great Awakening and the American Revolution, the two most important eighteenth-century events for the churches, had provided causes and a rationale for many of the separations of later years.

The nineteenth century marked a distinct era in American church history. From the Second Great Awakening at the start of that century to the controversy between "Modernists" and "Fundamentalists" at the end, American Protestantism experienced an age of spectacular successes and failures. Yet when Protestants in the nineteenth century divided, they did so for reasons that had already been established in American church history—conflicts over the essence of the faith, specific doctrines, particular practices, and due to the influence of powerful leaders.

Disciples and "Christians"

One of the most important separations of the nineteenth century began as a difference of opinion over specific doctrines and practices and ended with a new form of Protestant Christianity. Barton W. Stone (1772-1844) and Alexander Campbell (1788-1866) were two of the powerful leaders who tried to win the frontier for Christ. Although these men began their ministries as Presbyterians, they soon came to feel that Presbyterianism was not adequate for their revivalistic experience or for their theological views. Barton W. Stone took umbrage at the strict Calvinism of Presbyterianism's Westminster Confession. He looked askance at the hierarchical structure of the Presbyterian church. And he had grave questions about the nature of Presbyterian ordination. As a result of these differences, and in keeping with his passionate desire to recover a New Testament form of Christianity, he separated from the Presbyterian Synod of Kentucky in 1804 to organize groups that would answer to no name but "Christians."

Alexander Campbell believed that a strict distinction needed to be made between the Old and New Testaments and that Christian worship should include only those practices commanded by the New Testament. He too found American Presbyterianism uncongenial. In 1811 Campbell separated from Presbyterianism and struck up an uneasy alliance with a group of Baptists in the Ohio valley. When one of Campbell's followers, Walter Scott, began to proclaim Campbell's ideas evangelistically in the late 1820s, it became obvious that the Baptist fellowship could not contain the Campbellites. What had for a time appeared as a variation on Baptist and Presbyterian themes now emerged as a distinct perception of the gospel: faith was intellectual assent to the truth claims of Christianity, baptism obtained the removal of sin, local congregations were absolutely independent, and no important distinction separated "ministers" from the laity. In 1832 the followers of Stone and Alexander Campbell came into a loose alliance known as the "Christian" or "Disciples" movement. This new grouping—it was too intensely congregational to be a denomination in the traditional sense—had developed over significant differences in doctrine and practice. Stone and Campbell, vigorous leaders with a great ability to move people to action, had formed a new body into the shape they thought a church should have.

Other Separations Over Doctrine and Practice

The nineteenth century saw many other separations for doctrinal reasons. At least four of these led to the formation of groups which are still in existence. The Cumberland Presbyterian Synod of Kentucky separated from its parent body in 1813. These separating Presbyterians desired more active participation in the frontier revivals, looser educational standards for ordination, and a revision of the strictly Calvinistic Westminster Confession. The Free Methodists separated from the Methodist church in 1860 when they concluded that the Wesleyan doctrine of perfection was not receiving its proper attention. A small group of Episcopalians, calling themselves The Reformed Episcopal Church, divided from the Protestant Episcopal Church in the United States in 1873 in order to proclaim a more strictly Reformed theology. We have already noted in chapter 2 that other Methodists late in the century grew dissatisfied with the church's stand on Christian perfection and formed Holiness (e.g., The Church of the Nazarene) and Pentecostal churches (e.g., the Assemblies of God).

Other separations came about more directly over differences in practice. The practice of slavery divided churches before it divided the nation. In 1845, after the Baptist Board of Foreign Missions rejected the application of Georgian James E. Reeves because he was a slaveholder, Southern Baptists organized their own convention. In that same year the Methodist church also agreed to divide north and south because of differences over slavery. Northerners in the two denominations gave active or passive support to abolition. Southern believers defended slavery as a positive practice or argued that it was at least compatible with Christian teaching. The breach of fellowship in the "Christian" groups at the end of the century is only one of the other separations over practice during this period. The source of this disagreement was a difference of opinion concerning strict observance of original Stonite-Campbellite distinctives. Could there be musical instruments in the church when the New Testament did not command their presence? Could there be missionary or other similar organizations uniting the resources of several churches when the New Testament nowhere demanded the formation of such agencies? Members of the Churches of Christ answered these question in the negative, members of the Disciples of Christ in the affirmative. A separation in the first decade of the twentieth century was the result.

More complicated separations involving both doctrine and practice also dotted the nineteenth-century landscape. In 1843 a group of Methodists, harking back to original Methodist standards and calling themselves Wesleyan Methodists, divided from the main Methodist body. They did not feel that Methodists were preserving Wesley's teaching on total sanctification, nor did they think that Methodists should waver on the issue of slavery. The combination of doctrinal and practical concerns led directly to separation from the parent denomination.

The Lutheran Church experienced a more comprehensive division in 1864 but again one in which doctrinal and practical elements were thoroughly mixed. The split came in the General Synod of Lutherans in America between those who desired to accommodate European Lutheranism to American religious life and those who wished to retain the distinctive character of the European heritage. "Americans" like Samuel Schmucker (1799-1873) wondered if the Augsburg Confession should be modified, particularly in its statements on the sacraments. "Confessionalists" like C. P. Krauth (1823-1883) countered sharply with a vigorous defense of the traditional Lutheran views. "Americans" were quite satisfied with the increasing use of the English language in Lutheran churches and with the nature of American revivalism. "Confessionalists" saw no need to rush away from German and the Scandinavian languages and shied away from revivalistic practices. An ecclesiastical division resulted when these differences became too intense to be ignored any longer. The General Synod continued to represent mostly American views; a new General Council was formed for those who maintained the opposing viewpoint.

The Presbyterians

The most complex series of ecclesiastical separations in the nineteenth century involved the Presbyterians. By the mid-1830s, two distinct tendencies had developed within this body. The more traditional Presbyterian group was called the Old School; the group more willing to accommodate itself to the American climate was known as the New School. (No hard and fast connections existed between the Old Side of the eighteenth century and the nineteenth-century Old School or the New Side and the New School.) The Old School forces felt that Presbyterian church order was a part of the gospel that should not be disturbed. They felt that nineteenth-century revivalism and some contemporary theology were nearly heretical by the standards of the Westminster Confession. And they were concerned lest the church dissipate its force through excessive involvement in Christian social action. The New Schoolers were more flexible with regard to Presbyterian practices. They were not as strict doctrinally as the Old Schoolers, and they were more amenable to the less Calvinistic strains of nineteenth-century revivalism. The New Schoolers also felt very strongly that Christians should speak out on social issues, particularly slavery.

The 1836 General Assembly of the Presbyterian Church was controlled by the New Schoolers. It refused to consider doctrinal questions raised by the Old School concerning the revivalistic practices of the day. This Assembly endorsed the missionary activity of the broadly evangelical American Board of Foreign Missions rather than sticking strictly with its own denominational boards. It reaffirmed its working agreement with the Congregationalists on the frontier. To add insult to Old School injury, several New Schoolers joined that same year with Congregationalists to establish an independent theological seminary in New York as indirect competition to the denominational seminary at Princeton.

By the time of the 1837 General Assembly, however, the Old School had marshalled its forces. In firm control of the proceedings, the Old School returned the Presbyterian church to what it considered its proper course. It abruptly ended cooperation with Congregationalists on the frontier. It expelled four Western presbyteries in which the New

School was especially strong. And it ordered that Presbyterian missionary activity be carried out only through Presbyterian boards. An underlying source of controversy between the two Presbyterian groups was the contrasting attitude toward slavery. Although not all of the New Schoolers were ardent abolitionists, most of them thought that abolition was compatible with the Christian's social mandate. The Old Schoolers, on the other hand, were often uneasy about slavery, but they did not feel that distinctly Christian assaults on the institution were proper. As a result of the Assembly actions in 1837 and due to fundamental differences in attitude, American Presbyterians divided once again into two distinct bodies.

The separation of 1837 was further complicated by the coming of the Civil War since both New and Old Schools had members north and south. Over the distinctly practical issue of slavery, the New School divided north and south in 1858, the Old School in 1861. Old School and New School quickly resolved their differences in the South, where a Southern Presbyterian church uniting both parties was formed in 1864. A similar process occurred in the North after the war when New and Old School merged in 1869. The southern and northern arms of mainstream Presbyterianism have remained distinct until this day, although discussions between the two groups aimed at merger are presently being held. Since 1869, however, other separations from the two dominant Presbyterian bodies have been as interesting to Evangelicals as the efforts to reunite the two major bodies.

The nineteenth-century religious climate partook generously of the national mood. This was an energetic, dynamic, and vigorous era in American history that saw much fervor in the churches also. Given the many substantial issues in both doctrine and practice, and given the general willingness to "reform" Christian thought and behavior through separation, it is little wonder that so many separations divided the churches in the nineteenth century. Whether all of them were wise or necessary is debatable. Some certainly arose from the questionable willfulness of influential leaders. Others probably occurred over differences that could have been settled without division.

AMERICA'S GREAT DIVIDE AND SEPARATISM

Earlier chapters have described the momentous shifts taking place in American Christianity between the Civil War and World War I: urbanization, industrialization, Darwinism, higher criticism. The modernization of American society and of the American mind that was taking place between 1865 and 1914 posed serious questions to the churches. What place, if any, did modern scholarship have in the church? How reliable was the Bible and its description of God's plan for human salvation? What really was the truth about man's origins? Had the startling advances of the modern world enabled modern man to outgrow the religious "myths" of his adolescence?

Separation was put on a new footing through the varied responses to these questions that appeared in the churches. Christianity was also in a new relationship with American culture. Where the first half of the nineteenth century has justly been called "the golden day of democratic evangelism," the early years of the twentieth had lost the distinctly Christian cast. The values of American society were increasingly secular, decreasingly Christian. With this changed cultural backdrop, the place of Protestantism was radically altered. Where once it had held a place of prominence as the arbiter of cultural values, it now had become suspicious of American culture and hostile to much of it. This radical change, perhaps the most significant in American religious history, had much to say about the shape of separatism in twentieth-century America. The question of "worldliness" took on a new importance. No longer would separations develop out of strictly religious controversies. Now they would also arise as the specter of secular worldliness appeared in the traditional denominations.

Twentieth-century separatism has several distinct features. It has seen a proliferation of "independent" churches, schools, and mission agencies which, after separating from parent bodies, have not formed distinct new denominations. It has seen many powerful individuals stand up for what they think is right and lead "a faithful remnant" out of larger bodies. Roger Williams's seventeenth-century argument has also been revived with some believers parting ways over the issue of separatism itself.

Before looking at twentieth-century separatism, however, we should note that the modern period has also seen more reunifications than earlier centuries of American history. Some of these mergers, as that of the Northern and Southern Methodist churches in 1939, of the northern Presbyterian church and the United Presbyterian Church of North America in 1958, or of the Evangelical and Reformed Church and the Congregational Christian Church in 1959, have been among denominations that are not consistently or comprehensively evangelical. Others, such as the various Lutheran mergers since 1910, have involved many confessionally orthodox bodies. And some have taken place among groups of strictly evangelical character such as the merger of the Swedish Evangelical Free Church and the Norwegian-Danish

Evangelical Free Church Association in 1950 or that of the General Synod Reformed and the Evangelical Presbyterians in 1965. Although reunifications and mergers are no new thing in American religious history, ecumenical forces in the twentieth century, both within and outside Evangelicalism, have encouraged a greater number of unions and also more comprehensive ecclesiastical unions than had been the case earlier in American history.

SEPARATIONS IN RECENT YEARS

Presbyterians (1930s)

The separatist beat, nevertheless, goes on. In 1936 a group of Presbyterians under the leadership of J. Gresham Machen (1881-1937) separated from the northern Presbyterian church. The major issues in the minds of these separates were the increasingly imprecise convictions of the parent denomination and its willingness to send out missionaries who did not hold traditional doctrine. In Machen's view, separation was the only way to save the essence of the gospel, since the northern Presbyterian church was "very largely *dominated* by unbelief . . . it has made unbelief, in the form of a deadly Modernist vagueness, the determinative force in its central official life."[4]

No sooner had this separation taken place, however, than the separates themselves were rent by division in 1938. Several influential leaders of the separated Presbyterian body, among whom Carl McIntire (b. 1906) would become most well known, discovered that they leaned in a different direction than Machen. Most of the major sources for separation in American church history can be seen in these separations from the northern Presbyterian church and then among the separates themselves. Machen and McIntire felt that the gospel itself was in jeopardy within the northern Presbyterian church. However much these leaders agreed in their criticisms of the mother church, they disagreed considerably between themselves over doctrine, church government, and personal practice. Where Machen rejected the dispensationalism that had become popular in America since the 1870s, McIntire was willing to allow it a place in Reformed theology. Where Machen wanted strict denominational control of mission work, McIntire was willing to employ nondenominational agencies. And where Machen felt the Bible allowed moderate use of alcohol, McIntire argued that total abstinence should be a standard of the church. Machen, the doctrinal precisionist, was willing to allow some latitude in Christian practice. McIntire, the practical precisionist, was willing to allow latitude on Christian doctrine. Both were forceful individuals whose personal leadership played large parts in the separations. In 1938 the conflicts resulted in division. (As a footnote to this separation, the Bible Presbyterian Church, which separated from Machen's organization, itself divided in 1958 between Bible and Evangelical Presbyterians when the latter group rejected the policies of Carl McIntire, who had become the dominant figure in the denomination.)

Baptists

Baptists have also witnessed several divisions in the twentieth century, some of which have occurred over separatism itself. The same reaction to Modernism present in Presbyterian circles emerged in the Northern Baptist Convention. The Fundamentalist Fellowship and the Baptist Bible Union arose in the early 1920s to challenge liberal tendencies in that denomination. The Baptist Bible Union, formed in 1923, stated in its founding documents the desire "to purge our beloved denominations from such heresies [Modernism]. . . . [We] refuse henceforth to contribute funds administered by rationalistic modernist officials."[5] When the protests of these groups did not achieve the results that were desired, a new denomination came into existence in 1933. The new General Association of Regular Baptists (an offshoot of the BBU) protested the doctrinal liberalism of the Northern Baptist Convention. It also attacked the Convention for refusing to separate itself from modernistic positions.

Two decades later the Fundamentalist Fellowship also spawned a separatist group, the Conservative Baptists. Again the issue was the failure of the denomination to guarantee the theological orthodoxy of its mission agencies. In September 1943 a "Directive" to the American Baptist Foreign Mission Society pledged that no further support would be given to any missionaries

> who do not affirm faith in the Bible as the inspired Word of God; the deity of our Lord Jesus Christ, which includes his pre-existence, virgin birth, miracles, and His bodily resurrection from the dead; the substitutionary death of our Lord for sinners in atonement for their sins; His high priestly intercession at the right hand of God and His eternal sovereignty.[6]

The Conservative Baptist Foreign Mission Fellowship that emerged in 1946 was thus a result of doctrinal differences as well as disagreement over the kind of purity required in the church on earth.

Presbyterians and Lutherans (1960s and 1970s)

Differences over doctrine, practice, and personality continue to be sources of division to the present. Members of the new Presbyterian

Church of America defend their separation from the Presbyterian Church in the United States (PCUS, or southern Presbyterian church) in doctrinal terms. In 1975 one denominational official of the PCA put the case for separation like this: "By 1970 almost every evangelical doctrine held precious by Presbyterians had been denied or questioned by leaders in the PCUS. Official PCUS publications, programs and policies waged open warfare against the Biblical faith."[7]

The recent division within the Lutheran Church—Missouri Synod has taken place due to disagreements over the nature of the Bible and how it should be interpreted (see also chapter 4 on this dispute). In his address to the triennial meeting of the denomination in the summer of 1975, President Jacob A. O. Preus stated frankly: "One of the basic issues that has troubled us has been the matter of the inerrancy of the Bible. . . . Our doctrinal controversy has produced further problems which, while not specifically doctrinal, are certainly vexing to us."[8] These further problems included the presence of dissenting organizations within the denomination and the clash of powerful personalities in the "political" life of the synod. In December 1976, the more liberal forces broke clearly from the Missiouri Synod to form the Association of Evangelical Lutheran Churches.

Once again in American church history, an internal dissent within a denomination had led to an outright division. The thing that makes this separation different, however, is the nature of the "winners" and "losers" in the struggle. In a break with past practice, discontent by a more liberal group had led to their separation from a more conservative parent body. Such an event also took place in 1962 among black Baptists. In that year the more liberal Progressive National Baptist Convention "came out" of its more conservative parent body, the National Baptist Convention, U.S.A. Separations like this have not been the norm in American church history.

Practical differences also occasion separations in our day. A goodly number of United Presbyterians are distressed with the denomination's ruling in the summer of 1975 on the "Kenyon case." In this dispute a prospective minister was denied ordination when his opinion on the ordination of women was rejected by the church's judicial system. The practical action of that judiciary, rather than the differences on the substantive issue, has encouraged talk of separation.

Independents

The twentieth century, besides witnessing several separations that resulted in the formation of new denominations, has also seen separations of countless individual churches. The phenomenon of "independency" is by its very nature separatistic. Nurtured by a strong belief in the primacy of the local church, many independent congregations are separate merely due to the belief that this is the proper way to organize Christian churches. Other Independents separate more specifically over separation. This has been particularly the case among the self-avowed fundamentalistic wing of Evangelicalism. Representatives of militant Fundamentalism still refuse to cooperate with the Billy Graham Association, the National Association of Evangelicals, Youth for Christ, or other interdenominational groups because such groups have not cut themselves off from all impure groups. Militant Fundamentalists call such organizations the "New Evangelicals." New Evangelicals are condemned not so much for the things they do wrong as for their failure to separate thoroughly enough from the world. Charles Woodbridge, a spokesman for this kind of Fundamentalism, puts its case clearly: "New Evangelicalism advocates toleration of error. It is following the downward path of accommodation to error, cooperation with error, contamination by error, and ultimate capitulation to error."[9] In spite of differences in tone and emphasis, this type of thinking represents a reappearance of the spirit of Roger Williams in contemporary dress.

Although not all Independents are militantly fundamentalistic, the more thoroughly separatistic churches have had much success in recent years. Two very loose organizations of separatistic Baptists, the Baptist Bible Fellowship, International, and the Baptist Missionary Association, have grown very rapidly since the end of World War II. In the light of America's history of separation it is interesting to observe that these separatistic bodies place great stress on the dynamic leadership of a forceful pastor. They have learned one lesson well—the way to get a separatistic movement off the ground is to recruit an energetic pilot.

A BRIEF EVALUATION OF AMERICAN SEPARATION

No attempt at an evaluation of American separatism should be undertaken apart from a consideration of the nature of Christianity itself. Believers affirm that Christianity is based on truth and on truth-in-action. Hence it is proper that Christians show an active concern for orthodoxy ("straightness") in the content of beliefs and the practice of the Way. Because Christianity is a religion of truth in action, determined defense of truth is required by the very character of the faith.

It is one thing to say that Christianity requires a determined defense. It is quite another to know when such a defense necessitates separation from existing churches. A number of Christianity's own principles makes a decision to separate difficult. Christians affirm the fallibility of man. Even believers must confess personal sin and the limits of their own wisdom. This means that each one of a believer's actions, including separation from a church, needs to be examined for pride, selfishness, or other sinful characteristics. Christian teaching observes that even believers err in many ways. In America, it is possible that separating believers have made a mistake when they look on the church as the creature of personal preferences and when they disregard the positive values of comprehensive ecclesiastical bodies. Separating believers in American history have sometimes given the impression that they have attained the whole truth and thus are able to leave behind those whose wisdom and insight have not come up to par.

Separating Christians have also tended to overlook gradations of importance in Christian truth and practice. One of the great contributions of Fundamentalists early in the twentieth century was their effort to isolate the essential rudiments, the fundamentals of the faith. This is a task in which all believers should be engaged. It is one thing to divide a denomination over the sovereignty of God, the divinity of Christ, the supernatural character of regeneration, or the authority of Scripture. It may not be so important to divide over the exact meaning of the Lord's Supper. It is on another order altogether to divide over differences concerning the last day, or the type of singing to be used in the local church. In American history the tendency has been to lump differences of all relative weights together, and this had made some separations rather frivolous.

The bent toward separation should also be tempered by the positive commands of Scripture concerning Christian unity. The high-priestly prayer of the Lord Jesus himself suggests that the union of believers is a very important thing. His petition, "that they also may be one in us," pointed to a most significant result, "that the world may believe that thou hast sent me" (John 17:21). Christian unity, the Savior seems to say, is not a luxury but an essential part of the gospel.

Having outlined some of the restraints that should check the rush to separation, we nevertheless see that separation is sometimes the only way to rescue Christian faith from corruption or degeneration. The believer facing difficulties within a church must not neglect a balanced set of principles: concern for Christian truth and concern for Christian unity. If both of these concerns are present, and if there is a healthy scepticism about the purity of our own motives, the question of separatism will be better understood. When considering orthodox faith and practice, American church history has perhaps had too few separations. When considering Christian unity and Christian humility, it has had far too many.

PART III: EVANGELICALS IN THE WORLD

8

"God Bless America"

Evangelicals and the Nation

"America," said President Woodrow Wilson, "was born a Christian nation for the purpose of exemplifying to the nations of the world the principles of righteousness found in the Word of God."[1]

Like numerous presidents before and after him, Woodrow Wilson shared a vivid sense of America's special role in the ongoing course of history. But unlike many of the men elected to the nation's highest office, Wilson was a devoted Christian and his view of this nation's special destiny sprang from his belief in America's special place in God's plan of salvation for the world. As the son of a Presbyterian minister, Wilson expressed a conviction about his native land with which most evangelical Christians, both in his day and in ours, would agree wholeheartedly.

For that matter, the idea of a Christian America represents a major design throughout the tapestry of American religious history. From the Puritan mission to establish in America a city upon a hill to the flurry of campaigns that Evangelicals sponsored to rekindle Christian belief during the Bicentennial, the gospel in America has often resounded with the theme that this country has been an elect nation, a chosen people, "God's New Israel."

Until recent times a majority of Americans readily identified with America's religious, if not her distinctively Christian, origins and purpose. The Englishman G. K. Chesterton commented earlier in this century that the United States appeared to be a nation with the soul of a church. The pledge of allegiance claiming that we are a nation under God, the parades and ceremonies on Memorial Day and the Fourth of July, the honor bestowed the American flag and the National Anthem—these customs and patterns were as widely followed as they were deeply held.

In our own day, however, sizable cracks are evident in this standard interpretation of America's spiritual heritage. Particularly among the generation under twenty-five, the American flag seldom evokes the patriotic kind of emotion that borders on religious feeling: the strains of "America" no longer move an audience to solemn reverence and eyes remain dry. Even more disturbing for those who revere America's Christian heritage is the forceful attack upon traditional ideals and institutions of the nation. Instead of confidence and pride in our past, a new generation has pictured America as almost the embodiment of evil. Turning from that which made America a refuge and a beacon, they have pointed to themes of oppression, discord and slavery. And in the aftermath of Vietnam and Watergate, influential people have ridiculed the love of God and country, unfurling a new banner confessing that they are ashamed to be American.

Despite the force of this disenchantment, it is surprising how little it has affected the evangelical community. More than others, Evangelicals have continued to appreciate America—they are glad that the gospel can be preached freely; they have been thankful that many Americans of past generations remained true to Christ; they have recognized the material plenty of their land as a gift from God.

In the last decade, however, a small number of young believers, speaking in such journals as *The Other Side*, *Vanguard*, *Right On*, and *Sojourners*, warned that some Evangelicals have tended to identify too closely certain features of American life with Christianity itself. They were particularly worried about any uncritical acceptance of conservative politics, capitalist economics, individualistic life style, and American patriotism. Yet these self-styled prophets have not been greeted with open arms by other Evangelicals, and their attempts to disentangle faith and culture have gained little acceptance among most conservative churches, denominations, and publications. Far more typical is the recent confession by a well-known Baptist pastor to a national television audience: "In this church," he said, "we teach patriotism as synonymous with Christianity," or the motto of a new evangelical college, "American Heritage Education: For God and Country." Apparently, the last, best hope of the conviction that America has been and should be a Christian nation is the local church represented in the National Association of Evangelicals or the Independent Fundamentalist Churches of America, the sympathetic audiences of major evangelists such as Billy Graham and Oral Roberts, and the interdenominational activity of Campus Crusade for Christ, sponsors of "Here's Life, America," the most ambitious attempt by Christians during the Bicentennial to bring America "back to God."

EVANGELICALS AND THE BICENTENNIAL

Unfortunately, during the Bicentennial celebration many Evangelicals were not as wise as they might have been concerning their reflections about the nation's history and about their own relationships to the nation (a proper Christian patriotism). Rather, they with others, sometimes fell headlong into what scholars have called "civil religion"—a tendency to attribute great religious significance to the nation. During 1976, evangelical publishers turned out an array of titles along these lines: *America: God Shed His Grace on Thee, One Nation Under God,* and *Faith, Stars and Stripes.* Churches sponsored celebrations under banners "200 Years Lord of Our Nation" and "Let Christ's Freedom Ring." A host of evangelical magazines, many of which had little else in common, fell in step to extol America's Christian heritage, the Biblical origins of American government, and the spiritual insights of the founding fathers. "America," suggested one in typical fashion, "has a great past, a great present, and a great future, because America has a GREAT GOD."

Three interlocking assumptions shaped the response of most Evangelicals to the Bicentennial. First, many orthodox Christians used 1976 as an occasion to remind their neighbors that religion has been the dynamic of American history. The finest fruits of the Founding Fathers, we were told, can be traced to biblical roots. Evangelical Congressman John B. Conlan, running for the Senate in Arizona, campaigned on the premise that it was Christian principles that infused strength and vitality into the early Republic. Focusing similarly on the spiritual roots of our nation, Billy Graham sponsored the Virginia Bicentennial Festival of Faith highlighted by an hour-long, nationwide television appeal that Americans return to their spiritual heritage. "The men who signed the Declaration of Independence," said Graham, "were moved by a magnificent dream. . . . And this dream is rooted in the book we call the Bible."[2]

Christian magazines presented the same message in a collage of images and quotations from the Founding Fathers: George Washington praying at Valley Forge or in other places professing his dependence upon Providence, James Madison drafting constitutional principles drawn from his biblical training at Princeton, and Benjamin Franklin breaking a deadlock at the Constitutional Convention by calling for a prayer meeting. If all of this evidence still left some unconvinced that America was shaped by men of religious faith, they would be referred to articles suggesting that it was the revival of 1740 rather than the secular political philosophy of 1776 that insured American independence, to prayer bulletins informing us that it was "direct answer to prayer that led Sam Adams to establish the Committee of Correspondence," and to books revealing that it was Evangelicals who launched the Ivy League.

In the second place evangelical patriotism has been sustained by the conviction that in a special sense America is—or has been—a Christian nation, raised up and equipped for a decisive role in history. Undoubtedly Americans have played a significant role in supporting Christian witness around the world. But some have gone further and argued that American institutions stem from religious ideals and that these institutions were due to God's special grace poured out upon America.

This emphasis has been evident whether Christians have been reflecting on the impact of American foreign missions or projecting what kind of role various nations might play in events leading to the millennium and the end of history. In what other nation would Christians feel comfortable sponsoring a Bicentennial Conference on Prophecy with the dual purpose of honoring national heroes and charting the events of the end times? Or in what other country do believers accord the civil constitutions the kind of religious significance that has led American Christians to believe or to state as did a leading evangelist, that the United States Constitution is "nothing short of a miracle of God"? And certainly one would have to look long and hard to find Christians in another land who would launch evangelistic efforts not so much to bring their communities to God but *back* to God.

This sense of specialness, of national election, blends quite naturally into a third characteristic of evangelical patriotism underscored by the Bicentennial: the tendency to think of the boundaries of religious community primarily in national rather than ecclesiastical terms. During 1976, somehow permissiveness, materialism, and loss of faith in national institutions seemed to evoke more evangelical remorse than lukewarmness ever did within the church; and somehow we had more heart for calling for a national day of prayer and fasting (worthwhile enterprises to be sure) under the banner of 2 Chronicles 7:14 than most of us ever have for kneeling in repentance with Christian brothers and sisters.

In America, where so many diverse groups all stand for an evangelical message, it has always been easier to find the overall design of God's redemptive work in the broad movement of American Christianity rather than within the narrow confines of any given denomination, Baptist, Church of God, Nazarene, Methodist, or whatever. The host of denominations, the spirit of cooperation that has characterized much of their history, and the strength of nondenominational activities—all foster attitudes that attach great religious significance to American culture itself. *It* was the fertile soil that nurtured Christendom's finest flower; America has always seemed to its Christian citizens the most natural habitat of the gospel.

Reflecting on these themes, some evangelists during 1976 presented the gospel almost as if its chief value was as a means to preserve the nation, rather than being the power of God unto salvation for all, whether they be Chinese, French, Colombian, or Angolan. Not going that far, many others did give the distinct impression that the continuation of the American republic was the surest, if not the only, ongoing defense of Christ's kingdom.

The strength of civil religion in our own day suggests the value, even the necessity, of an historical understanding of this phenomenon. While many other nations similarly link religion and nationalism, the United States has been particularly prone to do so. "Americans," observed Max Lerner, "have tended to find their religious faith in various forms of belief about their own existence."[3] In divorcing at all costs the institutional arrangements of church and state, Americans at the same time have joined the civil and the sacred in a new union more intimate than the Old World ever knew. "Americans," noted the French visitor Alexis de Tocqueville in 1840, "have linked liberty and Christianity so closely in their minds that it is impossible for them to think of the one without the other."[4] For these Americans Christian worship was too closely related to the "worship" of the state. They did not have a healthy patriotism as judged from a Christian point of view.

History is far from static and while the vision of America as God's New Israel is as dynamic for some today as it was for John Winthrop and the Puritans of 1630, the nature of that vision has undergone significant change over time. What have been the different expressions of this idea throughout American history? More significantly, what different purposes has the vision served? The sense of being an elect people can prick the conscience and challenge men and women to strenuous action or it can sanctify complacency. American history offers rich examples of that entire spectrum.

"THE CITY UPON A HILL"

The watershed of the American sense of mission and destiny can be traced to Puritan England. Recent studies have emphasized the intense sense of religious patriotism that dominated seventeenth-century England—and particularly those of Puritan persuasion. An almost overwhelming sense of destiny drove the English Puritans to purge their nation of its sin and lukewarmness. The standard mythology, in the words of John Milton, was that God had revealed himself "as his manner is, first to his Englishmen"; they were to fulfill the Reformation by purifying themselves of the remaining corruptions of Roman Catholicism. By doing so, England would bring the seventh vial of judgment upon the head of Antichrist, the Pope, and thus herald Christ's millennial kingdom.

The Puritans who came to establish New England were even more intense in their conviction that God had chosen them. The theme that crossing the Atlantic was the Exodus for God's "New English Israel" runs throughout the early sermons of Massachusetts. John Cotton, the most influential minister of the new settlement, preached for an entire winter on the book of Revelation and predicted that the millennium would bring history to an end before 1700. According to his interpretation, New England was playing a major role in overthrowing Antichrist and bringing on that happy day; its pure churches were an example that the rest of the world would certainly follow.

The most important thing about the Puritan vision of being God's chosen is that it functioned as a powerful spur to action. The vision of their own destiny was a primary motivating force in the rigorous struggles necessary to plant a new community in the wilds of America. "God sifted a whole nation that he might send a choice grain into this wilderness," expressed one minister.[5]

The ideal of the New English Israel bordered on a revolutionary vision. And some ten years after the Puritans came to the new world, their closest friends in England actually instigated the king's overthrow during the English civil war of the 1640s. The vision of a godly society had a tremendous motivating force for Cromwell and his Ironsides. They fought with the sense that they were important actors on a cosmic stage. In New England the vision had different implications; but it called men with no less intensity to remake society according to a Christian model.

Colonists brought other religious traditions to America during colonial times which also affirmed that the course of empire was moving westward, shifting God's primary base of operations from the Old World to the New. Most Englishmen of that day agreed with the Puritans that the state was a desired partner of the gospel and one of them, the Quaker William Penn, struggled to establish a "holy experiment" on the banks of the Delaware River. He hoped to show how men of various religious and national backgrounds together could build a community of brotherly love. By 1750 Pennsylvania and its neighboring colonies became an intricate religious mosaic. State-supported traditions—Anglicans, Scottish Presbyterians, German Lutherans, Dutch Reformed—intermingled with Moravians, Mennonites, Dunkers and Shakers—to name a few of the European sects that sought in America an escape from the heavy-handed meddling of civil authority that they had known back home in Europe.

Even though many of these Christians kept to themselves as much as possible, shunning political involvement, the very fact that they were left alone gave rise to feelings that God had chosen America as a special religious haven, a refuge in which the gospel could flourish. Even the eccentric Mother Anne Lee, who led the Shaker sect in denouncing the evils of American politics, found herself predicting that the millennium would begin in America.

During the colonial period the strongest attack on the idea that America was a city on a hill came from the lips of Roger Williams, founder of Rhode Island and spiritual father of American Baptists. Williams was expelled from Puritan Massachusetts in 1636 because of his extreme ideas about separation (see chapter 7). In Rhode Island he came to reject the Puritan idea that the state should or could be distinctly Christian. He argued that the Puritans had corrupted the purity of the gospel by trying to use the Bible as a political handbook. Massachusetts, for instance, had patterned its first law code, *Moses, His Judicials*, explicitly on the Ten Commandments. Williams rejected this because in his view it sought to impose requirements upon all of society that only a true Christian could fulfill. In an innovative argument that does not seem striking today because it is so conventional, Williams insisted that there had been no holy commonwealth, no elect nation, since the destruction of Old Testament Israel. After the coming of Christ, there could be no "new Israel." Accordingly, Williams attempted to build the government of Rhode Island with moral principles upon which a variety of men could agree, Christian and non-Christian alike.

"NOVUS ORDO SECLORUM"

In the years prior to American independence, the dissenting voice of Roger Williams gave way to an ever stronger chorus that America was unique—and providentially so. In New England ministers continued to apply to their own colonies Old Testament texts addressed to Israel; they began also to address the Puritan founders by such names as Moses, Aaron, and Joshua. If other Americans considered Yankees a bit provincial because of this, they were soon relieved to find in the aftermath of the Great Awakening (a revival ignited throughout the colonies) that Jonathan Edwards announced that not just New England but all of America would be the center of Christ's millennial kingdom. And as the Americans took up arms against the French in the Seven Years' War (1756-1763), many agreed with the evangelical Presbyterian Samuel Davies from Virginia that defeating Catholic France would wound Antichrist sufficiently to bring on that long-awaited reign.

What does change in the period leading up to the American Revolution among laity and ministers alike is the reasons for which men thought they were God's elect. Early New England determined that they were God's chosen people because they had such pure religion. By the time of the American Revolution, however, men throughout the colonies were making statements that America was elect because of the heights of civil liberty that it had achieved. This is a significant shift, and in one way the foundation of civil religion; for it allowed men to express secular purposes in religious terms, as historian Alan Heimert has indicated:

> In the years between the Stamp Act and the Revolution the evangelical ministry often spoke in the phrases of Sam Adams—who in 1772 explained that the religion and public liberty of a people are so intimately connected, their interests are interwoven and cannot exist separately. Not the least of the consequences of such a blending of interests and issues was that elements of the Calvinist populace were allowed to think that they were defending religion when in fact they were doing battle for civil liberties.[6]

The following apocalyptic interpretation of the American Revolution by Samuel Sherwood, a Connecticut Evangelical, is not atypical:

> God almighty, with all the powers of heaven, is on our side. Great numbers of angels, no doubt, are encamping round our coast for our defense and protection. Michael stands ready, with all the artillery of heaven, to encounter the dragon, and to vanquish this

> black host. . . . It will soon be said and acknowledged that the kingdoms of this world are become the kingdoms of our Lord, and of his Christ.[7]

Sherwood went on to attack the British as "one of the last efforts and dying struggles of the Man of Sin"; he threatened those hesitant to join the Revolution that the vials of God's wrath would be poured out on anyone who did not oppose the anti-Christian tyranny of the British.

In this context, where sin became tyranny and righteousness the realization of liberty, it is not hard to understand the heightened millennial expectations that appeared after the Revolution in even the most secular minds in America. We can see how the often profane Benjamin Franklin could propose that the seal of the new republic be a picture of Joshua with his rod held over the Jordan River. At the time of the Revolution, the vision of America's destiny remained intense but with an altered foundation. Instead of motivating men to create a Christian society, it encouraged them to bring about a revolution that would ensure the reign of civil liberty.

Between the American Revolution and 1800, the United States underwent a major religious depression, probably the low ebb of religious vitality in the nation's history. Yet in contrast to the downward state of religion, millennial expectancy during these years rose to unparalleled heights. One minister triumphantly proclaimed that the advancing kingdom had delivered "the deadly shock to the last section of the Babylonish Image. . . . It trembles, it reels to and fro, and threatens to fall."[8]

But how could ministers rejoice in the success of the kingdom while their own churches lay devastated by the enemy? Their answer was that God, in their view, had shifted his primary base of operations to the arena of nations. In the ringing success of the American republic, they witnessed a model for the coming age: "No sooner had the *twenty years* of our political operation built for us this political temple," argued a Presbyterian in 1796, "than wisdom fell from God in respect to the millennial temple."[9]

In what would become the heart of American civil religion, Christians began to argue, as the Congregationalist John Mellen did in 1797, "that the expansion of republican forms of government will accompany that spreading of the gospel . . . which the scripture prophecies represent as constituting the glory of the latter days."[10] This shift greatly strengthened the American republic, endowing it with a new sense of lofty purpose. It had just the opposite effect upon the church, however, blunting its once authoritative mission. As Christian ministers became high priests of the new republic, they were less able to serve as prophets, discerning for their congregations what it meant to be in the world but not of it.

RIGHTEOUS EMPIRE

Evangelicals have not always been a beleaguered minority in American society. In fact, their attempt to Christianize American society in the nineteenth century is a remarkable success story. In contrast to their declining fortunes in the Revolutionary era (see chapter 1), Christians after 1800 accomplished so much that historians are led to describe that period of American history as an "Evangelical Empire."

"The first half century of national life," one has recently written, "saw the development of evangelicalism as a kind of national religion."[11] During these years the membership of evangelical churches not only kept pace with population growth; the percentage of church members actually doubled. From 1832 to 1854 the population of the nation increased 88 percent while the number of evangelical clergymen grew 175 percent. By 1840 Alexis de Tocqueville noted that "no country in the whole world existed in which the Christian religion retains a greater influence over the souls of men than in America."[12] And whereas at the time of the American Revolution the largest denominations represented the staid and formal traditions of the Anglicans, Congregationalists, and Presbyterians, by 1850 the fervent piety of Methodists and Baptists accounted for 70 percent of Protestant church members.

As Evangelicals increasingly came to shape the values of the nation, they were, in turn, even less able to distinguish between the kingdom of God and the republic. The civil religion that was born during the Revolutionary era grew to manhood as civic values such as freedom and democracy became inseparable from the message of evangelical faith that the nation gladly owned. The author of *Moby Dick*, Herman Melville, represented a whole generation in confessing: "We Americans are the peculiar chosen people—the Israel of our time; we bear the ark of the liberties of the world."[13]

A major impetus to this new union of church and state was, ironically, the separation of the old. As we have previously suggested (see chapter 6), the multiplication of denominations in this period reduced the exclusive claims of any one church and expanded the horizons of most Evangelicals to appreciate what God was doing in and through the republic. Barton W. Stone, for example, shortly after 1800 rejected the "traditions of men" that he found in the Presbyterian church. But in challenging his new movement, the "Christians" or the Disciples of Christ, to return to "New Testament Christianity," he saw no reason to throw out his conviction that God had chosen the American republic as a model for the millennial kingdom.

The blossoming evangelical interest in foreign missions is another example of this fusion of Christianity and national values. The prominent Evangelical Lyman Beecher viewed missions more as a national than an ecclesiastical task: "The millennium would commence in America," where "by the march of revolution and civil liberty, the way of the Lord is to be prepared. . . . From this nation shall the renovating power go forth. Only America can provide the physical effort and pecuniary and moral power to evangelize the world."[14] "Our heavenly Father," said William Williams in 1845, "has made us a national epistle to other lands."[15]

Even the Presbyterian Charles Hodge, who normally made a sharper distinction between the church and the nation, fell into step with his fellow Americans when he wrote in 1829 that "If the Gospel is to form our character and guide our power, we shall be a fountain of life to all nations."After reading a full complement of sermons and tracts written during this time of great missionary activity, the modern scholar Perry Miller has concluded that the motivation of evangelical missionaries cannot be divorced from their deep sense of "romantic patriotism."[16]

Others who have compared the motivations of American and British missionaries during the nineteenth century note the higher degree of loyalty to a distinctly national expression of the gospel among the former. It was not that they went forth proclaiming anything less than the high ideals of the gospel; it was that they proceeded with the equally high ideal of sharing the full benefits of American democracy, a task not carefully distinguished from the gospel.

It is important to note that in the nineteenth century the vision of America as God's chosen people still operated as a motive to vigorous action. The goal of Christianizing America stirred men and women not only to be active evangelists, but also to join in purging along with unbelief every form of social evil. In the wake of the revivals of Charles G. Finney, Evangelicals intent on preaching the gospel also were behind numerous societies for moral reform: antislavery, temperance, women's rights, education, poor relief, and prison and hospital reform. Knowing that their bountiful heritage as Americans required much of them, Evangelicals in the age of President Andrew Jackson struggled fervently to remake every part of their society according to Christian standards. On the eve of the Civil War nothing was safe from their burning gaze.

But there is a much less heroic side of this quest for a righteous empire. In addition to broadening minds to reform, the goal of a Christian commonwealth narrowed definitions of who should be included within the American community. On the verge of inaugurating a kingdom that was essentially Protestant, democratic, and Caucasian, many Evangelicals looked askance at anyone who threatened the solidarity of this image: Catholic immigrants, religious dissenters such as the Mormons, and most blacks and native Americans.

Even worse, this resentment of "foreign" elements could flare easily into open hostility or even violence. When Catholics objected to the explicit evangelical teaching in many public schools, they were denounced in many quarters as subversives. Lyman Beecher, for instance, joined with Samuel F. B. Morse, better known for his telegraph, to make public a supposed conspiracy by Catholics to undermine the liberties of the United States. In the wake of these fears, Protestants burned to the ground a Catholic convent in Boston and two churches in Philadelphia. In similar fashion, a virtual war was waged on Joseph Smith and the unconventional ideas of his Mormon followers, driving them from New York, Ohio, and Missouri, before an angry mob finally lynched Smith in Nauvoo, Illinois, in 1844.

Calling this kind of action a "tyranny of the majority," the observant Frenchman Tocqueville noted that Americans were more tolerant than Europeans within certain limits and less tolerant outside those boundaries. Americans opened their arms to groups that could be assimilated into a Protestant empire, but clenched their fists at others. While evangelical belief certainly was not the only factor in this intolerance, the idea of a Christian America too easily led Christians to attempt to purify the nation as well as the church.

The most striking illustration of civil religion's power during the nineteenth century is the Protestant reaction to the Civil War—the Southern attempt to divide the American Union. Numerous splits among Baptists, Methodists, and Presbyterians in the years preceding the war never evoked anything like the religious passion that erupted at the thought of dismembering America. Abraham Lincoln stands as an eloquent spokesman of this religious interpretation of the Civil War. He clearly looked to the United States for fulfillment of God's purposes in history; in 1861 he expressed confidence that "when the people rise in masses in behalf of the Union and the liberties of their country, truly it may be said, 'The gates of hell shall not prevail against them.'"[17] The ease with which he transferred to the nation Christ's promise to the church is convincing evidence that the United States had truly become a nation with the soul of a church.

MYTHS OF THE PAST

The last quarter of the nineteenth century witnessed a strange divorce among those who claimed the mantle of America's Christian heritage. On the one hand many Protestants were taken by the new directions of theological liberalism and began to define the task of the church primarily as the social renovation of industrial society. With a religious philosophy that has come to be known as the "social gospel," clergymen such as the Baptist Walter Rauschenbusch and the Congregationalists Washington Gladden and Josiah Strong proclaimed that the kingdom of God could be attained only by marshalling Christians to attack the ills of society. They cherished the ideal of a Christian America but were compelled by that vision to withstand the rising tide of poverty, ignorance, crime, and inhumanity to man in whatever form. They worked energetically, confident that Americans had a unique role to play in heralding the millennium.

But other American Protestants were not caught up in this postmillennial jubilation and its call for social reform. They were convinced that the message of the social gospel overlooked, if it did not deny, the heart of the gospel; they were not about to jump aboard. As the voice of Liberalism came to overwhelm all others in the mainline denominations, conservative Protestants mounted a new defense of the gospel. They countered the idea that human endeavor could bring on the millennium with the argument that only divine intervention could alter the course of history, and they deflected the call to social action by pointing out that only a few individual passengers could be saved from a sinking ship.

Yet in scurrying to establish at all costs a defense of the fundamentals of Christianity, these men and women—soon to be called by that name—did not surrender the idea that America was a Christian nation. But like the prophets of the Old Testament, they used the occasion as a reminder of the high standards from which the country had fallen. Repelled by Liberalism's preoccupation with remaking contemporary society along its own Christian principles, these defenders of orthodoxy increasingly fixed their gaze on the American past, when, supposedly, authentic Christianity informed every dimension of national life.

In its best form this focus on the past offered a much needed corrective to Americans who, in the age of the Scopes trial and H. L. Mencken, so easily ridiculed every form of orthodox Christianity from the Puritans to the Fundamentalists. The danger, however, was that embattled Christians unwittingly began to shade the history of America, not so much by outright distortion but by a process of selecting only those items that preserved the myth that at one time America had been an harmonious Christian commonwealth. In its worst form, this sense of the past became more myth than history and allowed Christians to find shelter from the difficulties of their own day by retreating to a Christian America that never existed at all.

Unfortunately, many Evangelicals in our own day have not gone beyond this misuse of history. For whatever reason, we have seen it necessary on the occasion of the Bicentennial to defend a view of early America that makes it an idealization of many of the goals we have not been able to obtain. Those were the days, we imagine, when Christian faith really mattered, when American politics reflected the principles of God's Word, and when the invisible hand of Providence overturned insurmountable odds to establish a nation under God. By a careful scissors-and-paste approach to the evidence, too many of us have projected upon the screen of the past what is little more than an ideal image of ourselves decked out in a powdered wig and a three-cornered hat.

A few examples will make the point clear. In the face of solid historical evidence that statesmen such as Thomas Jefferson, George Washington, and John Adams had rejected orthodox Christianity for a more liberal form of religion—what could be called Deism—evangelical publications have taken great relish in the Christian faith of the Founding Fathers. (There is no firm evidence, by the way, to sustain the myth that Washington knelt and prayed at Valley Forge.)

Worse still, we have drawn encouragement from the fact that at least the Founding Fathers recognized the importance of religion. We have failed to note that for them a variety of religions were, in the words of Jefferson, "all good enough." As long as religion supported political harmony, they were not so concerned with *what* a man believed. Benjamin Franklin, for instance, had no use for a particular evangelical minister because "he wanted to make men good Presbyterians rather than good citizens." Similarly, when George Washington stated in his farewell address that religion and morality were the "indispensable supports" of sound government, the force of his words was much the same as saying what you believe does not matter as long as you have faith.

There is no question that life in early America was more religious than it is today; but the nation was not, by evangelical standards, necessarily more Christian. Understanding this, we may be less inclined to see our political institutions as being of divine origin. This does not lead us to debunk our political institutions but to understand better the context of their creation.

"TO WHOM MUCH IS GIVEN, MUCH IS REQUIRED"

We have come full circle. By returning to the distinctive myths that Evangelicals have sustained during the Bicentennial, we are confronted with how differently the vision of a Christian America functions today than it has in the past. For the Puritans, it had radical implications, the task of carving a Christian community out of raw wilderness. During the American Revolution it convinced men that it was their Christian duty to take up the sword against constituted authority. For nineteenth-century Evangelicals, this vision led to an outpouring of evangelistic activity and social reform. In each case, the sense of God's special blessing upon the nation became a dynamic force, a powerful motivation.

How does the current civil religion among Evangelicals compare with this tradition? In the twentieth century the trend has been for Evangelicals to cling to the idea of a Christian America but reject what for most of American history has been a logical corollary: to purge from the nation that which flagrantly violates Christian principles. Patriotism among Christians has shifted its vision to the past where it finds ample, if selective, evidence that America did at one time fulfill most of our Christian and American ideals.

Drawing upon these themes, Evangelicals during the Bicentennial called us time and again to honor the flag, to discard despair and negativism about America. Some of their admonitions were commendable. Their challenge did not include, however, what so many of our Christian forefathers heard: marching orders to preach the gospel, relieve the hungry, serve the widows, care for the prisoners. Rather than calling us to serve in Christ's name those less fortunate than ourselves, messages in 1976 too often skimmed over the painful and ugly side of contemporary American life and took refuge in the myth of a golden age of Christian influence.

The irony of this situation is that Christians most vocal about a Christian America generally remain silent about the ills of that society, about applying Christian influence to America's thorny problems:

urban ghettoes, migrant workers, racial strife, New Yorkers who equate an electricity blackout with "Christmas"—a time to steal. We might expect this detachment from society and its problems from a Christian who rejected America's providential destiny or from a Christian living in a non-Christian culture, say, India or Saudi Arabia. But it is difficult to understand those who claim God's promises to this nation in one breath and in the next discount any personal responsibility to bring relationships throughout that society into line with the character of God. Whatever else, this direction of thought is exactly the opposite of those Christians throughout our history whom we honor for trying to build Christian principle into every nook and cranny of American life. They were not overwhelmed by the greatness of the task.

What, then, should be the Christian's attitude toward the American nation and its heritage? Four biblical principles, sketched in brief, will at least introduce a subject that deserves extensive treatment. In the first place, we must agree with Roger Williams that no nation since the collapse of Israel six hundred years before the time of Christ has been uniquely God's chosen people. The New Testament clearly teaches that Christ set aside national and ethnic barriers and that he has chosen to fulfill his central purposes in history through the church, which transcends all such boundaries. However much particular nations may be used at particular times to do God's work in the world, they are not the primary tools that he is now using. Similarly, the Lord of history has not aligned his purposes with the particular values of any given country or civilization.

Instead, God calls out his people to be strangers and pilgrims, as many of America's early settlers knew so well. He calls them to repent of their sins and to avoid conformity with the world. We are to be good citizens, but we must remember that our real home, that city with foundations, is beyond our own culture. Our renderings to Caesar, while they must be taken seriously, are to follow the values of that kingdom that stands above all earthly authority. These priorities, rather than those of our culture and nation, demand our unfettered loyalty.

The second principle for evaluating attitudes toward our nation is that for any given generation God is primarily concerned with the present rather than the past. In the Old Testament, the prophets were constantly warning Israel that what had been a fine garden had become a wilderness, that what had been fine gold had become ugly and tarnished. God was not interested in a past commitment of the nation to him; his concern for each age focuses on the present and the nature of that generation's obedience. We find the same principle also present in the New Testament. Christ condemned the Pharisees for relying on the fact that Moses was their father. In the book of Revelation he angrily denounced one church because they had lost their first love and another because they were lukewarm.

Applying this principle to a modern nation, we can say that at the present time God has interest in what is Christian in America's heritage only as it evokes contemporary obedience. American Christians must see the rich history of God's faithfulness to this country as a stewardship of which much is required. Without question God in his providence has blessed this nation with remarkable spiritual and material riches, and the people of America have manifested an unusual generosity in sharing both of these treasures with the rest of the world. But these good gifts have come from our Creator. Much has been given; much more is required of us. The Christian heritage of America should not allow us a safe retreat into the past; it should sharpen our concern and move us to action.

The third principle is that God has no interest in religion *per se*. There are strong indications, in fact, that he hates religion that is not truly Christian more than the absence of religion. Christ condemned the Pharisees because not only were they blind, but as religious leaders they misled others. "I hate the sound of your solemn assemblies," God informed religious men and women of the Old Testament, when they used their religion as an excuse not to face the Lord himself. One of the biggest dangers of civil religion in America is the temptation to condone religion *per se* as the means to the ends of national solidarity and stability.

There is the implicit tendency among uncritically patriotic Christians to confirm any religion that tends to uphold the basic principle of American morality. Where is the prophetic voice that condemns all religion that does not have its ultimate end in God? We must recognize that the American civic faith constantly repeats the chorus that any religion is good enough and that none should claim exclusive truth. Against this tenet, we must be willing to stand as lonely prophets whose hearts are not glad with a rise in religiosity not centered in God. Jehovah demands exclusive loyalty.

The fourth principle is that God judges men not according to what they say they believe but according to their real faith commitments. God always is very practical in this respect. You are a liar, he says, if you say you love God and hate your brother. Similarly, when Israel would parade her religiosity, God would remind her people of the social injustice that was everywhere practiced. This is the message of the book of James. Real Christian faith can always be evaluated by the fruit it bears. Real Christian faith will produce works, or it is not genuine faith. According to this principle, it seems that we should evaluate the righteousness of any society not merely by the religious professions that people make, but also by the extent to which Christian principles are realized in the society.

The basis for judging the righteousness of this nation at any point is not solely to examine the membership roles of the churches to see how many claim to be Christian. Let there be no doubt; professions of faith are important. But we must also look at the extent to which believers are engaged in the task of applying Christian love and justice to every facet of life. What is really important is not the claims of our society to be Christian, the invoking of the rhetoric of the "New American Israel"; what will stand in the final analysis is how many Americans knew that deep-seated commitment to God that proves its faith by its works.

9

"Work, for the Night is Coming"

Evangelicals in Society

One of the most interesting interpretations of history in the twentieth century is called the "Halévy Thesis." Around the turn of the century a Frenchman, Elie Halévy, proposed a comprehensive interpretation of English society, thought, and institutions at the time of the Napoleonic wars. In his book, *England in 1815,* Halévy puzzled over the stability and continuity of English institutions in contrast to the revolutionary instability of his native France, and he spent considerable energy addressing the logical, but complex question: what factors were responsible for the survival of English traditions? Halévy finally concluded that the English escaped the kind of social turmoil experienced in the French Revolution at least in large part because of the social impact of the evangelical revival in the middle of the eighteenth century. The effectiveness of the early Methodists in meeting the needs of the urban poor and in organizing significant numbers of them into responsible communities made a notable impact on the nature of eighteenth-century English society. Halévy argued that the dynamic force that flowed from John Wesley's compassion for the needy spread and multiplied until the entire complexion of the English working class was changed. Furthermore, he argued that the revival was a dominant force in mobilizing a group of influential political figures to crusade for needed reform in English society. Prominent among these was William Wilberforce (1759-1833) whose lifework as a politician culminated in the abolition of the slave trade, and eventually of slavery itself, within the British empire.

Whether or not Halévy is correct in attributing such massive results to the English Methodists, no historian who examines the first years of Methodism can escape the intense social concern demonstrated by John Wesley and his followers. From his student years at Oxford, where his Holy Club was maligned due to its methodical religious activity, Wesley unceasingly hammered at the theme that Christians must daily be involved in charity. "To withhold money from the poor," he taught, "is to buy poison for ourselves." For him the ownership of goods was not meant to serve personal ends, but the fulfillment of a moral purpose in society. Those who hold property for reasons other than this Christian ethic, said Wesley, were robbing God, embezzling their Maker's goods, corrupting their own souls, and violating the rights of the community. "If therefore you do not spend your money in doing good to others, you must spend it to the hurt of yourself."[1] The point is not that Wesley advocated poverty, for he did not. He merely practiced and preached a gospel of compassion that compelled him to search out the suffering and the needy. Wesley was always aggressive in looking for people who required help. "The Gospel of Christ knows no Religion but Social, no Holiness but Social Holiness."[2] Wesley and his followers taught this principle and lived it out in daily experience.

What a striking contrast if we compare the early Methodists with much of the contemporary evangelical church in America. "Ethical commitment," say the sociologists Rodney Stark and Charles Glock, "is seemingly not the typical product of American religious devotion."[3] They find that the more intense Americans are in their religious beliefs, the less likely they are to have any real concern for the poor and the more likely they are to manifest racial prejudice. Many other students of the contemporary religious scene come to conclusions that are similar if not quite so bleak. The point remains: Christian piety too frequently serves to comfort, reassure, and validate rather than to challenge, judge, and demand commitment.

Even more disturbing are studies that find a correlation between orthodoxy in theology and an absence of compassion for the less fortunate. Conservatives in theology, like their political counterparts, generally have felt uneasy around poor people, perhaps assuming that anyone who cannot afford a ranch home in the suburbs is somehow not trying very hard. The striking thing about this tendency is that it focuses on Christian attitudes to the poor, not on attitudes to government relief. It is one thing to oppose the government's welfare program, arguing that it has usurped the responsibility of the church and of

Christian individuals. It is quite another to manifest indifference to visible human problems. This dichotomy, between Christian belief on the one hand, and a retreat from human need on the other, appears to be a serious problem for Evangelicals in this country today. Despite a few rumblings to the contrary, the overall evangelical witness stands rebuked by the early Methodists, or for that matter, by any number of Christians who since the time of Christ have brought compassion to a decaying world. How did we arrive at the present state? What happened that Evangelicals in America have misplaced this distinctive?

By taking a broad historical view of the problem of social concern in America, we shall find how strikingly out of step we are with our evangelical forebears. The Puritans, for example, were committed to bringing all of life—economics, vocation, social relations, government—under the piercing scrutiny of biblical norms. The gospel that saved a man's soul was supposed to transform every facet of his life. During the nineteenth century, revivalists like Charles G. Finney consoled sinners with the promise of being born again, but then fired them with a zeal to attack every form of slavery, poverty, cruelty, and injustice. No evil in American society was safe from the burning gaze of these redeemed men and women. The story of evangelical social concern also has a less heroic side, however. Evangelicals have been apathetic toward slavery, or even defended it; we have joined the unbridled and unsanctified scramble for wealth. During the fundamentalist period early in this century, we largely withdrew from responsibility for the world beyond our own portals. Yes, there is much in this heritage to cherish but much also to regret. But all of it should bring perspective to those of us called to live as biblical Christians in American society during the last two decades of this century.

PURITANS AND SOCIETY

How difficult it is for anyone to change gears and to try to understand a society in the past that thinks and behaves in a manner very different from our own. We are individualists and approach any subject with the assumption that all values, rights, and duties originate in the individual. But the Puritans, like most Europeans in the seventeenth century, did not think that way. As we noted in chapter 6, they saw society as an organism, a body, a commonwealth. The good of the whole was always a primary consideration. Society did not exist primarily to allow the individual to develop his or her full potential; it had a meaning and identity of its own to which the individual was challenged to relate. Thus whenever the Puritans spoke of choosing a vocation, they emphasized the necessity of a calling that tended to public good. Theirs was a society where unity, order, and stability were the primary social virtues.

Chapter 6 elaborated further this social philosophy. Here it is important to relate Christian social ethics to the Puritan point of view. For all intents and purposes the social values of that culture exemplified Christian ideals. Whether a man looked at himself as a citizen or as a Christian, the responsibility to live for the public good was the same. In at least three significant respects, Puritan social ethics can offer a challenge to our own.

The first area is that of stewardship. The Puritan view of vocation grew out of the conviction that everything belongs to God. As Englishman Richard Baxter (1615-1691) put it, "God is the Owner." The Christian served God as a steward and was accountable for time, talents, and possessions. Despite what is popularly said about the "Protestant ethic," the Puritans, like Calvin before them, kept their Christian scruples when engaged in business. It is quite true that the Puritans were diligent about whatever they set their hands to accomplish, but they certainly did not work hard solely to build a fortune. As one scholar has written, "Puritan writers had a name for the appetite that craved profit without end or final purpose and it was covetousness; and a name for economic individualism, and it was pride."[4] The English Puritan divine John Preston (1587-1628) deflated the self-made man by telling him that riches, like every good gift, came from above. They must be used for God's glory and the public good. Preston, whom American Puritans honored as a father in the faith, called it rebellion when men failed to realize that possessions came as a free gift just like God's grace.

Although many Puritans in both England and America became wealthy, their riches evoked more godly fear than placid assurance. Richard Baxter, one of England's most respected pastors, exhorted men in this way: "Riches are in themselves but dross, which will leave thee at thy grave poor as any. And as to their usefulness, they are but thy Master's talents, and the more thou hast, the greater will be thine account." If the full weight of this responsibility were felt, Baxter went on to say, "it will quench your thirst after plenty and prosperity . . . you will become more concerned to use well what you have than to get more."[5] The Puritan idea of stewardship led quite naturally into helping those in need.

The second emphasis of Puritan teaching was the ready admission that a fallen world contained "worthy poor." That is, the Puritans felt poverty was not always a result of personal sloth or God's anger. New England's Samuel Willard was only one of those who argued that poverty is not a sign of God's displeasure. Riches or poverty were in themselves not tokens of God's attitude toward us. Although the Puritans had no sympathy for the "idle poor," those who refused to work, they did recognize full well that God might afflict one man with poverty just as he would appoint another to wealth. The responsibility of the latter, obviously, was to meet the needs of his neighbor and thus to bring health to the whole society. Although Puritan pocketbooks did turn out to be less generous than Puritan sermons might lead us to believe, New England did take remarkable care of its poor for at least a century. By not attaching a moral stigma to poverty, the Puritans were able to sustain a deep concern that expressed itself in tangible charity for the downcast.

A third characteristic of Puritan social concern was that its ministers applied biblical norms to a full range of social issues. What is important is not the particular stands they happened to take on specific issues. What is important is that laymen received regular exhortation to evaluate every dimension of life according to Christian principles.

A good example is the way Richard Baxter instructed Christians about their vocations. It was not enough, he began, for someone merely to shun unlawful means of accumulating wealth. Addressing the lawyer, Baxter warned:

> Be sure that you make not the getting of money to be the principle end in the exercise of your function but the promoting of justice. . . . He is a lover of money more than justice that will sweat in the cause of the rich that pay him well and will slubber over and starve the cause of the poor because he getteth little by them.[6]

He also admonished physicians:

> Be sure that the saving of men's lives and health be first and chiefly your intention before any gain or honor of your own. . . . Be ready to help the poor as well as the rich. . . . Let not the health or lives of men be neglected because they have no money to give you.[7]

In similar fashion, Baxter exhorted businessmen that in making a bargain or contract, they must set their hearts upon the true love of their neighbor and ask: "How would I be dealt with myself, if my case were the same with his? Instead of thinking how much his own gain, he must remember how much he will lose by sin."[8] Baxter also spoke about responsibility to the public: "It is not lawful to take up or keep up any oppressing monopoly or trade which tendeth to enrich you by the loss of the commonwealth or the many."[9] Thus, we see that a Puritan minister attempted to develop a comprehensive biblical ethic. From our perspective we can criticize these stern saints of another day for tolerating slavery and the plundering of Indian lands. Yet we must also acknowledge that they put us to shame in the gallant effort to bring all of life into subjection to the Word of God.

REVIVALISM AND SOCIAL REFORM

Two decades ago, the respected evangelical historian Timothy L. Smith wrote a prize-winning book, *Revivalism and Social Reform: American Protestantism on the Eve of the Civil War.* Smith argued persuasively that nineteenth-century revivalism released a mighty reforming force which revamped American society. He goes on to suggest that direct links tie the social gospel, which appeared late in the century, and this earlier tradition of evangelical reform: "The Power which earliest opposed the organized evils of urban society and stretched out hands of mercy to the poor was sanctified compassion."[10] As a newspaper commented in 1855, "Infidelity makes an outcry about its philanthropy but religion does the work."[11]

Whether Professor Smith can demonstrate such a close connection between Evangelicalism and social gospel, he has shown indisputably that genuine social concern and activity resulted directly from persons being converted in the revivals. "Nothing short of the general renewal of society ought to satisfy any soldier of Christ," proclaimed one revivalist.[12] He joined the most significant evangelical figures of the day—Charles G. Finney, Albert Barnes, Lyman Beecher, Matthew Simpson, and Samuel Schmucker, among others—in forging a tight bond between personal salvation and community improvement. They called Christians to feed the poor, educate the unlearned, reform the prisons, humanize treatment for the mentally ill, establish orphanages, gain women's rights, abolish slavery, and take on numerous other works of charity. By 1837, the editor of the *New York Evangelist* broadcast the agenda that many Christians found compelling: "Devoted to Revivals, Doctrinal Discussion, Religious Intelligence Generally, Practical Godliness, and Human Rights."[13]

In *Revivalism and Social Reform,* Professor Smith documents the surprising extent of social activity that issued from the revivals. By 1850, over 2,500 home missionaries had scattered through the West into communities without churches. The American Sunday School Union listed over 3,700 different schools and enrolled some one-seventh of the nation's total population of children between the ages of five and fifteen. The most effective abolitionists preached against slavery as sin under the auspices of the American Antislavery Society. Like their tireless leader, Theodore Dwight Weld (1803-1895), many of these reformers had been converted in the revivals of Charles G. Finney. The same evangelical zeal led Christians to tackle the growing problems of the cities, where numerous agencies began serving the poor. In New York seventy-six missions were operating by 1860. In Philadelphia five hundred volunteers representing scores of different churches and agencies divided the city into sections for relief of the indigent. In Boston the Evangelical Edward Norris Kirk began the YMCA with the goal of helping men "grow in the love of God, in the faith of Christ, and in zeal for human welfare."[14] At the time of the Civil War, the conviction had become commonplace among Evangelicals that society must be reconstructed through the sanctifying power of the gospel.

This spirit of reform among Christians certainly did not bring on the millennium, as many had hoped. This very real benevolence was limited by its boundless optimism and its inability to retain momentum after the Civil War when chronic social problems thrust themselves upon the consciousness of the country for the first time. And, earlier on, all Evangelicals had not joined this train. Conservative Presbyterians and Lutherans, for instance, argued against social reform that did not carry a specific scriptural warrant. Nevertheless, Evangelicals in the age of Finney were in general intensely committed to a variety of society's needs. In this sense, Christian social values became the norm that judged those of the nation; when it found them wanting, Christians zealously sought to bring the society into line with divine standards.

AMERICAN SLAVERY AND THE LIMITS OF REFORM

It is perhaps the greatest irony in American history that at the time this nation was being "conceived in liberty and dedicated to the proposition that all men are created equal," it held some 20 percent of its own population in slavery. At the time of the Declaration of Independence, half a million blacks in America already knew by experience the kind of slavery that patriotic Americans went to war to avoid for themselves. By the time of the War between the States, the number of Afro-Americans had grown to four million, most of them still in bondage. The Revolution of 1776 did bring about a gradual emancipation in the North, where slaves were few and incidental to the economy, but failed to bring about a frontal assault on forced labor in the South.

An even more tragic story is the position of evangelical Christians regarding chattel slavery. Men and women of evangelical conviction were certainly in the forefront of the attack on "the peculiar institution" from the Revolution until the Civil War. But that is only one-third of the story. Equally devout Christians, with handy proof texts from Philemon, marshalled a biblical defense: "The Scriptures not only fail to condemn slavery," argued the southern Presbyterian J. H. Thornwell, "they as distinctly sanction it as any other social condition of man."[15] Most Evangelicals, North and South, remained somewhere in between these extremes and, whatever their personal preferences on the matter, were inclined to proclaim a gospel that did not meddle with such controversial affairs. George Whitefield, for example, the Grand Itinerant of America's first Great Awakening in the 1740s, actually proposed that slavery be introduced into the new colony of Georgia, where it had been originally forbidden, so that his much-acclaimed orphanage might reap the benefits. "Had negroes been allowed," he concluded, "I should now have had a sufficiency to support a great many orphans without expending half the sum that has been laid out."[16] Although Whitefield did attack the cruelty of some slave owners—"Masters of Barbarity"—he did not challenge the system of slavery nor promise anything more than spiritual liberty to the many slaves that heard him preach.

The relationship of Evangelicals to slavery does point up several characteristic limitations of how Christians in America have related the gospel to society. We shall mention three: the assumption that evangelism alone will be a sufficient salt for society, the fact that evangelical growth can just as readily dilute as strengthen ethical convictions, and the tendency for reformers to attack evils from which they consider themselves delivered.

The Gospel and Social Ills

As we have suggested, most American Christians have lived somewhere in between the few prophets of each generation who have attempted to reconstruct society according to the gospel and the few priests who have proposed an explicit biblical defense of the status quo. More typically American, perhaps, is the Christian who has thought that preaching the gospel is the only effective means to remedy social ills. A large body of concerned believers in this country has always argued that society can be revamped only by converting individuals. It is a question of means rather than ends; the heart of the individual remains the heart of the problem. Unfortunately, the story of Christian attitudes toward slavery in America shows that conversion does not automatically bring about Christian convictions in society.

No better example of this point exists than the career of John Newton (1725-1807) who, although he was an Englishman, shared many of the attitudes of his American counterparts in the 1700s. Newton was an infamous slave trader, who, after his conversion in 1748, became a beloved pastor, confidant of Wesley, and author of such well-known hymns as "Amazing Grace" and "Glorious Things of Thee Are Spoken." Newton also became an adamant opponent of the slave trade. In 1788 he published *Thoughts Upon the African Slave Trade,* a stinging attack upon slavery that makes scenes from Alex Haley's *Roots* seem mild by comparison. Like Haley, Newton contrasted the peaceful and relatively law-abiding life of the African with the cruelty and barbarity perpetrated in the slave trade.

What is instructive about Newton's experience is how he came to view slavery as a sin. The surprising twist in Newton's experience is that he became a slave captain *after,* not before, his conversion. A deserter from the Royal Navy in 1743, Newton had become a virtual slave himself on the Windward Coast of Africa before he was rescued in 1748. On the trip back to England, this lost seaman was converted and for the next six years pursued two matters intently: a diligent study of the Scriptures and a profitable term as a captain of a slave ship. Newton penned the beloved hymn "How Sweet the Name of Jesus Sounds in a Believer's Ear" during the leisure time afforded by a voyage from Africa to the West Indies. But how could this devout Christian revel in the comfort of the gospel—"it soothes his sorrows, heals his wounds and wipes away his tear"—while black men and women, chained in squalor below, were cursing the day they were born!

The answer to this question is complex in the extreme. But Newton does assist us by reflecting on this ethical dilemma in his 1788 denunciation of slavery. "I am bound in conscience," he admitted, "to take shame to myself by public confession, which however sincere, came too late to prevent or repair the misery and mischief to which I have, formerly, been accessory."[17] Although Newton had considered his role disagreeable, it never crossed his mind that his responsibility might extend beyond merely being a "Christian" slave captain:

> But I never had a scruple upon this head at the time; nor was such a thought once suggested to me by any friend. What I did I did ignorantly, considering it as the line of life which Divine Providence had allotted me, and having no concern, in point of conscience, but to treat slaves, while under my care, with as much humanity as a regard to my own safety would admit.[18]

Newton's conviction about the evils of slavery came years later, when, as the spiritual advisor of William Wilberforce, he fell under conviction about his previous behavior. By 1788 Newton considered it "criminal" to remain silent and not inveigh with evangelical fervor against the entire slave system. This conviction did not arise automatically upon his conversion, but from ethical deliberations that Wilberforce set in motion. Just as Christians, under the tutelage of Scripture, must wrestle with teachings about the Atonement, sanctification, the Holy Spirit, evangelism, and the church, so they must give serious attention to biblical ethics, not assuming that the mind of Christ in this matter will necessarily blossom spontaneously in their hearts.

Success and Social Action

Another limitation of evangelical social responsibility is evident in viewing what happens when revival does break out. Evangelistic success, more often than not, has diluted ethical concern and erased many stern convictions that might not sit well with the world that is to be evangelized. Finney and the abolitionists were able to keep evangelism and controversial ethical positions as parts of the same gospel message, but many others have not been so successful.

The experience of the Baptists and Methodists in the two generations after the American Revolution is sobering. Both of these communions at the time of the Revolution were extremely small in numbers and influence, and both of them roundly denounced black slavery. As early as 1780 the Methodist Episcopal Church condemned slavery as "contrary to the laws of God, man, and nature . . . contrary to the dictates of conscience and pure religion."[19] The Baptists in Virginia even went out on a limb and welcomed blacks into their churches. This prophetic stance, which effectively forbade the holding of slaves among church members, was simple enough at the time of the Revolution when one could count Methodists and Baptists in the hundreds. But, like a prairie fire out of control, Methodist and Baptist evangelistic zeal swept the advancing frontier. By 1844 the Methodists had become the most numerous religious body in America with over a million members, four thousand itinerant preachers, and over seven thousand local pastors. Their closest competitor, the Baptists, had grown at least tenfold in the same period. With this kind of explosive growth, these Evangelicals were, in the words of Bernard Weisberger, slaying "their thousands while the other denominations counted their hundreds." This was far and away the most successful evangelistic campaign on American soil.

Yet this success did something to the original intention of forbidding slavery absolutely. Methodists and Baptists in the South came, in fact, to defend it quite openly. By 1845, twenty-five thousand Methodist laymen held slaves, as did some twelve hundred clergymen. Methodist Bishop James O. Andrew of Georgia and the Baptist leader Richard Furman of South Carolina defended in biblical terms the slave system that other Southerners justified economically. During the 1840s, Methodists and Baptists in the South withdrew to form their own denominations and thus prevent Northern meddling in the Southern way of life. In the North these communions were not so obviously swayed by their culture; but, despite the antislavery convictions of a few, most rank and file members were content to lay aside such disruptive issues. Should not revivalism go forward without such pesky stumbling blocks? In 1841 the Wesleyan Methodist Church was founded by a few stalwarts who resisted this "lukewarmness" and who sought to continue the tradition of preaching in righteous anger against human slavery.

Thus, we see that in the South and on the western frontier evangelistic success blunted rather than sharpened the witness of Evangelicals in society. By enlarging their number, these Evangelicals did not transform society but came instead to endorse existing social arrangements. It had been far easier to speak out against unchristian features of American life before Methodists and Baptists themselves became pillars in society.

The "Mote and Beam" Complex

A third limitation of Evangelicals in American society is a problem by no means unique to these shores. It is the tendency for groups as well as individuals to take such offense at the mote in their brother's eye that they forget the beam in their own. As Reinhold Niebuhr put it, "Reformers have the habit of confessing the sins of a group from which they imagine themselves emancipated." It is hardly accidental, for instance, that movements to abolish slavery in America took deep hold in areas where slavery was marginal. Now there were notable exceptions, like the Grimké sisters from South Carolina, or James G. Birney from Kentucky; but they were just that—exceptions. More broadly speaking, what did it cost New England Congregationalists or Pennsylvania Quakers in the Revolutionary era to mount an attack against slavery in areas where slaves numbered fewer than 5 percent of the population? Or what did Christians in Boston, New York, or Detroit have to lose when, half a century later, they offered a hearty amen to Harriet

Beecher Stowe's runaway best seller *Uncle Tom's Cabin*? At home they had nothing to attack but complacency about reform, hardly a deadly sin. Their righteous indignation was reserved for the moral callousness of their cousins below the Mason-Dixon line.

While flaying away at the sin of slavery, however, northern reformers found it much more difficult to speak about other social problems that could have drawn their fire—the relentless displacement of the American Indian and the angry persecutions of immigrants and religious minorities, for instance. Slavery, no doubt, was the most serious moral dilemma for Americans to face in the nineteenth century, but the fact that northern reformers centered their attention upon it also reflects that it was an external problem. Their sense of moral outrage all too easily justified and confirmed their own way of life.

The same New England ministers who championed the liberation of the slaves often watched the destruction of Indian civilization without shedding a tear, often rationalizing the relentless acquisition of Indian lands as a providential design: "I cannot but look back and adore the dealings of Heaven," explained the Reverend Amos Adams in 1769, "in gradually cutting off the barbarous nations, to make room for us. The iniquity of the Canaanites was full, and for their idolatry and wickedness, God caused the land to spue out its inhabitants. . . . I am ready to think that, not only the extension of our settlements, but all our attempts to civilize these barbarians, will be found hereafter, as they always have been, to hasten their utter destruction. This is the Lord's doings and it is marvellous in our eyes."[20] In pointing out this kind of ambiguity, the intent is not to sit in judgment upon reformers of an earlier day. They could not transcend flesh and blood, after all, and their blindspots do not invalidate the authentic message of their reform. Their difficulty was, and ours is, to ferret out those social sins of which we ourselves, and not just our neighbors, are guilty. It continues to be easier to tell others about charity than to begin to practice it at home.

A DECOROUS WORLDLINESS

During the second half of the nineteenth century, the spirit of reform that had characterized ante-bellum Evangelicals ground almost to a halt. The longstanding assumption that society should be constrained and reformed in accordance with the gospel gave way in general to a defense of the status quo. After the Civil War a decorous worldliness seemed to fall upon Protestantism at large as Christians grew much more comfortable with prevailing cultural norms. The difference in climate was as great as the difference between Charles G.

Finney and the best-known revivalist of the Gilded Age, Dwight L. Moody. Finney preached a gospel that called its converts to crush social evil wherever it might be found. In contrast, Moody said, "I look upon this world as a wrecked vessel. God has given me a lifeboat and said to me, Moody save all you can."[21] Although Moody was personally concerned about the poor and downtrodden, he had confidence that individual conversion would solve the problems of rich and poor alike. The gospel he preached asked for little more in response from wealthy supporters like Cyrus McCormick and John Wanamaker than from the urban poor of Chicago. His answer to Chicago's Haymarket Riot of 1886 was simple and direct: "Either these people are to be evangelized or the leaven of communism and infidelity will assume such enormous proportions that it will break out in a reign of terror such as this country has never known."[22]

These sentiments had great appeal for most American Protestants a century ago. Having partaken of the bounty of American life and having grown accustomed to a degree of affluence, they were upset by growing social unrest. They approved of the old Wesleyan injunction to gain and save wealth and agreed with the consolation of a Massachusetts clergyman: "Material prosperity is helping to make the national character more joyous, more unselfish, more Christ-like."[23] But the second part of the Methodist command, to love not the world and to care for the needy and oppressed, seemed far too meek and mild for this age of steam and steel.

A NEW ORDER OF SOCIAL PROBLEMS

What factors help to explain the complacency that was so infectious among Christians in the Gilded Age? Let us first deal with the massive social problems of the time and then with new ideas that found their way into evangelical thinking. In the last half of the nineteenth century America moved out of the ranks of agricultural nations and joined that of the world's major industrial powers. Textile production jumped 700 percent in fifty years; iron and steel grew tenfold. From 1860 to 1890, national wealth increased from sixteen to eighty-seven billion dollars, and half of the latter amount was held by one-third of one percent of the population. Intricately related to this explosive economy was the burgeoning city. In 1860, six million Americans were urban dwellers; by 1900 it was thirty million. During the three decades from 1860 to 1890, the population of Detroit and Kansas City jumped fourfold, Memphis and San Francisco fivefold, Cleveland sixfold, Chicago tenfold, and Los Angeles twentyfold. Much of this new growth came from massive waves of European immigration, six million between 1875 and 1890. Eighty percent of these were unskilled and about the same ratio settled in cities.

The reaction of Protestants to the mushrooming city with its hoards of immigrants, largely Roman Catholic, was too often simply flight to the suburbs. Two hundred thousand immigrants, for example, moved into lower Manhattan during the two decades after the Civil War, and seventeen Protestant churches moved to the suburbs. In Boston one ward with twenty-two thousand people could boast only one Protestant church. One of the results of this massive exodus was that Evangelicals lost any strong witness among the urban poor. As one observer noted in 1887, "Go into an ordinary church on Sunday morning and you see lawyers, physicians, merchants, and business men with their families; but the working man and his family are not there."[24] Thus began the problem that many have called the "suburban captivity of the church." This problem was compounded by the polity of American denominations, characteristically decentralized and democratic. As local churches followed their constituency out of the central cities, there was no institutional structure that could step into the gap and manifest a continued presence in an area of intense need.

In this context evangelical attitudes changed profoundly. Most importantly, evangelical pulpits generally ceased to deal seriously with social issues. Ministers no longer concentrated on relating the gospel to political and economic decisions that laymen had to make. By focusing on personal godliness as the primary, if not the only responsibility of Christian in the world, Evangelicals became imitators rather than people of vision. Sidney Mead has well summarized this point:

> But since men, if not given instruction and guidance in such matters as citizenship and conduct in business by ministers and theologians in their churches, will nevertheless be instructed and guided by some prevailing code, the effectual abdication of the Protestant churches meant the ideas and ideals of the emerging acquisitive society were generally accepted without criticism.[25]

A NEW ORDER OF SOCIAL ATTITUDES

What were those ideals that Evangelicals began to assimilate? Certainly the most important was the doctrine of rugged individualism, the belief that each person was captain of his or her own fate and should be left alone to sink or swim. In keeping with this philosophy was the assumption that the welfare of all would best be served by each one pursuing his own interest. Earlier in the nineteenth century, Evangelicals had championed this idea to an extent. But in stressing the freedom of the individual, they were also constrained by a higher commitment, to engage all powers to serve the present age. As time went by, increasingly these ideals of individualism became an end in themselves. Francis Wayland, the president of Brown University and a firm believer in the older form of Christian social involvement, denounced this trend:

> One man asserts that his religion has nothing to do with the regulation of his passions, another that it has nothing to do with business, and another that it has nothing to do with his politics. Thus while the man professes a religion which obliges him to serve God in everything, he declares that whenever obedience would interfere with his cherished vices, he will not serve God at all. The pulpit has failed to meet such sentiments at the very threshold, with its stern and uncompromising rebuke.[26]

This accommodation became even more dangerous as strands of Social Darwinism (see chapter 2) began to fortify the already intense American individualism. From this perspective individualism was not just beneficial, it was absolutely essential, the only system in tune with the governing laws of the universe. Interference in the competitive arena must not be allowed, for distributing the gains of the rich to the poor would slow down the overall development of civilization. The most blatant example of this way of thinking was the steel magnate Andrew Carnegie and his book *The Gospel of Wealth*. Carnegie crusaded for the sacredness of private property and competition. "We accept . . . great inequality of environment, the concentration of business, industrial and commercial, in the hand of a few, and the law of competition between these, as being not only beneficial, but essential for the future progress of the race."[27] From those few who rose to the top, Carnegie did demand that money be used for public purposes—but in a way that fulfilled his doctrine of rugged individualism. He never gave money directly to the poor, for that might deter them from embarking upon the road of the self-made man. Carnegie, instead, brought libraries to every kind of town in America. These could be used by young people to improve themselves.

A similar and more clearly evangelical example of this sort of accommodation is found in the career of the famous Baptist preacher Russell H. Conwell, founder of Temple University. Conwell was well known for his sermon "Acres of Diamonds," an address that catapulted him to the forefront of the lecture circuit and made him a wealthy man. Conwell's theme was crystal clear, that men had a moral responsibility to become wealthy. "It is your duty to become rich. . . ," he said, "because you can do more good with money than without it. . . . To live and let live is the principle of the gospel and the principle of every-day common sense."[28] The tragic part of Conwell's analysis is his view of poverty:

> Some men say, don't you sympathize with the poor people? Of course I do, or else I would not have been lecturing these years. I won't give in but what I sympathize with the poor, but the number of poor who are to be sympathized with is very small. To sympathize with a man whom God has punished for his sins, thus to help him when God would still continue a just punishment, is to do wrong. . . . While we should sympathize with God's poor . . . let us remember that there is not a poor person in the United States who was not made poor by his own shortcomings or by the shortcomings of someone else. It is all wrong to be poor anyhow.[29]

From this we can now see how a doctrine of rampant individualism could sever the taproot of social concern. Starting with the premise that each person is solely responsible for his or her own fate, American Christians have easily attached a moral stigma to the down-and-outs that makes them the object of disgust rather than of concern. The notion of a "worthy" poor becomes a contradiction in terms.

THE GREAT REVERSAL

Despite this bleak picture, the early twentieth century witnessed considerable evangelical social concern. A goodly number of theological conservatives—increasingly identifying themselves as fundamentalists—actually promoted a social witness among the urban poor. A. J. Gordon, founder of the Boston Missionary Training Institute, now Gordon College, and A. C. Dixon, editor of *The Fundamentals*, both were quite active with urban relief programs. A. B. Simpson founded the Christian and Missionary Alliance at the turn of the century not only to promote missions but also to serve the largely forgotten poor of the city.

What takes place, however, early in this century is a drying up of those springs that remained. The situation of A. C. Dixon (1854-1925) is typical. In 1901 he became pastor of a Boston church which administered a million dollar endowment set aside for the social service of the parish. After three years of distributing food, clothing, rent, and medicine, Dixon decided that the aid did not square with his primary goal, the winning of converts. He made the decision to "dispense with the whole business and get back to first principles." He soon began to attack the "false evangelism, which hoped to save society in bulk by means of humanitarian effort." By 1919, the newly founded Christian Fundamentalist Association, meeting in Philadelphia, heard William B. Riley call for mobilization against such modern subversions as "social service Christianity." In contrast to Puritan teaching that Christians must build moral principles into society, and to the message of reform in the days of Finney, Fundamentalists began to argue that Christian involvement in society actually denied rather than fulfilled the gospel.

This stance differed from Evangelicals even in the Gilded Age. Moody and Conwell had sustained some vision of bringing relief to the needy. For them it was largely a question of means. Preaching the gospel and emphasizing individual responsibility was the only effective instrument in transforming society. By 1920, however, many Fundamentalists felt compelled to withdraw from an evil world and abandon hope that this wrecked vessel could or should be salvaged at all. The purpose of Christianity was to save souls not society.

Why did this black and white dichotomy between personal salvation and social concern take hold? Why did the vibrant evangelical tradition relating Christian faith to society succumb to what Timothy Smith and sociologist David Moberg have called "the Great Reversal"? What was the catalyst that crystallized the individualistic heritage of the late nineteenth century into the explicit teaching that service to mankind did not really follow from the gospel?

We can begin to answer these elusive questions by understanding the extent to which orthodox Christians in these years thought that everything for which they stood was under attack. They perceived a frontal assault on their most cherished beliefs. Between the Civil War and World War I, Evangelicals had seen their position in society change from one of influence and esteem to that of an increasingly despised minority. Massive waves of immigration, largely from central and southern Europe, threatened Protestant dominance in America. American higher education, once a bastion of orthodoxy, now popularized "the new science": Darwinism, Freudian pyschology, and naturalistic explanations of religion such as William James's *Varieties of Religious Experience.* These seemed to share an identical purpose—to sever rudely the taproot of supernaturalism. All of life, man's origins, his development, even his religion, could now be explained in natural terms.

Making matters worse, the assault on Fundamentalism was as much real as it was imagined. Self-assured prophets of Modernism, having renounced the shackles of orthodoxy, attacked with a vengeance the "superstitions" from which they considered themselves delivered.

By the 1920s, an age that coined the word "debunk" in its quest to deflate accepted traditions, the popular press joined the academic critique of America's evangelical heritage. Columnists such as the influential H. L. Mencken associated Fundamentalism with bigotry, ignorance, and intolerance. What is striking about the famous Scopes trial of 1925, which dramatized the conflict between Fundamentalism and Modernism, was the extent to which William Jennings Bryan was maligned, jeered, and cast in the role of fanatic and crank. The *New York Times* strategically misquoted Bryan on the first day of the trial and referred to him in editorials as "prodigiously ignorant" and a man with a "poorly furnished brainroom."

The popular image of the Fundamentalist as an intolerant bigot was hard enough for orthodox Christians to swallow. But they felt an even more acute sense of loss as they watched Modernists in theology dismantle orthodoxy from within. One after another the major Protestant seminaries—Congregational, Methodist, Baptist, Presbyterian, Disciples, Episcopal—began to tolerate, if not champion, religious liberalism: an optimistic view of man, the higher criticism of the Bible, questioning the exclusive claims of Christianity, and a concern for the humanity of Christ and the need for rapprochement between theology and evolutionary theory. Orthodox Christians were dumbstruck. Under the banner of Christianity the gospel was being snuffed out: "A God without wrath brought man without sin into a kingdom without judgment through the ministration of Christ without a cross."[30]

Uncomfortable with traditional dogma, Liberals increasingly made ethical imperatives the heart of their program. A strong emphasis on ethical instruction accorded with their liberal view of man and led them to identify the social gospel with their modernist theology. The Social Gospel movement had its origins in the 1880s when it functioned as a small vanguard calling the church to consider the problem of evangelical conviction. The original movement included persons of evangelical conviction, but in the twentieth century, as historian Robert Linder has suggested, "The social gospel was detached from its evangelical roots by theological liberals looking for a *raison d' être* as they watched their young men leave the ministry and their constituency drift away because of the theological sterility of their position."[31]

In this context, we can begin to understand why Fundamentalism became caught in a pattern of reaction against modern scholarship, against humanistic concepts of religion, and against the social gospel. The controversy between orthodoxy and liberalism, which Sydney

Ahlstrom calls "the most fundamental controversy to wrack the churches since the time of the Reformation," fostered a "siege mentality" among Fundamentalists, a brittle defensiveness that often spent more time reacting to evil than proclaiming the good news of the gospel. In the trauma of the times, many Fundamentalists too readily accepted the way the Liberals defined issues and wound up promoting whatever would oppose their theological enemies. In stark contrast to the social appeal and humanistic orientation of Liberalism, therefore, Fundamentalists called for a gospel of individual piety that besought men and women to separate from this evil world until Christ returns. The mention of concern for the poor raised for many a terrible specter—"the poison of the social gospelers."

STIRRINGS AND COMPLACENCY

The most powerful legacy of the Great Reversal has been the characteristically complacent attitude of Evangelicals toward the unhealed social wounds of their country. Seeing no reason to meddle with the status quo, most Evangelicals have found it necessary to extend the gospel to include political and social issues only when danger from the left appeared in the form of communism abroad or socialism at home. Otherwise, Evangelicals have generally celebrated the traditional virtues of America—staunch individualism, self-reliance, and patriotism—and challenged their countrymen to return to the halcyon days when Christian belief made this nation great. The striking problems of race relations, urban and rural poverty, unequal educational opportunity, migrant workers, and world hunger have not been decisively addressed by churches and institutions that are theologically conservative. These too often have been fortresses for the kind of rugged individualism that is either oblivious or immune to social compassion.

This is not to say that Evangelicals have been remiss in acts of personal kindness or in generosity, expressed particularly in generous giving to world missions and evangelism at home. There they shine—even as the blindspot for community and national problems remains.

In recent years, however, a small but articulate vanguard within the evangelical community has called for a reconsideration of these matters. Drawing upon earlier critiques of evangelical apathy made by Carl Henry *(The Uneasy Conscience of Modern Fundamentalism*, 1947) and Edward J. Carnell *(The Case for Orthodox Theology*, 1959), this new movement came into its own in the 1960s as younger Evangelicals began to rethink the responsibility of Christians in society. Journals began to spring up: *Freedom Now*—later called *The Other Side, The*

Post-American—later renamed *Sojourners*, *Vanguard*, and *Radix*. All of these called for a fresh biblical lifestyle that would not retreat from ugly social issues. An unexpected difficulty encountered by the editors of these journals is that their own countercultural positions can becloud their Christianity in much the same way that the cultural commitments of more conservative Christians influence theirs. Thus, where traditional Evangelicals sometimes dispense with biblically commanded good works in their focus on individual faith, these more socially alert believers run the opposite risk of overstressing good works at the expense of justifying faith.

Books such as Richard Pierard's *The Unequal Yoke: Orthodox Christianity and Political Conservatism* (1970), David Moberg's *The Great Reversal: Evangelism Versus Social Concern* (1972), Donald Dayton's *Discovering an Evangelical Heritage* (1976), and Ronald Sider's *Rich Christians in an Age of Hunger* (1977) proclaimed this new perspective that calls the orthodox to dust off their heritage of active social concern. A major step in this reassessment came in 1973, when the Thanksgiving Workshop on Evangelical Social Concern in Chicago issued a major declaration. This statement reaffirmed the evangelical faith of the signers, confessed past sin, and proclaimed: "So we call our fellow evangelical Christians to demonstrate repentance in a Christian discipleship that confronts the social and political injustice of our nation."[32] Prophetic voices do abound, then, calling Evangelicals to rethink their biblical ethics. But have these calls and this rethinking been translated into anything more than just talk?

While it would be rash to suggest that the slumbering giant of America's forty-odd million Evangelicals has awakened to social responsibility, it is safe to speak of a committed remnant—vibrant and growing that seeks to apply the balm of the gospel to society. In a number of places Evangelicals have actually remigrated to the cities in order to wrestle with the problems of crime, poverty, and family disintegration. At Grace and Peace Fellowship in St. Louis, the Church of the City in Philadelphia, and LaSalle Street Church in Chicago, to name a few, the so-called suburban captivity of the church has been strikingly reversed. Evangelical seminaries such as Gordon, Eastern Baptist, Calvin, Covenant, and Fuller have revised their curriculums to include training in urban ministry. American Evangelicals in the next decades will increasingly have to come to grips with these brothers and sisters who are calling for those who are "born again" to replace a life style of success with one of compassion and service.

One of the most resourceful and effective evangelical movements in society in recent years has been the Voice of Calvary in Mendenhall, Mississippi. For the last fifteen years, John Perkins and his associates have attempted to build a multiracial Christian community that would help move the poor of Mississippi out of their economic paralysis. No detached crusader, Perkins himself grew up as a black in rural poverty in Mississippi. After his older brother was gunned down by a marshall for standing in a line at a theater "closed" to blacks, Perkins left for California vowing never to return. On the West coast he worked his way up to a very responsible job that afforded a comfortable living. But during this time John Perkins became a disciple of Jesus Christ and felt compelled to return to Mississippi to minister in the name of his Lord.

In Mississippi John and Vera Perkins realized early that their evangelistic work among children and their Bible studies in homes were only a partial answer to the chronic problems of the rural poor. Confronted with the desperate "felt" needs of the people that they worked with—illiteracy, inadequate health care, wretched housing and diet—the Perkins began to struggle with human development in a comprehensive way. Over the years the Voice of Calvary has used the cooperative principle to help the poor move out of a hopeless economic trap. In addition to founding a Bible institute, participants have built apartments, formed buying clubs for materials such as fertilizer, set up a cooperative store, health-care center, and a credit union.

The Perkins have not always been appreciated by those who wield power in Mississippi. In February 1971 Perkins and several associates were surrounded by twelve highway patrolmen and beaten and tortured for most of a night. At other times death threats, Klan intimidation, and general ostracism have been their lot. But in the face of opposition, the Voice of Calvary has continued to expand its ministry. In Jackson, the Center for Continuous Christian Community, the Jackson Bible Institute, and Peoples' Development, Inc. have been established to promote other indigenous movements aimed at community development on a biblical model.

Most of America's Evangelicals live a long way from Mendenhall, Mississippi, probably a greater distance figuratively than by the map. For most of us being born again means peace with God, strength to cope with uncertainty, hope for heaven, and the conviction that nothing can be taken from us that will not be replaced with greater reward. But we are not very often cut to the quick by the ethical demands of God's Word. It is much too easy to drink deeply of spiritual ideas that comfort us and only sip warily at truths that taste bitter.

ROADBLOCKS TO EVANGELICAL SOCIAL CONCERN

In conclusion, let us mention five continuing problems that hinder the evangelical church from serving as light to the world and salt in the earth. In the first place, it is far too easy in our society to structure one's life so that everything foul and discomforting is safely hidden from view. Too many Evangelicals, having achieved the comfort and success of the American dream, make sure that they remain "unspotted" by anything in the world, particularly poverty, unemployment, disease, and malnutrition. Except for disconcerting newscasts, we often live out our professional, church, and family lives only dimly aware that this planet is under a curse. We disregard human need not so much out of brazen insensitivity as out of virtual isolation. We need to heed the call to expose evil wherever it might be found and to do good to all men.

Secondly, Evangelicals are not in the habit of listening to the church for ethical instruction. The American church is prone to a message of comfort rather than commitment. This is particularly true in an evangelical context that stresses faith rather than works as the means to salvation. The forgiveness of sins through Christ must certainly be preached, but the converted person's responsibilities as a Christian in the world must be proclaimed as well. It is here that biblically based sermons on racism, materialism, and injustice need to be heard from evangelical pulpits, and Christian principles for responsible action need to be developed and discussed.

A third problem is that the continuing tradition of rugged individualism makes it difficult for men and women to perceive the effect of forces outside themselves. The person who attributes success solely to his or her own determination naturally applies the same categories to the disadvantaged and concludes that such a condition is due to that person's shortcomings. The same principle applies to racism. If we interpret society solely from the perspective of the individual, we do not readily admit social forces that can deprive men of viable opportunity. Thus in seeing that blacks, native Americans, or Mexican-Americans are collectively disadvantaged, many conclude that it must be some racial shortcoming. But this violates the Christian belief that all people share equally in the very image of God.

A fourth danger is what has been called the "miracle motif." This is the idea that if everyone were converted to Christ, social ills would disappear. We know ourselves, however, that sin remains in our lives even after conversion. Certainly when people are converted, they normally begin to work more conscientiously and to care more about their families. Evangelicals have been correct in stressing this. Evangelicals have been much weaker, however, in proposing distinctly Christian solutions to large-scale social problems. Issues such as equality of educational opportunity, the renewal of the cities, or the role of the government as social engineer have not received sustained, biblically guided thought. All too often Evangelicals leave these concerns to others by default. A stress on conversion is proper, but it should not eliminate our desire to apply biblical ethics to society's most difficult problems.

A final danger is that of the moral cliché which embodies high principles that practically everyone endorses but very few put into practice. A recent survey in California churches is a good example. Ninety-one percent of the church members polled agreed with the statement that "love thy neighbor means that we should treat all races the same." Virtually the same proportion also approved of the statement that "Negroes ought to have the same rights and opportunities as others." But on the same page of this questionnaire, nearly a third of the people said they did not want to have blacks in their church, and more than forty percent said that they would leave if several black families moved into their block. This is the kind of rhetoric which calls men to pursue the vision of a just society but never reaches down to alter day-to-day life.

Christians, of all people, must break through the haze of the moral cliché and translate high purpose and good intention into tangible effort. No less than in the days of the apostle James do we need to heed the injunction: "Be doers of the word, and not hearers only, deceiving yourselves" (1:22 RSV).

"To God Be the Glory"

Epilogue

The story of the gospel in America is really almost two stories. It is an inner history of the Holy Spirit's work in the lives of millions upon millions of people who have called the United States home. But it is also an outer history of how these Christians have lived in America—how they have helped mold their culture and how, in turn, they have been molded by it. In one sense, it is easier to describe the first history than the second. We know beyond question that God has called many Americans to himself, has transported them from the kingdom of darkness to the kingdom of his Son, has given them a new birth through the Word. We know, also beyond question, that the Holy Spirit has led these believers in their walk with God, has caused them to grow in grace, has produced his fruit in their lives. And we know that spiritual battles—defeats as well as victories—have occurred in the life of every Christian. So the story of the *gospel* in America is, in one sense, simply the old, old story of Jesus and his love, the story of the kingdom of Christ at war with the kingdom of Satan. In this respect it is much the same as the story of the gospel in Europe, Asia, Africa, or elsewhere in the Western hemisphere.

The story of the gospel *in America* needs to be described in different terms. The Evangelicals that this book has talked about have been both believers and Americans. Sometimes the two have gone together well; sometimes the life of faith and the culture of the United States have gone separate ways; sometimes being an American has stood in the way of being a Christian.

It is hard to sum up a story that includes such diverse figures as Benjamin Warfield and Barton Stone, Carl F. H. Henry and Carl F. W. Walther, Phoebe Palmer and Charles Hodge. Yet a few things do stand out. From a religious perspective, American Evangelicals have been generally orthodox, professedly biblical, and eagerly evangelistic.

Orthodoxy, "straight teaching," is often in the eye of the beholder. In general, however, American Evangelicals have preserved the biblical faith that was handed down to the early church and then renewed in the Reformation. Evangelicals, that is, have believed in man's fall, God's grace in Christ, the necessity of the new birth, and the supreme authority of Scripture. To be sure, the Calvinists of the nineteenth century thought Charles Finney's idea of salvation gave too much credit to man. Modern separatists think Billy Graham has altogether too much fellowship with deviant, so-called (they would say) Christians. From Roman Catholics and Eastern Orthodox outside Evangelicalism, and from the Lutherans and Reformed inside, criticism is raised about the evangelical slighting of baptism and the Lord's Supper. Yet in spite of these areas of controversy and many more, the defining characteristics of Evangelicalism—convictions about justification by faith, about the Bible, and about the necessity for Christian living—have not been lost. And these have provided a voice for Christian orthodoxy, spoken to be sure with competing accents, throughout United States history.

American Evangelicals have read their Bibles differently, but they have read their Bibles. Until the late 1800s, very few questions were raised about the full authority and truthfulness of Scripture. After that time, belief in the Bible became a distinguishing characteristic of Evangelicals. Heated discussions among Evangelicals in recent years about the Bible's exact character and role testify to its importance, for why else would so much energy and effort be poured into the debate unless Evangelicals believed that the Bible contained the words of life?

American Evangelicals, as their very name suggests, have also been interested in evangelism—spreading the good news that the gift of God is eternal life through Jesus Christ. Some, even within evangelical circles, would say we have evangelized too much—at the expense of personal growth in grace, church stability, and our influence in society. None would deny, however, that the line from Jonathan Edwards and George Whitefield through Dwight, Finney, Moody, and Sunday to Billy Graham has been a kind of scarlet thread in evangelical history. Parallel lines in missionary evangelism would have been a major concern of this book if only we could have made it longer. Where

Evangelicals have not been working for conversions, for revival of one sort or the other, they have regularly prayed for them.

The whole other aspect of the evangelical story is the relationship between its orthodoxy, its biblicism, and its evangelism and American society. From this perspective Evangelicals have been characteristically activistic, individualistic, and down to earth.

Just as activism has been of great benefit to the American nation, so evangelical activism has reaped a bountiful harvest. In America there have been churches to build, souls to win, reforms to support, schools to construct, journals to publish, causes to proclaim, arguments to settle—and the Evangelicals have taken to the work with a vengeance. The tangible results of all this activity cannot be gainsaid. The churches, converts, reforms, schools, journals, causes, and arguments of the American Evangelicals are a wonder in the religious world. Yet there has been a price to pay for all this activity. The virtues of contemplation, of meditation, of long-term stability, of calm and reflective study, of steady vision over the long haul have often been absent among Evangelicals. And so it is hard to pick the right image for our activity—is it Nehemiah rebuilding the walls, diligent in the work of the Lord? Or is it Martha busy with her preparations, missing the rewards that come from sitting quietly at the feet of the Savior?

Evangelical individualism also has its positive and negative sides. The American glorification of the individual has made it relatively easy for Evangelicals to stress personal piety, personal evangelism, personal reform. We, as indeed all Americans, have been less successful when it comes to institutions. As liberating as it has been for evangelical leaders to strike out on their own when infidelity or lukewarmness compromised the old institutions, there has been a price to pay here as well. And that has been an inability to deal with big problems in a big way. Our social reforms focus on individual acts and leave institutionalized evil untouched. Our preaching speaks to the individual heart but does not coordinate a Christian response to society. Our churches—as centers of fellowship and places where individuals are heartened for Christian life in the world—are strong. But our churches—as sources of Christian stability and life-directing authority—are weak. With the good of individualism comes also the bad.

Evangelicals are down to earth as well. The simple gospel message of Billy Graham, the simple ethical principles of Bill Gothard, the simple future view of Hal Lindsey are not at all new in evangelical life. Except for the Puritans, we have not gone in for thorough theology in a big way. Except for representatives of the older European churches, we have simplified the sacramental lives of our churches. Except for Jonathan Edwards and a very few others, we have not been distinguished for intellectual profundity. But we have known how to travel from place to place preaching the gospel, to send our missionaries across the seas, to take a stand against drunkenness and other sins of the flesh. While these do not take the place of more profound wrestling with what it means to be a Christian in the world, they are not to be sneered at.

The activism, individualism, and down-to-earth quality of evangelical life all point to the influence of America herself. To an amazing degree the concerns of American life and the concerns of Evangelicals have followed each other closely. Were eighteenth-century Americans concerned about order in society and liberty? So were the Evangelicals. Did Americans champion the common man in the Jacksonian age of the first half of the nineteenth century? So did the Evangelicals. Did Americans leave the cities for the suburbs in the late nineteenth century? So did the Evangelicals. This intimate connection between Christian life in America and American influence on the Christians has led to problems. Particularly when Evangelicals have regarded the United States—its government, its economy, its social practices—as the highest stage of Christian civilization, it has been time to fear that the faith in country has replaced faith in God. Again, however, the negatives do not tell the whole story, for who can neglect the liberating breathing space that the United States has given its Christians? In this country we have enjoyed the privileges of organizing ourselves, worshiping as we think best, speaking for Christ without official reprisal. We hope this book has shown that these positive contributions of America to Evangelicals have not lead to a Christian utopia. But we hope also that it has honestly recognized their value.

The Christian view of history is absolutely certain about the most important things. We know that God appeared in Christ reconciling the world to himself. We know that this same Jesus will come again in power and great glory to rule world without end. On many of the historical details in between, however, Christians see less clearly. We don't usually know, for example, if national calamities are punishments for sin or trials given by God to test the faith of believers. We don't know whether national blessings are signs of God's approval or temptations that he allows to test believers with prosperity. What we do know, in this time between the first and second comings of Christ, is that God is pleased when his name is honored, when the gospel is proclaimed, when his people are one, when works of mercy are done in his name, when we are salt in our society. We know also that God is not pleased when the name of Christ is besmirched, when Christians fall out among themselves, when the minds of believers are conformed to this world, when Christians believe in word but not in deed.

The standards that God gives for us to evaluate ourselves are not primarily concerned with national success or failure. They can be summed up in simple questions: do we love him with our whole hearts? do we obey his commandments? do we love our neighbors as ourselves? No amount of freedom, prosperity, or worldly success can help the church in America or anywhere else if these questions must be answered negatively. No amount of oppression, poverty, or worldly failure can harm the believers who answer "yes" to these questions. Evaluated in this light, the history of America's Evangelicals is marked by both success and failure. Our story in the future depends entirely on the answers our lives give to these questions. This side of the grave, we may not know exactly how the story comes out, but God our Father does—to whom with the Son and the Holy Spirit be all honor and glory in America and throughout the world both now and forever.

Notes

Chapter 1

[1]Sydney E. Ahlstrom, "Theology in America: A Historical Survey," *The Shaping of American Religion,* ed. J. W. Smith and A. L. Jamison (Princeton: Princeton U Pr, 1961), p. 265.

[2]Ibid., p. 270.

[3]Eugene E. Genovese, *Roll, Jordan, Roll: The World the Slaves Made* (New York: Random, 1972), p. 283.

Chapter 2

[1]William R. Hutchinson, ed., *American Protestant Thought: The Liberal Era* (New York: Harper & Row, 1968), p. 31.

[2]Sydney E. Ahlstrom, "Theology in America: A Historical Survey," *The Shaping of American Religion,* ed. J. W. Smith and A. L. Jamison (Princeton: Princeton U Pr 1961), p. 293.

[3]Walter Rauschenbusch, *Christianity and the Social Crisis* (1907; reprint, New York: Harper & Row, 1964), p. 349.

[4]Hutchinson, *American Protestant Thought,* pp. 91-92.

[5]Edgar Youngs Mullins, *Christianity at the Crossroads* (Philadelphia: Judson, 1924), p. 275.

[6]Walter Lippman, *A Preface to Morals* (New York: Beacon, 1929), p. 32.

[7]Sydney E. Ahlstrom, *A Religious History of the American People* (New Haven: Yale U Pr, 1972), p. 912.

[8]J. Gresham Machen, *Christianity and Liberalism* (Grand Rapids: Eerdmans, 1923), p. 53.

[9]John Roach Straton, *The Salvation of Society* (Baltimore: Fleet-McGinley, n.d.), pp. 11, 13.

[10]George M. Marsden, *The Evangelical Mind and the New School Presbyterian Experience* (New Haven: Yale U Pr, 1970), p. 179.

[11]Hunter Dupree, *Asa Gray* (Cambridge: Harvard U Pr, 1959), p. 360.

[12]Ibid., p. 365.

[13]Charles Caldwell Ryrie, *Dispensationalism Today* (Chicago: Moody, 1965), p. 46.

Chapter 3

[1]Kenneth Kantzer, "Buswell as Theologian," *Presbyterian: Covenant Seminary Review,* II (Spring-Fall, 1976), p. 69.

[2]Carl F. H. Henry, *Fifty Years of Protestant Theology* (Boston: Wilde, 1950), p. 88.

[3]Winthrop S. Hudson, *Religion in America,* 2nd ed. (New York: Scribner, 1973), p. 277.

Chapter 4

[1]Robert Preus, *The Inspiration of Scripture: A Study of the Seventeenth Century Lutheran Dogmaticians* (Edinburgh, 1957), p. 77. For the perspectives of Reformed theologians, see John Robinson, "The Doctrine of Holy Scripture in Seventeenth Century Reformed Thought" (Unpublished doctoral thesis: Faculté de Théologie Protestante, Strasbourg, 1971).

[2]John Whitgift, *The Works of John Whitgift, D. D.*, ed. J. Ayre (Cambridge: At the University Press, 1851), Tract II, p. 190.

[3]Ibid., p. 189, p. 191.

[4]See Willard's discussion of the Bible in his *Compleat Body of Divinity . . .* (Boston, 1726). See also William Ames's comments on scriptural authority and infallibility in his *Marrow of Theology,* ed. John D. Eusden (Philadelphia: United Church, 1968), chapter 34, pp. 185-189. Ames's text was used widely at Harvard College in the seventeenth century.

[5]Carlos Baker, "The Place of the Bible in American Fiction," *Theology Today,* 17 (1960), p. 57.

[6]Carl Bridenbaugh, *Myths & Realities: Societies of the Colonial South* (New York: Atheneum, 1963), p. 174.

[7]Timothy Dwight, *Theology Explained and Defended in a Series of Sermons by Timothy Dwight . . .* , ed. Seveno E. Dwight (Edinburgh, 1831), pp. xxiii-xxiv.

[8]Ibid., p. xxiv.

[9]Ibid., pp. 399-400.

[10]Elhanan Winchester, *The Universal Restoration* (London, 1788), pp. xvii-xviii.

[11]Jerry Wayne Brown, *The Rise of Biblical Criticism in America, 1800-1870: The New England Scholars* (Middletown, Conn.: Wesleyan U Pr, 1969), p. 49.

[12]George Marsden, *The Evangelical Mind and the New School Presbyterian Experience: A Case Study of Thought and Theology in Nineteenth-Century America* (New Haven: Yale U Pr, 1970), p. 144.

[13]Ibid., p. 145.

[14]Charles Briggs, *Biblical Study* (New York: Scribner, 1883), pp. 212-213.

[15]Ibid., p. viii.

[16]William Warren Sweet, *The Story of Religions in America* (New York: Harper & Row, 1930), p. 492. The Social Gospeler Washington Gladden noted in 1891 that Protestant lay people in America believed that the Bible was "free

from all error, whether of doctrine, of fact, or of precept." He wrote: "Such is the doctrine now held by the great majority of Christians. Intelligent pastors do not hold it, but the body of the laity have no other conception" (*Who Wrote the Bible? A Book for the People* [Boston & New York: Houghton, Mifflin, 1891], p. 357.

[17]Dennis Okholm, "Biblical Inspiration and Infallibility in the Writings of Archibald Alexander," *Trinity Journal,* 5 (Spring, 1976), p. 84. See also Archibald Alexander, *Evidences of the Authenticity, Inspiration and Canonical Authority of the Holy Scriptures* (Philadelphia: Presbyterian Board of Publications, 1836), p. 230.

[18]Norman Maring, "Baptists and Changing Views of the Bible, 1865-1918, Part I," *Foundations,* 1 (July, 1958), pp. 52-53. See Hovey's comments on the infallibility of the Bible's original autographs in his *Manual of Systematic Theology and Christian Ethics* (Philadelphia: American Baptist Publication Society, 1877), pp. 77-84.

[19]See Charles Briggs, *The Authority of Holy Scripture: An Inaugural Address* (New York: Scribner, 1891).

[20]L. W. Munhall, *The Highest Critics vs. The Higher Critics* (New York: Revell, 1892). p. 5.

[21]Charles Hodge, *Systematic Theology,* vol. 1 (New York: Scribner, 1871), p. 187.

[22]See A. A. Hodge's discussion of Scripture in his *Outlines of Theology: Rewritten and Enlarged* (New York: Carter, 1879).

[23]Charles Briggs, *Whither? A Theological Question for the Times* (New York: Scribner, 1889), p. 68.

[24]Alexander Carson, *The Inspiration of the Scriptures . . .* (New York: Fletcher, 1853), p. 136.

[25]Hunter Dupree, *Asa Gray* (Cambridge: Harvard U Pr, 1959), p. 377.

[26]Ibid.

[27]Hodge, *Systematic Theology,* I, pp. 184, 188.

[28]Franz Pieper, *Christian Dogmatics* (St. Louis: Concordia, 1950), I, p. 275.

[29]B. B. Warfield, *The Inspiration and Authority of the Bible,* 2nd ed. (Nutley, N.J.: Presbyterian and Reformed, 1948), pp. 210-212.

[30]Norman Maring, "Baptists and Changing Views of the Bible, 1865-1918, Part II," *Foundations,* 1 (October, 1958), p. 39.

[31]Ibid., pp. 56-57.

[32]Ibid., p. 50.

[33]Timothy Weber, "Fundamentalism and *The Fundamentals,*" (Unpublished paper, U of Chicago, 1973), pp. 12-13. Professor Weber's paper captures well the spirit behind the writing of *The Fundamentals.*

[34]Ibid., p. 21.

[35]Ibid., p. 23.

[36]On this controversy, see James E. Adams, *Preus of Missouri and the Great Lutheran Civil War* (New York: Harper & Row, 1977).

[37]Ernest Sandeen, *Toward an Historical Understanding of the Origins of Fundamentalism* (Philadelphia: Fortress, 1968), p. 14. See also Ernest Sandeen, "The Princeton Theology: One Source of Biblical Literalism in American Protestantism," *Church History,* 31 (September, 1962), p. 307-321. On the

other hand, Professor Jack Rogers places the creation of the doctrine of inerrancy in the last decades of the sixteenth century. See Jack Rogers, ed., *Biblical Authority* (Waco: Word, 1977), pp. 29-31.

[38]Charles Elliott, "Subjective Theory of Inspiration," *The Princeton Review* (July-December, 1881), p. 192. For Luther's adherence to biblical authority and inerrancy, see M. Reu, "Luther and the Scriptures," *The Springfielder* (August, 1960), pp. 9-111. For Calvin's viewpoint on the same subjects, see Kenneth Kantzer, "John Calvin's Theory of the Knowledge and the Word of God" (Unpublished doctoral thesis: Harvard University, 1950).

[39]"A New Third World," *Time* (October 18, 1976), p. 63.

Chapter 5

[1]Frank Beardsley, *A History of American Revivals* (New York: American Tract Society, 1912), p. 17.

[2]Carl Bridenbaugh, *Myths & Realities: Societies of the Colonial South* (New York: Atheneum, 1963), p. 32.

[3]Catherine Cleveland, *The Great Revival in the West 1797-1805* (Gloucester, Mass.: Smith, 1959), p. 40, note 2.

[4]James B. Finley, *Autobiography of Rev. James B. Finley . . .* , ed. W. P. Strickland (Cincinnati: Printed at the Methodist book concern for author, 1859), pp. 172-173.

[5]Winthrop Hudson, *Religion in America,* 2nd ed. (New York: Scribner, 1973), p. 154.

[6]Jonathan Edwards, *A Faithful Narrative of the Surprising Work of God* (New York: American Tract Society, 18—), p. ix.

[7]Charles Finney, *Lectures on Revival* (Virginia Beach, 1978 [1835]), p. 27.

[8]Beardsley, *History of American Revivals,* p. 227.

[9]G. W. Hervey, *Manual of Revivals . . .* (New York: Funk & Wagnalls, 1884), p. xi.

[10]Ibid., p. xiv.

[11]George C. Bedell et al., *Religion in America* (New York: Macmillan, 1975), p. 171.

[12]James Johnson, "Charles G. Finney and a Theology of Revivalism," *Church History,* 38 (September, 1969), p. 357. On Moody's theology of revival, see James F. Findlay, Jr., *Dwight L. Moody: American Evangelist 1837-1899* (Chicago: U of Chicago Pr, 1969), pp. 227-261; Stanley Gundry, *Love Them In: The Proclamation Theology of D. L. Moody* (Chicago: Moody, 1976).

[13]R. A. Torrey, *How to Promote and Conduct a Successful Revival With Suggestive Outlines* (Chicago, New York: Revell, 1901), p. 3.

[14]Ibid., pp. 15-16.

[15]Vinson Synan, *The Holiness-Pentecostal Movement in the United States* (Grand Rapids: Eerdmans, 1971), pp. 95-96

[16]William T. Ellis, *"Billy" Sunday: The Man and His Message* (Philadelphia: Winston, 1917), p. 291.

[17]Ibid., p. 292.

[18]William McLoughlin, Jr., *Billy Graham: Revivalist in a Secular Age* (New York: Ronald, 1960), pp. 3-4.

[19]John Blum et al., *The National Experience: A History of the United States,* 2nd ed. (New York: HarBraceJ, 1968), p. 836.

[20]John R. Rice, *We Can Have Revival Now* (Wheaton, Ill.: Tyndale, 1950), p. 10.

Chapter 6

[1]John Winthrop, "A Modell of Christian Charity," in Perry Miller and Thomas J. Johnson, eds., *The Puritans* (New York: Harper & Row, 1938), pp. 195-199.

[2]Stephen Foster, *Their Solitary Way: The Puritan Social Ethic in the First Century of Settlement in New England* (New Haven: Yale U Pr, 1971). p. 100.

[3]Ibid., p. 15.

[4]Ibid., p. 100.

[5]Winthrop, "Modell of Christian Charity," p. 195.

[6]Foster, *Their Solitary Way,* pp. 155-172.

[7]Mark A. Noll, "Believer-Priests in the Church: Luther's View," *Christianity Today,* XVIII, no. 2 (October 26, 1973), pp. 4-7, quotation on p. 4.

[8]John Calvin, *Institutes of the Christian Religion,* vol. 2, ed. John T. McNeill (Philadelphia: Westminster, 1960), p. 1016.

[9]Ibid., p. 1019.

[10]Alexis de Tocqueville, *Democracy in America* I (New York: Random, 1945), p. 51.

[11]Charles G. Finney, *Memoirs* (New York: Revell, 1876), pp. 42, 45-46, 54.

[12]Sidney E. Mead, "The Rise of the Evangelical Conception of the Ministry," in H. Richard Niebuhr and Daniel D. Williams, eds., *The Ministry in Historical Perspective* (New York: Harper & Row, 1956), p. 223.

[13]John Williamson Nevin, "The Sect System," in James Hastings Nichols, *The Mercersburg Theology* (New York: Oxford U Pr, 1966), pp. 104-105.

[14]Ralph E. Morrow, "The Great Revival, the West and the Crisis of the Church," in John F. McDermott, ed., *The Frontier Re-examined* (Urbana, Ill: U of Illinois Pr, 1967), p. 73.

[15]Mead, "Evangelical Conception of Ministry," p. 218.

[16]Sidney E. Mead, *The Lively Experiment: The Shaping of Christianity in America* (New York: Harper & Row, 1963), pp. 114-115.

[17]Sidney E. Mead, "The Nation With the Soul of a Church," *Church History* XXXVI (1967), pp. 262-283.

[18]Ibid., p. 262.

[19]Nathan O. Hatch, *The Sacred Cause of Liberty: Republican Thought and the Millennium in Revolutionary New England* (New Haven: Yale U Pr, 1977), pp. 170-175).

[20]Will Herberg, *Protestant-Catholic-Jew: An Essay in American Religious Sociology* (New York: Doubleday, Anchor Books, 1956), pp. 1-33.

Chapter 7

[1]Edmund S. Morgan, *The Puritan Dilemma: The Story of John Winthrop* (Boston: Little, 1958), p. 117.

[2]Perry Miller, *Orthodoxy in Massachusetts, 1630-1650* (New York: Harper & Row, Torch, 1970), pp. 157-158.

[3]Edwin Scott Gaustad, *The Great Awakening in New England* (Chicago: Quadrangle, 1968), p. 90.

[4]George P. Hutchinson, *The History Behind the Reformed Presbyterian Church Evangelical Synod* (Cherry Hill, N.J.: Mack, 1974), p. 213.

[5]George F. Dollar, *A History of Fundamentalism in America* (Greenville, S.C.: Bob Jones U Pr, 1973), p. 163.

[6]Bruce L. Shelley, *A History of Conservative Baptists* (Wheaton: Conservative Baptist Pr, 1971), pp. 32-33.

[7]Paul G. Settle, "God's Instrument for Renewal," *The Presbyterian Journal*, XXXIV (May 14, 1975), p. 7.

[8]"Preus: God Has Helped Us," *Lutheran Witness: Reporter Edition*, XCIV (July 20, 1975), p. 1.

[9]Dollar, *History of Fundamentalism*, p. 205.

Chapter 8

[1]Martin E. Marty, *Righteous Empire: The Protestant Experience in America* (New York: Dial, 1970), on first printed page preceding Contents page.

[2]"Celebration of Faith," *Decision*, XVII, no. 5 (May, 1976), p. 16.

[3]Max Lerner, *America as a Civilization*, vol. 2 (New York: Simon & Schuster, Clarion, 1957), p. 715.

[4]Nathan O. Hatch, *The Sacred Cause of Liberty: Republican Thought and the Millennium in Revolutionary New England* (New Haven: Yale U Pr, 1977), p. 174.

[5]Thomas Foxcroft, *Observations Historical and Practical . . .* (Boston: Printed by S. Kneeland and T. Green for S. Gerrish, 1730), p. 23.

[6]Alan Heimert, *Religion and the American Mind From the Great Awakening to the Revolution* (Cambridge, Mass.: Harvard U Pr, 1966), p. 359.

[7]Hatch, *Sacred Cause of Liberty*, pp. 21-22.

[8]Ibid., p. 149.

[9]Ibid., p. 151.

[10]Ibid., p. 139.

[11]Marty, *Righteous Empire*, p. 57.

[12]Alexis de Tocqueville, *Democracy in America*, vol. 1 (New York: Random, 1945), p. 303.

[13]Marty, *Righteous Empire*, p. 46.

[14]Hatch, *Sacred Cause of Liberty*, pp. 172-173.

[15]Sidney E. Mead, *The Lively Experiment: The Shaping of Christianity in America* (New York: Harper & Row, 1963), pp. 151-152.

[16]Perry Miller, *The Life of the Mind in America From the Revolution to the Civil War* (New York: HarBraceJ, 1965), pp. 49-58.

[17]Sidney E. Mead, "The Nation With the Soul of a Church," *Church History*, XXXVI (1967), pp. 279-283.

Chapter 9

[1]Warner J. Wellman, *The Wesleyan Movement in the Industrial Revolution* (New York: Russell, 1967), p. 208.

[2]Ibid., p. 211.

[3]Charles Y. Glock and Rodney Stark, *Religion and Society in Tension* (Chicago: Rand, McNally, 1965), P. 87.

[4]Winthrop S. Hudson, "Puritanism and the Spirit of Capitalism," *Church History*, XVIII (1949), pp. 3-17.

[5]Ibid., p. 14.
[6]Ibid., p. 10.
[7]Ibid., p. 10.
[8]Ibid., pp. 10-11.
[9]Ibid., p. 11.
[10]Timothy L. Smith, *Revivalism and Social Reform: American Protestantism on the Eve of the Civil War* (New York: Harper & Row, Torch, 1965), pp. 148-171.
[11]Ibid., p. 176.
[12]Ibid., p. 154.
[13]Ibid., pp. 34-44.
[14]Ibid., p. 175.
[15]Martin E. Marty, *Righteous Empire: The Protestant Experience in America* (New York: Dial, 1970), p. 64.
[16]Stephen J. Stein, "George Whitefield on Slavery: Some New Evidence," *Church History,* XLII (1973), pp. 243-256, quotation on p. 245.
[17]John Newton, "Thoughts Upon the African Slave Trade," in *The Posthumous Works of the Rev. John Newton,* vol. 2 (Philadelphia: Woodward, 1809), p. 228.
[18]Ibid., p. 229.
[19]Donald G. Mathews, *Religion in the Old South* (Chicago: U of Chicago Pr, 1977), p. 68.
[20]Amos Adams, *A Concise, Historical View . . .* (Boston: Kneeland & Adams, 1769).
[21]Marty, *Righteous Empire,* p. 184.
[22]Ibid., p. 184.
[23]Ibid., p. 150.
[24]Sidney E. Mead, *The Lively Experiment: The Shaping of Christianity in America* (New York: Harper & Row, 1963), pp. 134-155.
[25]Ibid., p. 138.
[26]Ibid., p. 137.
[27]Andrew Carnegie, *The Gospel of Wealth and Other Timely Essays,* ed. Edward C. Kirkland (Cambridge, Mass.: Harvard U Pr, Belknap, 1962), pp. 16-17.
[28]Russell H. Conwell, *Acres of Diamonds* (1915; reprint ed., New York: Revell, 1960), pp. 18, 21, 27.
[29]Ibid., p. 21.
[30]Robert D. Linder, "The Resurgence of Evangelical Social Concern (1925-75)," in David F. Wells and John D. Woodbridge, *The Evangelicals: What They Believe, Who They Are, Where They Are Changing* (Nashville: Abingdon, 1975), pp. 189-210.
[31]Ibid., p. 198.
[32]Ibid., p. 205.

Bibliography

This list contains two types of works: those that the authors drew on directly in writing the various chapters and those that contain more thorough coverage of the various subjects. No one should consider this a full bibliography of American Evangelicalism, for that would require a book even larger than this one. Although some books were used in the preparation of more than one chapter, we have listed each one only once in the interest of saving space.

General

Ahlstrom, Sydney E. *A Religious History of the American People.* New Haven: Yale U Pr, 1972.

Bloesch, Donald G. *The Evangelical Renaissance.* Grand Rapids: Eerdmans, 1973.

Burr, Nelson R. *Religion in American Life.* Goldentree Bibliographies in American History. Arlington Heights, Ill.: AHM Pub., 1971.

Cairns, Earle E. *Christianity in the United States.* Chicago: Moody, 1964.

Dayton, Donald. *Discovering an Evangelical Heritage.* New York: Harper & Row, 1976.

Dollar, George F. *A History of Fundamentalism in America.* Greenville, S.C.: Bob Jones U Pr, 1973.

Frazier, Edward Franklin, and Lincoln, C. Eric. *The Negro Church in America,* and *The Black Church Since Frazier.* New York: Schocken, 1974.

Handy, Robert T. *A History of the Churches in the United States and Canada.* New York: Oxford U Pr, 1976.

Hudson, Winthrop S. *Religion in America,* 2nd ed. New York: Scribner, 1973.

Kelley, Dean M. *Why Conservative Churches Are Growing.* New York: Harper & Row, 1972.

Marty, Martin E. *Righteous Empire: The Protestant Experience in America.* New York: Dial, 1970.

Mead, Sidney E. *The Lively Experiment: The Shaping of Christianity in America.* New York: Harper & Row, 1963.

Meyer, F. E. *The Religious Bodies of America,* 4th ed. St. Louis: Concordia, 1961.

Mouw, Richard J. "New Alignments: Hartford and the Future of Evangelicalism," *Against the World for the World,* ed. P. L. Berger and R. J. Neuhaus. New York: Seabury, 1976.

Quebedeaux, Richard. *The Young Evangelicals.* New York: Harper & Row, 1974.

Ramm, Bernard L. *The Evangelical Heritage.* Waco: Word Bks, 1973.

Smith, Hilrie Shelton et al. *American Christianity: An Historical Interpretation With Representative Documents,* 2 vols. New York: Scribner, 1960, 1962.

Sweet, William Warren. *The Story of Religion in America,* 2nd ed. New York: Harper & Row, 1950.

Synan, Vinson. *The Holiness—Pentecostal Movement in the United States.* Grand Rapids: Eerdmans, 1971.

Wells, David F., and Woodbridge, John D., eds. *The Evangelicals: What They Believe, Who They Are, Where They Are Changing.* Nashville: Abingdon, 1975.

Chapters 1-3—Theology

Ahlstrom, Sydney E. "The Scottish Philosophy and American Theology," *Church History,* XXIV (September 1955), pp. 257-272.

———. "Theology in America: A Historical Survey," *The Shaping of American Religion,* ed. James Ward Smith and A. Leland Jamison. Princeton: Princeton U Pr, 1961.

———, ed. *Theology in America: The Major Protestant Voices From Puritanism to Neo-Orthodoxy.* Indianapolis: Bobbs-Merrill, 1967.

Berk, Stephen E. *Calvinism Versus Democracy: Timothy Dwight and the Origins of American Evangelical Orthodoxy.* Hamden, Conn.: Archon, 1974.

Carter, Paul A. *The Spiritual Crisis of the Gilded Age.* DeKalb, Ill.: Northern Illinois U Pr, 1971.

Chiles, Robert E. *Theological Transition in American Methodism: 1790-1935.* Nashville: Abingdon, 1965.

Cross, Robert D., ed. *The Church and the City.* Indianapolis: Bobbs-Merrill, 1967.

Dupree, Hunter, *Asa Gray.* Cambridge: Harvard U Pr, 1959.

Edwards, Jonathan. *Selections,* ed. Clarence H. Faust and Thomas H. Johnson. New York: Hill & Wang, 1962.

Foster, Frank H. *A Genetic History of the New England Theology.* Chicago: U of Chicago Pr, 1907.

The Fundamentals: A Testimony to the Truth, 4 vols. Los Angeles: Bible Institute of Los Angeles, 1917.

Genovese, Eugene E. *Roll, Jordan, Roll: The World the Slaves Made.* New York: Random, 1972.

Haroutunian, Joseph. *Piety Versus Moralism: The Passing of the New England Theology.* New York: Harper & Row, 1932.

Heimert, Alan, and Miller, Perry, eds. *The Great Awakening.* Indianapolis: Bobbs-Merrill, 1967.

Hollenweger, W. J. *The Pentecostals,* trans. R. A. Wilson. Minneapolis: Augsburg, 1972.

Holmes, Arthur F. *Christian Philosophy in the Twentieth Century.* Nutley, N.J.: Craig, 1969.

Hopkins, C. Howard. *The Rise of the Social Gospel in American Protestantism: 1865-1915.* New Haven: Yale U Pr, 1940.

Hutchinson, William R., ed. *American Protestant Thought: The Liberal Era.* New York: Harper & Row, Torch, 1968.

Kantzer, Kenneth S. "Buswell as Theologian," *Presbyterian: Covenant Seminary Review,* II (Spring-Fall 1976), pp. 67-94.

McLoughlin, William G. *The American Evangelicals, 1800-1900: An Anthology.* New York: Harper & Row, 1968.

Marsden, George M. "From Fundamentalism to Evangelicalism: A Historical Analysis," *The Evangelicals,* ed. David F. Wells and John D. Woodbridge. Nashville: Abingdon, 1975.

May, Henry F. *The Enlightenment in America.* New York: Oxford U Pr, 1976.

Meyer, Donald H. *The Instructed Conscience: The Shaping of the American National Ethic.* Philadelphia: U of Pa Pr, 1972.

Middlekauf, Robert. *The Mathers: Three Generations of Puritan Intellectuals 1596-1728.* New York: Oxford U Pr, 1971.

Miller, Perry. *The New England Mind,* 2 vols. Boston: Beacon, 1961 (1939, 1953).

Russett, Cynthia Eagle. *Darwin in America: The Intellectual Response 1865-1912.* San Francisco: W H Freeman, 1976.

Ryrie, C. C. *Dispensationalism Today.* Chicago: Moody, 1965.

Schlesinger, Arthur M., Jr. *A Critical Period in American Religion 1875-1900.* Philadelphia: Fortress, 1967.

Simonson, Harold. *Jonathan Edwards: Theologian of the Heart.* Grand Rapids: Eerdmans, 1974.

Simpson, Alan. *Puritanism in Old and New England.* Chicago: U of Chicago Pr, 1955.

Smith, James Ward. "Religion and Science in American Philosophy," in *The Shaping of American Religion,* ed. James Ward Smith and A. Leland Jamison. Princeton: Princeton U Pr, 1961.

Smith, Timothy L. "Slavery and Theology: The Emergence of Black Christian Consciousness in Nineteenth-Century America," *Church History,* XLVI (December 1972), pp. 497-512.

Wells, David F. "The Stout and Persistent 'Theology' of Charles Hodge," *Christianity Today* (August 30, 1974), pp. 10-12, 15.

Chapter 4—The Bible

Baker, Carlos. "The Place of the Bible in American Fiction," *Theology Today,* 17 (1960), pp. 53-76.

Brown, Ira V. "The Higher Criticism Comes to America, 1880-1900," *Journal of the Presbyterian Historical Society,* 38 (December 1960), pp. 193-211.

Brown, Jerry Wayne. *The Rise of Biblical Criticism in America, 1800-1870.* Middletown, Conn.: Wesleyan U Pr, 1969.

Frei, Hans. *The Eclipse of Biblical Narrative: A Study in Eighteenth and Nineteenth Century Hermeneutics.* New Haven: Yale U Pr, 1974.

Lindsell, Harold. *The Battle for the Bible.* Grand Rapids: Zondervan, 1976.

Maring, Norman H. "Baptists and Changing Views of the Bible 1865-1918," *Foundations,* 1 (July 1958), pp. 52-75; 1 (October 1958), pp. 30-61.

Preus, Robert. *The Inspiration of Scripture. A Study of the Theology of the Seventeenth Century Lutheran Dogmaticians.* Edinburgh: Oliver and Boyd, 1955.

Sandeen, Ernest R. *The Roots of Fundamentalism: British and American Millenarianism 1800-1930.* Chicago: U of Chicago Pr, 1970.

_____. *The Cambridge History of the Bible.* Cambridge: Cambridge U Pr, 1963-1970.

Walvoord, John F. *Inspiration and Interpretation.* Grand Rapids: Eerdmans, 1957.

Weber, Timothy, "Fundamentalism and *The Fundamentals.*" Unpublished paper, U of Chicago, 1973.

Chapter 5—Revival

Cleveland, Catherine C. *The Great Revival in the West, 1797-1805.* Gloucester, Mass.: Peter Smith, 1959.

Findlay, James F. *Dwight L. Moody: American Evangelist 1837-1899.* Chicago: U of Chicago Pr, 1969.

Finney, Charles G. *Memoirs of Rev. Charles G. Finney Written by Himself.* New York: Revell, 1903.

Gaustad, Edwin Scott. *The Great Awakening in New England.* Chicago: Quadrangle, 1968.

Gundry, Stanley N. *Love Them In — The Proclamation Theology of D. L. Moody.* Chicago: Moody, 1976.

McLoughlin, William G. *Modern Revivalism: Charles Grandison Finney to Billy Graham.* New York: Ronald, 1959.

Miller, Perry. *Jonathan Edwards.* Toronto: William Sloane Associates, 1949.

Orr, J. Edwin. *Campus Aflame: Dynamic of Student Religious Revolution.* Glendale, Calif.: Regal, 1971.

Smith, Timothy L. *Revivalism and Social Reform in Mid-Nineteenth Century America.* New York: Abingdon, 1957.

Chapter 6—The Church

Gaustad, Edwin S. *Historical Atlas of Religion in America,* rev. ed. New York: Harper & Row, 1976.

Hofstadter, Richard. *Anti-Intellectualism in American Life.* New York: Random, 1962.

Mains, David. *Full Circle: The Creative Church for Today's Society.* Waco: Word Bks, 1971.

Marsden, George M. *The Evangelical Mind and the New School Presbyterian Experience.* New Haven: Yale U Pr, 1970.

Smith, Timothy L. *Called Unto Holiness; The Story of the Nazarenes: The Formative Years.* Kansas City, Mo.: Nazarene, 1962.

Snyder, Howard. *The Problem of Wineskins: Church Structure in a Technological Age.* Downers Grove, Ill.: Inter-Varsity, 1975.

Stedman, Ray C. *Body Life.* Glendale, Calif.: Regal, 1972.

Tocqueville, Alexis de. *Democracy in America,* 2 vols., ed. Bradley and Phillips. New York: Random, 1944.

Winslow, Ola E. *Meetinghouse Hill, 1630-1783.* New York: Norton, 1972.

Chapter 7—Separatism

Adams, James E. *Preus of Missouri and the Great Lutheran Civil War.* New York: Harper & Row, 1977.

Bumsted, J. M., and Van De Wetering, John E. *What Must I Do to Be Saved? The Great Awakening in Colonial America.* Hinsdale, Ill.: Dryden Pr, 1976.

Goen, C. C. *Revivalism and Separatism in New England, 1740-1800.* New Haven: Yale U Pr, 1962.

Hutchinson, George P. *The History Behind the Reformed Presbyterian Church Evangelical Synod.* Cherry Hill, N.J.: Mack Pub., 1974.

McLoughlin, William G. *Isaac Backus and the American Pietistic Tradition.* Boston: Little, 1967.

Morgan, Edmund S. *Roger Williams: The Church and the State.* New York: HarBrace World, 1967.

Noll, Mark A. *Christians in the American Revolution.* Grand Rapids: Eerdmans, for the Christian U Pr, 1977.

Shelley, Bruce L. *A History of Conservative Baptists.* Wheaton: Conservative Baptist Pr, 1971.

Chapter 8—Nation

Cherry, Conrad, ed. *God's New Israel: Religious Interpretations of American Destiny.* Englewood Cliffs, N.J.: Prentice-Hall, 1971.

Handy, Robert. *A Christian America: Protestant Hopes and Historical Realities.* New York: Oxford U Pr, 1971.

Hatch, Nathan O. *The Sacred Cause of Liberty: Republican Thought and the Millennium in Revolutionary New England.* New Haven: Yale U Pr, 1977.

Jorstad, Erling. *The Politics of Doomsday: Fundamentalists of the Far Right.* Nashville: Abingdon, 1970.

Mead, Sidney E. *The Nation With the Soul of a Church.* New York: Harper & Row, 1975.

Niebuhr, H. Richard. *The Kingdom of God in America.* New York: Harper & Row, 1937.

Strout, Cushing. *The New Heavens and New Earth: Political Religion in America.* New York: Harper & Row, Torch, 1975.

Tuveson, Ernest L. *Redeemer Nation: The Idea of America's Millennial Role.* Chicago: U of Chicago Pr, 1968.

Chapter 9—Society

Bready, J. Wesley. *England: Before and After Wesley: The Evangelical Revival and Social Reform.* London: Hodder & Stoughton, 1938.

Cairns, Earle Edwin. *Saints and Society: The Social Impact of Eighteenth Century English Revivals.* Chicago: Moody, 1960.

Davis, David B. *The Problem of Slavery in an Age of Revolution, 1770-1823.* Ithaca, N.Y.: Cornell U Pr, 1975.

Irwin, Grace. *Servant of Slaves* (John Newton). Grand Rapids: Eerdmans, 1961.

Linder, Robert D. "The Resurgence of Evangelical Social Concern (1925-75)," in *The Evangelicals: What They Believe, Who They Are, Where They Are Changing,* ed. David F. Wells and John D. Woodbridge. Nashville: Abingdon, 1975.

Mathews, Donald G. *Slavery and Methodism: A Chapter in American Morality.* Princeton: Princeton U Pr, 1965.

Moberg, David. *The Great Reversal: Evangelicals Versus Social Concern.* Philadelphia: Lippincott, 1972.

Mouw, Richard. *Political Evangelism.* Grand Rapids: Eerdmans, 1973.

Perkins, John M. *Let Justice Roll Down.* Glendale, Calif.: Regal, 1976.

Pierard, Richard. *The Unequal Yoke: Evangelical Christianity and Political Conservatism.* Philadelphia: Lippincott, 1970.

Yoder, John Howard. *The Politics of Jesus: Vicit Agnus Noster.* Grand Rapids: Eerdmans, 1972.

Index of Persons

Index of Subjects

Index of Titles